Namibia: Conquest to Independence
Formation of a Nation

Godfrey Mwakikagile

Copyright © 2015 Godfrey Mwakikagile
All rights reserved.

Namibia: Conquest to Independence:
Formation of a Nation

Godfrey Mwakikagile

First Edition

ISBN 978-9987-16-044-0

New Africa Press
Dar es Salaam, Tanzania

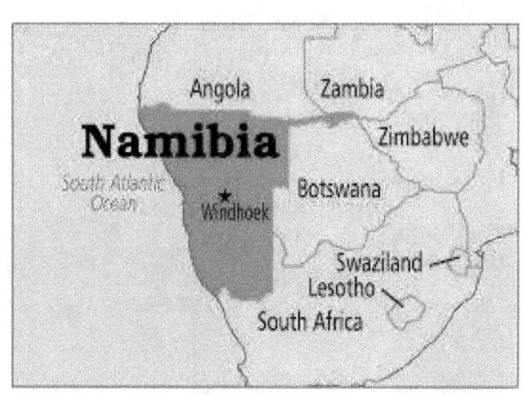

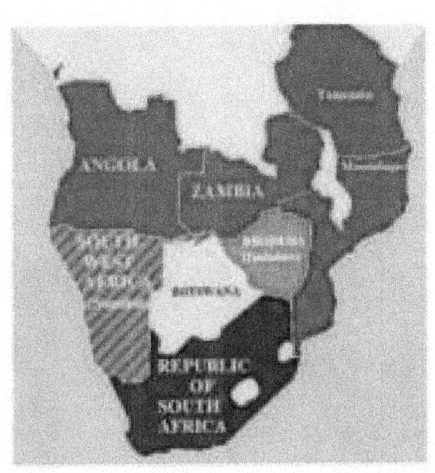

Contents

Acknowledgements

Introduction

Part One:
Namibia: An Overview

Part Two:
Namibia: Founded on Genocide

Part Three:
The Struggle for Independence

Part Four:
The People: Unity in Diversity
Comparative Analysis

Appendix I:
Amid Namibia's White Opulence, Majority Rule Isn't So Scary Now

Appendix II:
Mass participation limited by English as sole medium

Appendix III:
A Muzungu in Namibia

Appendix IV:
Averting Namibia's own holocaust

Appendix V:
Land claims turn tribal in Namibia

Appendix VI:
Insult reflects tribal division in Namibia

Appendix VII:
SWAPO retains power

Acknowledgement

SPACE does not allow me to name the individuals and institutions to whom I am deeply indebted for helping me make this work possible. But I must express my profound gratitude to all the sources I have cited to document my work. They are given full attribution in the book.

The brevity of this acknowledgment should not in any way be misconstrued as a deliberate attempt to ignore or minimise the contribution made by different scholars and others whose works I have used to fortify my thesis. It is, rather, a genuine attempt to convey the depth of my indebtedness to each and everyone of them, including some of whom I may have inadvertently omitted, however indirect their contribution may be. They have all equally contributed to the success of this effort.

Writing a book of this nature is a cooperative effort. It is a product of cumulative knowledge gathered through the years by different people in different fields. We can see far only because we stand on the shoulders of others. But the analysis is mine. And I take full responsibility for whatever mistakes and shortcomings may be found in my work while credit for its success goes to others.

Introduction

THIS work is a study of Namibia's identity and evolution as a sovereign entity. It is also an introductory text on the young nation.

The people who collectively constitute the nation of Namibia and their separate identities as ethnic and racial groups have formed a national identity which is one of the most fascinating developments in the history of post-colonial Africa.

Even in contemporary times, Namibia continues to inspire admiration, especially after emerging from brutal racial oppression which lasted for many years. But the country is also trying to consolidate her national identity in an imaginative way after the end of white minority rule which traumatised her people even during its last years in the last decade of the 20th century because of its brutal nature.

Namibia entered the new millennium with hope and excitement inspired by the ideals which fuelled and sustained her struggle against racial oppression and other injustices perpetrated against non-whites when the country was under the apartheid regime. It was, for all practical purposes, a colony of South Africa during the apartheid era.

She emerged from that era scarred, yet undaunted in her quest for peace and stability, and in her determination to build a truly multiracial society in which everybody has equal rights under the law. But she still has a long way to go in spite of the success she has had in many areas.

Namibia today is a good example of what other African countries can do, or attempt to do, in their quest for peace and prosperity, and for justice and equality, in spite of the challenges it continues to face across the spectrum. It is a country that embodies the ideals and aspirations which are shared by millions of Africans across the continent.

As an African, I feel that it is my duty, as much as it is the duty of other Africans, to write about our countries in order to help the rest of mankind learn about us as much as they can.

We don't have to wait for foreigners to write about us or define us. And we don't have to be indigenous to the countries we write about. We can write about any African country as long as we have the necessary knowledge to do so. We are all Africans and Africa is one.

Part One

Namibia: An Overview

NAMIBIA is one of the largest countries in Africa in terms of area. It is also one of the most sparsely populated because of its arid and semi-arid conditions. Much of the country is desert. And its name comes from the Namib Desert.

It's the least populated country in the world after Mongolia. It's also one of the most uninhabitable in most of its parts because of the harsh climate. And it has very little water.

The climate is arid in the western part of the country, semi-arid and sub-humid in the central and northeastern parts. Namibia also has long droughts. It gets rain mainly from November to March.

But in spite of its harsh climate, Namibia has a wide variety of plants and wildlife. It is also is one of the most popular destinations for tourists and one of the most stable countries in Africa.

Located in the southwestern part of continent, it was

once known as South West Africa and was a German colony before South Africa assumed control of the territory.

It's bordered by the Atlantic Ocean in the west; by Angola in the north, Zambia and Zimbabwe in the northeast, Botswana in the east, and by South Africa in the south and southeast.

Its largest city is Windhoek which is also the nation's capital. Windhoek also has a reputation as one of the cleanest and safest cities in Africa.

Namibia has an area of 318,696 square miles and a population of only about 2.2 million in such a vast expanse of territory. Partly because of that, but mainly because of its relative wealth, the country has one of the highest per capita incomes in Africa. Its per capita income was about 8,780 US dollars in 2014.

The country is well-endowed in terms of natural resources contrasted with many other African countries. But in spite of the country's wealth, more than half of its people live below the poverty level. Namibians are some of the poorest people in Africa and in the entire world because of income disparities. Disparities in income in Namibia are some of the worst in the world.

The country has 11 ethnic groups, most of them indigenous. There is also a small white minority population, mainly German, Afrikaner and British. Black Africans of Bantu stock constitute the vast majority of the population.

The Ovambo constitute almost 50 per cent of the country's population; the Kavango, about 9 per cent; Herero 7.5 per cent; Damara, 7.5 per cent; Whites, almost 6.5 per cent; Nama, almost 5 per cent; Coloureds, about 4 per cent; Caprivian, almost 4 per cent; San, almost 3 per cent; Baster, 2.5 per cent; and the Tswana, about 0.6 per cent. People of other ethnicities constitute almost 1 per cent.

The Ovambo, Kavango, and East Caprivians who live

in the northern part of Namibia which has a significant amount of water and fertile areas, are mostly farmers and herders. Historically, they were stayed in their own areas and did not have much interaction, if any, with the Nama, Damara, and Herero, who lived the central part of the country competing for land. But they were all brought together under one rule by the Germans and collectively constituted a colony which, in German, was known as *Deutsch-Südwestafrika* (DSWA).

German colonial rule weakened the tribes by oppressing them. But it did not destroy or erase their ethnic identities and traditional institutions and ways of life, although the indigenous people were subjected to all kinds of brutalities and indignities by their conquerors.

One of the saddest chapters in Namibia's and in Africa's history was the near-extermination of the Herero and the Nama, but mostly the Herero.

From 1904 to 1907, the Herero together with the Nama took up arms against their oppressors. The German colonial rulers responded with brute force.

Figures vary but up to 100,000 Hereros – about a third of the entire Herero population – were killed. And more than 10,000 Namas, who constituted half of the Nama population, lost their lives.

Tens of thousands of Hereros and a significant number of Namas were driven into the desert, without food and water, where they perished.

The extermination of the Herero and the Nama by the Germans is said to be the first genocide in the 20th century. The German government apologised to the people of Namibia in 2004 for this horrendous tragedy but refused to pay compensation for the atrocities.

People from northern Namibia have migrated to other parts of the country in recent years in search of jobs, providing cheap labour. As a result of that, they have been able to integrate with members of other tribes, leading to a more integrated nation.

The integration has also been facilitated by urbanisation and education, making Namibia's urban centres some of the most integrated parts of the country.

Besides their shared national identity and traditional values so prevalent in indigenous cultures across Africa, the people of Namibia are also united by language, although it is a tenuous bond. The official language is English. Most Namibians who can read and write speak or know some English. But most Namibians don't know English.

Other languages spoken in Namibia are German, Afrikaans, and Portuguese. Portuguese is new, spoken by immigrants from neighbouring Angola. But it is the indigenous languages which are dominant in a predominantly black country, especially in the rural areas, where the vast majority of the people live.

Oshiwambo, a language of the Ovambo ethnic group, is the most widely spoken black African language in Namibia. It is also one of the major African languages spoken in neighbouring Angola.

The majority of the people in Namibia are Christian. Most Namibian Christians are Lutheran. But there are also significant numbers of Roman Catholic, Methodist, Anglican, Jewish, African Methodist Episcopal, and Dutch Reformed Christians in the country.

Indigenous religious practices are also prevalent. Even a significant number of people who have converted to Christianity have not entirely abandoned indigenous religious beliefs and practices. Also, many of them don't see a conflict between the two and justify this dual allegiance on grounds of cultural fusion or integration.

Although Namibia is mainly desert, the country still has a thriving agricultural sector because of the relatively developed nature of its economy in sharp contrast with many other African countries.

Minerals, tourism, and livestock constitute the backbone of Namibia's economy.

Education and services have been extended, in varying degrees, to most rural areas in recent years.

Although the literacy rate is quite high – estimated to be 85 per cent – the number of Namibians who have skills needed in the labour market is significantly lower than that.

Like most of the countries on the continent, Namibia has suffered from the devastating impact of the AIDS epidemic, reducing economic growth, especially in the agricultural sector which is labour-intensive. The mineral and tourism sectors have not suffered as much because they are not heavily dependent on manual labour provided by a large segment of Namibia's indigenous population.

In many parts of the country, agricultural growth is low because of the harsh climate.

Namibia's landscape is divided into five distinct regions: the Central Plateau, the Namib Desert, the Escarpment, the Bushveld, and the Kalahari Desert.

Although Namibia's climate is extremely dry in most cases, there is a strong influence over some parts of the country coming from the Benguela current. It is a cold current flowing north from the Atlantic Ocean, causing low precipitation over a number of areas in the country.

The Central Plateau runs from north to south. It is a wide area and is bordered by the Skeleton Coast in the northwest, by the Namib Desert and its coastal plains in the southwest, the Orange River in the south, and by the Kalahari Desert in the east.

The highest point in Namibia is also in the Central Plateau. It is an elevation of 8,550 feet at Königstein.

Also the majority of Namibians live in the Central Plateau. The region is also the nation's economic hub. Most of the economic activities in Namibia take place in this region. And most of the country's arable land is in the Central Plateau. The Central Plateau is also home to the nation's capital, Windhoek.

Although arable land occupies only one per cent of

Namibia's vast land area, it provides a large and strong economic base for the country, employing about half of the entire population in the agricultural sector.

The Central Plateau is also a region of remarkable contrasts in terms of climate. Frosts are common during winter. And summer temperatures can reach as high as 104°F.

The Namib Desert is another prominent geographical feature and region of Namibia which is also one of the most outstanding on the entire Africa continent.

It is a vast expanse of extremely arid gravel plains and dunes stretching along the entire coastline of Namibia on the Atlantic ocean. It varies in width from 60 miles to hundreds of miles and has the largest sand dunes in the world. There is very little vegetation in the desert.

Another important geographical region of Namibia is the Great Escarpment. It has an elevation of more than 6,560 feet with varying temperatures. As you go further inland away from the coast whose weather and climate is influenced by the cold currents from the Atlantic Ocean, the temperature goes higher and higher. The coastal area is also known for its fog.

The Great Escarpment is rocky and has poor soil. But it is more productive than the Namib Desert. Vegetation along the escarpment ranges from dense woodlands to shrubs with scattered trees.

The Bushveld is in the northeastern part of Namibia along the border with Angola and in the Caprivi Strip. The Bushveld gets more precipitation than other parts of the country. It also has cooler temperatures between 50°F and 90°F. The region is mostly flat. It also has sandy soils, making it almost impossible to retain water.

Adjacent to the Bushveld in north-central Namibia is one of the most outstanding geographical features in the world: the Etosha Pan.

It is a huge alluvial basin, 75 miles long, which once had a saltwater lake. Most of the time every year, it is a dry, saline wasteland. But during the rainy season, the area is transformed into a shallow lake covering more than 3,700 square miles.

There is not much water available except on the edges of the Etosha Pan. But the area is able to sustain abundant wildlife – antelope including gemsbok, impala, and springbok – as well as zebra, and elephants which are the biggest attraction in the region.

Herds of elephants are found in the dense mopane woodland on the south side of the pan.

There are many other species of wildlife. The Etosha National Park is one of the most prominent animal sanctuaries in Africa in the same category with well-known parks in South Africa, Tanzania, and Kenya. It is also one of the biggest tourist attractions in Namibia.

During the wet season, the Etosha Pan also becomes a breeding ground for flamingoes, providing a spectacular sight for tourists and others visitors. It is also home to a large number of other birds and animals.

Yet another major geographical area in Namibia is the Kalahari Desert. The desert is shared with Botswana and South Africa.

One of the most important areas in the Kalahari Desert is the Succulent Karoo. An entire third of the world's succulents are found in the Karoo. The Karoo is in Namibia and South Africa but not in Botswana.

Namibia's coastal desert is one of the world's oldest. Its sand dunes are also the world's highest. The Namib-Naukluft National Park is located there.

The coastal desert area is extremely rich in diamonds, making Namibia one of the world's largest producers of the mineral. It also has other minerals including gold, uranium, copper, lead, silver, tin, zinc, lithium, cadmium, tungsten and salt.

Namibia may also have large deposits of oil, coal and iron ore, based on preliminary findings.

In 1974, natural gas was discovered in the Kudu Field

at the outlet of the Orange River. The field is believed to have more than 1.3 trillion cubic feet of reserves.

The country also has hydroelectricity but not enough for its needs.

It also has abundant coastal and marine resources which have not been exploited. And there are large quantities of fish in its territorial waters in the Atlantic Ocean.

But there is no question that the country is heavily dependent on the mining sector as the driving force of its economy. It earns much-needed foreign exchange.

Mining accounts for 8 per cent of Namibia's gross domestic product (GDP) but provides more than 50 per cent of foreign exchange earnings.

The country's rich alluvial diamond deposits also make Namibia not only a primary source of gem-quality diamonds but also of diamonds which surpass those mined in many other parts of Africa in terms of quality.

Namibia ranks fourth in the production and export of non-fuel minerals on the continent. It is also the fifth-largest producer of uranium in the world and produces large quantities of lead, zinc, tin, silver, and tungsten.

The country also has natural stones such as granite and marble in significant quantities. It also has semiprecious stones which are are extracted in smaller amounts.

Although minerals play the biggest role in Namibia's economy, only about 3 per cent of the country's population is engaged in the mining sector.

About 70 per cent of the Namibian population depends on agriculture, mostly in the subsistence sector dominated by peasants.

The commercial sector of agriculture is dominated by whites who are mainly engaged in livestock ranching in the central and northern parts of Namibia. Goat and sheep farming is mostly in the arid parts of the south.

The northern regions of Namibia are the country's "food basket," although their potential has not been fully harnessed. In addition to a variety of crops, the area is also known for its cattle.

The Orange River in the south also plays a significant role in the agricultural sector. Grapes grown along its banks are an important commodity in the commercial sector of agriculture which provides much-needed jobs to many seasonal labourers.

Compared with many other African countries, Namibia's agricultural sector is relatively strong. But it is not large and productive enough to meet the country's needs. And because of inadequate supplies, the country is forced to import about 50 per cent of its cereal requirements. It also imports other foods.

Food shortages are a major problem in many parts of Namibia especially in the rural areas, especially during drought.

For historical and economic reasons, the Namibian economy has been inextricably linked with the South African economy for decades. Even its currency is dominated by South Africa, with the Namibian dollar being pegged one-to-one to the South African rand. Also 80 per cent of Namibia's trade is conducted with South Africa. Most of its exports and imports go through South Africa.

Namibia's manufacturing sector is vibrant by African standards. But its growth is small because it has a small domestic market and faces strong competition from South African manufacturers.

In terms of infrastructure, Namibia is surpassed only by South Africa on the continent. The country also has excellent port facilities.

Namibia's fishing industry, concentrated in Walvis Bay, is well-developed. Walvis Bay is one of the best deep-water ports on the continent and may become a major gateway to other countries in southern Africa.

The country's road and railway network is modern; so is its aviation facilities, unlike in most African countries with the exception of South Africa and a few others such as Mauritius.

Tourism plays a very important role in Namibia's economy. It employs many people and is the third-largest foreign exchange earner surpassed only by mining and fisheries.

The subterranean economy also plays a big role as a source of income for many Namibians who can not get jobs in the formal sector; it is a continental phenomenon.

A large number of Namibians seeking employment in the formal sector can not get jobs because they don't have the necessary skills or training. Jobs are also scarce.

Namibia's economy has bright prospects if it is diversified, especially in the areas of tourism, fisheries, manufacturing and agriculture. It is expected that foreign investment will play a major role in diversifying the economy.

It is one of the ironies of history, at least in the African context, that some of the most developed countries are also some of the least developed; Namibia being a prime example, besides pockets of affluence and high levels of modernisation which rival those in the West and other parts of the industrialised world. While Namibia's modern sector – especially mining – produces a substantial amount of wealth which is in the hands of a minority, the traditional sector produces less but supports the majority of the population especially in the rural areas. And while it is true that the country's per capita income is very high, the poverty that is rampant across the country especially in the rural areas makes those statistics meaningless in terms of real benefits for the average Namibian.

And although the vast majority of the people depend on subsistence agriculture and herding, and are basically unskilled, there are more than 200,000 skilled workers and a small but highly significant and well-trained professional and managerial class.

The contrasts are glaring, even more so when

compared with other African countries.

Namibia is a member of the Southern African Development Community (SADC), the richest economic bloc on the continent mainly because of the membership of South Africa, the continent's economic "super power," and of resource-rich countries such as Angola, the Democratic Republic of Congo (DRC), Zimbabwe, Mozambique, Zambia and Tanzania.

South Africa's economic influence on Namibia is demonstrated in many ways, including the circulation of its currency, the rand, in its former colony, as legal tender. But the Namibian dollar is not legal tender in South Africa.

This asymmetrical relationship is a product of South Africa's economic might in the region which continues to tip scales in its favour even after the end of apartheid.

Yet, in spite of such dependence on South Africa, Namibia's economy is still one of the strongest and most prosperous on the entire African continent. The country also has one of the highest standards of living on the continent; clearly demonstrated by the large number of people who have migrated to Namibia from all parts of the continent seeking employment and better living conditions. Their other prime destinations are South Africa and Botswana.

Part Two

Namibia:
Founded on Genocide

THE area that is now known as Namibia was first occupied by the San who are also known as Bushmen, a derogatory term coined by Europeans to describe them. Other people who later entered the region included the Damara and the Namaqua who are also simply known as the Nama.

All these groups were later overwhelmed by the members of Bantu ethnic groups. Today, they constitute only a small percentage of Namibia's population, contrasted with those of Bantu stock.

Members of the Bantu ethnic groups who moved into the region were the Ovambo and the Herero. They migrated from the north, the area that is now Angola and Congo, in the 1300s A.D.

Therefore Namibia has a long history as an inhabited region. But it does not have a very long history as a country, a product of imperial conquest when European powers staked out claims in southern Africa, creating countries which exist there today.

The first Europeans to explore the region were Portuguese in the 1480s. But they did not stake out claims to the territory or declare the region as a Portuguese possession. And unlike most of sub-Saharan Africa, the area was not extensively explored by Europeans until the 1800s.

The inhospitable Namib Desert constituted a formidable barrier to European exploration.

The area was later explored by European travellers, traders, hunters, and missionaries.

Walvis Bay was taken by the British in 1878 on behalf of the Cape Colony in South Africa. The Cape Colony itself was a British possessions. In 1884, Walvis Bay was incorporated into the Cape of Good Hope and remained an integral part of South Africa even after Namibia won independence more than a hundred years later. In 1994 South Africa renounced her ownership of Walvis Bay and the area became a part of Namibia.

In 1883, a German trader, Adolf Lüderitz, claimed the rest of the coastal region of Namibia after negotiations with a local chief. He is acknowledged as the founding father of German South-West Africa. There is a coastal town that bears his name.

He was also known for using questionable tactics to swindle Africans out of their land. He used unfair treaties African chiefs were duped into signing, giving away their land; reminiscent of what another German, Carl Peters, did in German East Africa – now mainland Tanzania – of which he is considered to be the founder.

Also, Carl Peters was so cruel when he was a colonial administrator in German East Africa that he was nicknamed "mkono wa damu," which means "bloody hand" in Kiswahili, because of the cruel punishment he inflicted on the "natives" even for minor infractions or none at all, including hanging; a practice that was in conformity with his racial views as a Social Darwinist who believed in the superiority of the white race over blacks and members of other races. He was even posthumously honoured by Hitler because of his white supremacist views shared by the Nazis, some of the most dangerous exponents of the doctrine of white supremacy the world has ever known.

In Namibia, besides the "agreements" Lüderitz signed with the Africans, other negotiations followed, between the United Kingdom and Germany, resulting in Germany's annexation of the coastal region, excluding Walvis Bay which remained under British control. The region already had well-established communities of Africans. But they meant nothing to the colonsers. As Dominik J. Schaller states in *Empire, Colony, Genocide: Conquest, Occupation, and Subaltern Resistance in World History*:

"When Southwest Africa became a German dependency in April 1884, a handful of powerful Herero chiefs competed with each other for the rank of paramount chief. Although the Herero were originally pastoralists, they depended in the first half of the nineteenth century almost solely on hunter-gathering and horticulture for their subsistence. But while the Herero fought successful trade wars and secured their position of power in Namibia, they started building up huge cattle herds and soon became (sic) to be known as *the* outstanding cattle breeders in Southwest Africa.

The economy of the Nama peoples in southern and central Namibia relied likewise on cattle, but mainly on trade with farmers from the Cape Colony.

Northern Namibia – inhabited by the Ovambo – remained for the most part untouched by the Germans, although this region was officially part of their colony. The Ovambo lived in centralized and highly stratified kingdoms that depended economically on agriculture, fishery, and trade with other Ovambo groups in Portuguese Angola.

Due to the lack of reliable data it is difficult to estimate the exact population figures. However, Most historians agree that about 80,000 Herero, 20,000 Nama, and 450,000 Ovambo were living in the region the Germans claimed as their colony." – (Dominik J. Schaller, in A. Dirk Moses, ed., *Empire, Colony, Genocide: Conquest, Occupation, and Subaltern Resistance in World History*, Brooklyn, New York; Oxford: Berghahn Books, 2008, pp. 298 – 299).

The British also played a role in defining the boundaries of the German colony during that period when European powers were competing for territory in Africa. In 1884, they acknowledged the area claimed by Germany as Germany's sphere of influence. They were not interested in acquiring the territory.

Twenty years later, the massacre of the Herero – and the Nama – further legitimised Germany's control of the territory, a vast expanse where Germany's imperial might found full expression, virtually unchallenged by the indigenous people who had learned their lesson well from the genocide.

On 1 July 1890, the Caprivi Strip was incorporated into German South-West Africa following an agreement signed by the two colonial powers. The Anglo-German agreement, also known as the Heligoland Treaty, was a compromise between the two powers. It enabled Britain to acquire Zanzibar which had been under German control. In return, Germany acquired Heligoland, an island in the North Sea which had been under Britain control.

When the Germans assumed control of South-West Africa (Namibia), they named the colony – Deutsch-Südwestafrika. And they went on to consolidate their rule, leading to brutal oppression of the indigenous people. Among the injustices perpetrated against them was expropriation of prime grazing land which was given to white settlers.

The injustices triggered a backlash from the indigenous people. The land belonged to the Herero, of Bantu stock, and the Nama, a Khoikhoi group. They took up arms against the German rulers in an uprising which lasted from 1904 to 1908. The conflict led to a genocide which is one of the most forgotten chapters in the history of imperial conquest of Africa.

The genocide took place during the Scramble for Africa when European powers were claiming and competing for territory on the continent.

The uprising started on 12 January 1904 when the Herero under the leadership of Samuel Maharero, their chief, took up arms against their colonial oppressors.

It was a total mismatch. The Herero were far outgunned by the Germans. The technological theory of imperialism was validated in the most ruthless way by the outcome of this conflict.

In August the same year, Lothar von Trotha, a German general who led the brutal campaign, defeated the Herero and drove them into the desert of Omaheke, one of the regions of Namibia, where most of them died of thirst and starvation.

And in October 1904, the Nama also rose against the Germans, with equally tragic consequences.

The water wells used by the Herero and the Nama were also poisoned by the Germans.

The conflict between the Germans and the indigenous people of Namibia, especially the Herero and Nama, was a classic case of imperialism at its best: total subjugation of a conquered people. And it's important to look at this conflict in a much broader context to understand what happened. As Torben Jørgensen and Eric Markusen state in "Genocide of the Hereros," in the *Encyclopedia of Genocide*:

"The Herero people, like their neighbors, the Namas, were cattle-herding nomadic peoples....

At the beginning of the twentieth century, most of the approximately 4,500 German settlers in the country were cattle ranchers whose inland farms were connected to the seacoast by railroad lines. The railroad lines and the adjacent land were off limits to the native population, which disrupted their nomadic lifestyles. Moreover, under German rule the Hereros and the Namas were largely without civil or political rights and were frequently attacked by German settlers.

In 1903 the Hereros decided to rebel after learning of a German plan to concentrate them on reservations and build a major new railroad. On January 12, 1904, led by Chief Maharero, the Hereros launched a military campaign that killed approximately 100 Germans and captured most of Hereroland. The Germans counterattacked, and by mid-August, had destroyed most of the Herero military forces. The surviving Herero, including many women and children, were driven by the Germans into the Omaheke Desert, where they died of thirst and starvation.

The genocide of the Hereros has also become famous for one of the drastic devices used by German General Lothar von Trotha, in poisoning the water holes of the Hereros. The Germans also attacked all native villages, including the Namas. Approximately 80 percent of the Herero people, or 65,000, and approximately 50 percent of the Namas, or 10,000, perished.

According to Bridgman and Worley, there were many protests in Germany, including government agencies that refused to support the actions, and demands that the slaughter be stopped before all Hereros were killed.

The slaughter of the Hereros was recognized by the UN Whitaker Commission as one of the first genocides of the twentieth century." – (Torben Jørgensen and Eric Markusen, "Genocide of the Hereros," in Israel W. Charny, ed., *Encyclopedia of Genocide, Volume 1*, The Institute on the Holocaust and Genocide, Jerusalem; ABC-CLIO, Inc., Santa Barbara, California, USA, 1999   pp.

288 - 289).

Racism did play a major role in making the decision to to exterminate the Hereros in order to enable the German settlers to acquire the land and other natural resources. It was also justified on Darwinian grounds not only to give it scientific respectability but to legitimise the natural differences among the races, especially between blacks and whites, with whites being on top. And because the differences were "natural," they could not be overcome, thus giving whites the right to rule Africans and other non-whites perpetually because they were incapable of even ruling themselves.

It was in Africa where Social Darwinism was practised most ruthlessly, and most effectively, to justify imperialism and colonisation of the indigenous people, the Herero being some of the most unfortunate victims of this racist ideology and philosophy.

Social Darwinism also justified genocide because members of "the lesser breed" such as the Herero and other blacks were "unfit" to live. As David Maybury-Lewis states in "Genocide against Indigenous Peoples" in *Annihilating Difference: The Anthropology of Genocide*:

"Imperialist genocide against indigenous peoples was...of two kinds. It was practiced in order to clear lands that invading settlers wished to occupy. It was also practiced as as part of a strategy to seize and coerce labor that the settlers could not or would not obtain by less drastic means.

It was often inspired furthermore by the rulers' determination to show who was master and who was, if not slave, then at least obedient subject; and it was often put into effect as deliberate policy where the masters felt that their subjects had to be taught a lesson. Acts of resistance or rebellion were often punished by genocidal killings.

A classic example of this, out of scores that might be cited, was the German extermination of the Herero in South West Africa (see Drechsler 1980; Bridgman 1981)....The German administration argued that it was in the interests of higher development and virtually a part of natural law that indigenous peoples become a class of workers in the service of the whites." – (David Maybury-Lewis, "Genocide against Indigenous Peoples," in Alexander Laban Hinton, ed., *Annihilating Difference: The Anthropology of Genocide*, University of California Press, Berkeley and Los Angeles, 2002, pp. 47 – 48. See also E.N. Anderson and Barbara A. Anderson, *Warning Signs of Genocide: An Anthropological Perspective*, Lexington Books, Lanham, Maryland, USA; Plymouth, UK, 2013. They contend, like others do, that the extermination of the Herero was the first genocide in the twentieth century, p. 101:

"Actual genocide in settler wars seems to occur when a long history of back-and-forth fighting has made the settler group particularly hostile, *and* when the government is openly racist. This occurred, for instance, in the United States in the 1850s, in Australia (locally) in the nineteenth and early twentieth centuries, and in Brazil at intervals throughout its history. The more social hate is mobilized against such groups, the more the danger.

It also occurred when Lothar Von Trotha and his troops massacred the Herero in southwest Africa, and arguably set off the modern escalating spiral of genocide. This, the first twentieth-century genocide, was also one of the last of the settler wars. In this case, the Herero tried to resist German conquest. The Germans eventually concluded that only extermination of the Herero people could solve the problem. Some sixty thousand Herero and ten thousand Nama were killed (Schaller, 2011: 37), almost ending the Herero as a people."

See also Mahmood Mamdani, *When Victims Become Killers: Colonialism, Nativism, and the Genocide in*

Rwanda, Princeton University Press, 2001, pp. 12 – 13:

"The genocide of the Herero was the first genocide of the twentieth century. The links between it and the Holocaust go beyond the building of concentration camps and the execution of an annihilation policy and are worth exploring. It is surely of significance that when General Trotha wrote...of destroying 'African tribes with streams of blood,' he saw this as some kind of a Social Darwinist 'cleansing' after which 'something new' would 'emerge.' It is also relevant that, when the general sought to distribute responsibility for the genocide, he accused the missions of inciting the Herero with images 'of the bloodcurdling Jewish history of the Old Testament.'

It was also among the Herero in the concentration camps that the German geneticist, Eugen Fischer, first came to do his medical experiments on race, for which he used both Herero and mulatto offspring of Herero women and German men. Fischer later became chancellor of the University of Berlin, where he taught medicine to Nazi physicians. One of his prominent students was Josef Mengele, the notorious doctor who did unsavory genetic experiments on Jewish children at Auschwitz.

It seems to me that Hannah Arendt erred when she presumed a relatively uncomplicated relationship between settlers's genocide in the colonies and the Nazi Holocaust at home: When Nazis set out to annihilate Jews, it is far more likely that they thought of themselves as natives, and Jews as settlers. Yet, there is a link that connects the genocide of the Herero and the Nazi Holocaust to the Rwandan genocide. That link is *race branding*, whereby it became possible not only to set a group apart as an enemy, but also to exterminate it with an easy conscience."

See also Adam Jones, *Genocide: A Comprehensive Introduction*, Routledge, 2010, p. 81:

"An advantage of a comparative and global-historical approach to genocide is that it allows us to perceive important connections between campaigns of mass killing and group destruction that are widely separated in time and space. Scholarship on the genocide against the Herero provides an excellent example. It is increasingly acknowledged not only that this was the first genocide of the twentieth century, but that it paved the way, in important respects, for the prototypical mass slaughter of that century - the Jewish Holocaust. As summarized by Madley:

'The Herero genocide was a crucial antecedent to Nazi mass murder. It created the German word *Konzentrationslager* [concentration camp] and the twentieth century's first death camp. Like Nazi mass murder, the Namibian genocides were premised upon ideas like *Lebensraum* [living space], annihilation war [*Vernichtungskrieg*], and German racial supremacy. Individual Nazis were also linked to colonial Namibia. Hermann Goering, who built the first Nazi concentration camps, was the son of the first governor of colonial Namibia. Eugen Fischer, who influenced Hitler and ran the institute that supported Joseph Mengele's medical 'research' at Auschwitz, conducted racial studies in the colony. And Ritter von Epp, godfather of the Nazi party and Nazi governor of Bavaria from 1933 – 1945, led German troops against the Herero during the genocide.'")

Although the German settlers in Namibia and many of their fellow countrymen in Germany considered the Herero and other Africans to be inferior to whites, there were practical considerations, as well, which played an important role in reaching the decision to exterminate them.

The decision was also made public. The Herero themselves were told, in their own language, that they were going to be exterminated by the Germans. As Jeremy Sarkin states in his book, *Germany's Genocide of the Herero: Kaiser Wilhelm II, His General, His Settlers, His Soldiers*:

"It is nearly unanimously agreed today that between 1904 and 1907 to 1908 Germany conducted genocide, as legally defined, of the Herero of then German South West Africa (GSWA), today Namibia.

The Herero genocide is unique in that the order to annihilate the Herero was publicly proclaimed and specifically made known to the target group in their own language.

The official proclamation initially sought the extermination specifically of the Herero. However, other groups, especially the Nama, were later targeted because of their rich land holdings and their intransigence against the Germans. The severe treatment meted out to the Nama and the major reduction in their population numbers may also fit the definition of genocide.

German settlers in the territory who wanted the land and cattle of the indigenous Herero and the public in Germany, incited by propaganda that the Herero were conducting a race war, bayed for Herero blood.

German troops, many of whom had previously exercised brutal treatment on indigenous populations in different parts of the world, killed men, women and children without distinction. Many other atrocities were committed, including the rape of Herero women.

These events initially occurred under the command of General Adrian Dietrich Lotha von Trotha, most likely at the instruction of of Kaiser Wilhelm II – both had a history of ordering and conducting brutal extermination-type practices. Von Trotha embarked on a planned, announced, systematic and indiscriminate extermination of the Herero community." – (Jeremy Sarkin, *Germany's Genocide of the Herero: Kaiser Wilhelm II, Hi General, His Settlers, His Soldiers*, UCT Press, Cape Town, South Africa; James Currey, London, 2011, pp. 233 – 234).

The extermination of the Herero had great historical

significance not only in the history of Namibia and of the continent as a whole but of the entire world. As Sarkin goes on to state:

"The order to wipe out the Herero community became the first genocide of the twentieth century. Between, 60,000 and 100,000 people, almost all civilians and non-combatants, many of them women and children, were executed by German troops in various ways or were forced into the desert to die of starvation and thirst or by drinking water at water wells poisoned by German troops. May be 20,000 of the original Herero population of about 100,000 were left in the end.

The extermination order (*Vernichtungsbefehl*) was issued on 2 October 1904. Due to pressure on him, Kaiser Wilhelm reluctantly and after a long delay rescinded the order in December 1904. But the genocide not only took place in those few months from October 1904 to December 1904, when the official extermination order was operative. A policy of taking no Herero prisoners was in force before the official order was proclaimed and the genocide began at least as early as August 1904. Furthermore, the eradication of the Herero continued after the genocide order was lifted.

Initially, the genocide of the Herero was achieved by means of German bullets and clubs, by hanging, by burning the huts where they lived or by forcing them into the desert to die. When the order was amended, the extermination continued in a less overt manner.

A few thousand Hereros were captured and placed in concentration camps, where thousands died due to ill treatment, disease and starvation. Different and smaller diet rations were given to Herero prisoners than to prisoners from other communities.

In addition, they were used as slave labour for both public and private enterprise. Some of the concentration camps were run by the colonial authorities, whereas others were run by private companies, such as Woermann shipping lines." – (Ibid., pp. 234 – 235. See also, cited by Jeremy Sarkin: Zimmerman has called the events in GSWA 'perhaps the first explicitly genocidal policy ever.' A. Zimmerman, "Adventures in the skin trade: German anthropology and colonial corporeality," in H.G. Penny & M. Bunzl, eds., *Worldly Provincialism: German Anthropology in the Age of Empire*, University of Michigan Press, Ann Arbor, Michigan, USA, 2003, p. 157; J. Sarkin, *Germany's Genocide of the Herero: Kaiser Wilhelm II, Hi General, His Settlers, His Soldiers*, p. 234).

The genocide of the Herero has been amply documented. What is clear is that it was pursued as official policy, sanctioned by the German government, and ruthlessly implemented by the German settlers and soldiers in South-West Africa who espoused the doctrine of white supremacy which they used to justify their total disregard for the lives of black people whom they considered to be members of the lesser breed on the lowest rung of the racial hierarchy. As Sarkin states:

"The experience of the Herero – while consistent with European and German colonial policy at the time – is among the most devastating endured by an indigenous people in Africa at the turn of the twentieth century." – (J. Sarkin, ibid., p. 237).

German imperial policy knew no bounds. That was during the time when the inferiority of non-whites, especially Africans, was widely accepted as a "scientific" fact, used to justify their conquest. They were an expendable commodity. They did not have any rights even in their own homeland, not even the right to life. Their property, including land, could be seized at will; and it was, to satisfy imperial ambitions.

Genocide was acceptable as a viable option, especially

with regard to "inferior" people; the extermination of the Herero being an indispensable exercise that also prepared Germany for another genocide on her own soil years later when six million Jews were exterminated by the Nazis.

Like those of other imperial powers, German expansionist ambitions were also justified on other grounds: to spread civilisation among savages. In reality, it was to exploit the indigenous people in the name of civilisation for the benefit of white settlers in Africa and for the betterment of Europe; although Africa's contribution to the development and industrialisation of Europe is deliberately ignored.

Dr. Walter Rodney, in his book *How Europe Underdeveloped Africa* which he wrote in the early seventies when he taught at the University of Dar es Salaam in Tanzania, addressed the subject well. And his work continues to stimulate and fuel debate almost four decades after it was first published by Bogle-L'Ouverture Publications, London, in 1972; and by Tanganyika Publishing House (TPH) in Dar es Salaam in 1973.

Although Germany did not have many colonies in Africa – it had only four – it ruthlessly exploited her possessions just like the other colonial powers did theirs. Besides German East Africa (Deutsch-Ostafrika) which was one colonial entity comprising Tanganyika, now mainland Tanzania, Ruanda and Urundi, what is now Namibia was the other prized possession of Germany on the African continent. It was, in fact, Germany's most prized colonial territory in Africa. And the German government had big plans for it.

The other German colonies on the continent were Togo and Cameroon. But even when combined with German East Africa, they were all dwarfed by German South-West Africa (GSWA) in terms of importance to Germany:

"GSWA was more than a distant acquisition to the German state. Rather, Germany considered it a second

Fatherland, an emigration destination for German settlers in search of more farmland and a *tabula rasa* upon which to impose German culture. This single-minded focus – among German colonial administrators and the German people at home and abroad – accounts for Germany's ruthless grip on the territory, regardless of the costs....

Berlin's investment in the territory, as well as that of German corporations at the time, demonstrate GSWA's vaulted status within Germany. As early as 1898, German capital dominated the GSWA economy, necessitating the protection of the German government. Germany responded to the call by investing 278 million marks in GSWA between 1884 and 1914, more than its expenditures in Cameroon, Togo and German East Africa combined. The years preceding and following the Herero rebellion witnessed the most intense spending." – (Jeremy Sarkin, *Germany's Genocide of the Herero: Kaiser Wilhelm II, His General, His Settlers, His Soldiers*, ibid., pp. 237).

Right from the beginning, Germany was determined to establish a racially stratified society, rigid in every conceivable way, in which the indigenous people would be at the mercy of the white settlers. But she also had other goals in order to consolidate white power over the black population:

"German deployed a disproportionate amount of troops to GSWA in comparison to its other colonies. Moreover, African conscripts were not permitted to serve in GSWA, unlike in Germany's other colonies, because of the sensitivity of the settler population.

Also, military forces were not the only people recruited to live in GSWA: from 1878, German colonial planners actively recruited German women to relocate to the province as an incentive to draw German men, but, more importantly, to end the proliferation of interracial relationships that had begun from the moment the first

Germans arrived.

Relations between German settlers and local women threatened, through the creation of a mixed race, to dilute the Reich's authority in the colony and the very 'Germanness' of the new state. Germany promptly passed edicts outlawing interracial marriages.

It was Governor Leutwein's and the Herero's resistance to Germany's plan to create a German state in Southern Africa that ignited the desire for outright extermination of the tribe. Correspondence from the settlers to Berlin in the years leading up to the genocide indicated the emigrants' increasing fatigue with the Governor's lax policies toward the Herero, including restrictions on the acquisition of Herero land.

The settlers saw such policies as a direct threat to their economic and cultural livelihoods in this 'new Germany' and threatened to take matters into their own hands should Berlin remain idle." – (Ibid., pp. 237 – 238).

The stage was set for a deadly confrontation. It was clear from the beginning that the German settlers in what is now Namibia were as much responsible for the genocide of the Herero, and the Nama, as the German government itself was. And it provided them with the help they needed to achieve their goals in the new colony, although there were some people in Germany who were opposed to their government and to the racist policies which were being pursued in German South-West Africa.

Another factor which motivated Germany to seek and establish colonies in Africa was the international situation during that period. It was the era of imperialism, hence expansionism, when European powers were competing for glory and global influence, for land, natural resources especially raw materials, and for markets, outside Europe. Two powers, Britain and France, had already claimed vast expanses of territory across the African continent and Germany did not want to be left out of the race.

The Berlin conference itself which led to the partition of the African continent during the Scramble for Africa was held in Berlin, Germany, from November 1884 to February 1885. As Sarkin states with regard to Germany and the international politics during that period, especially at the turn of the twentieth century:

"The political landscape in the international arena, as well as in the German state, also drove Germany's aggressive behaviour in its colonies. In the early 1900s, colonies were a means by which Western states achieved stature on the international stage. This fuelled Germany's race to acquire and retain as much land as possible outside of Europe.

Germany built its colonies upon two distinct models: those for trade and those for settlement....GSWA fell into the latter category and thus merited the harsh rule that Germany imposed upon indigenous people who threatened its aims. However, Germany's barbaric treatment of its settlement holdings led to it being the first state to lose its possessions after World War I.

Moreover, Germany was not in the same league as other Western powers, such as Great Britain and France, when it came to the race to colonise the New World. As a result of Germany's late entry into the colonial race, it engaged in particularly brutal methods to acquire sufficient territory – in size and prestige – in order to place it on par with its European brethren. This inferiority complex is partly to blame for Germany's atrocious treatment of its colonies, as it sought to acquire trade routes, emigration space and new cultural outposts.

Thus, when the Herero dared to rise up against German oppression in 1904, colonial soldiers, administrators and settlers responded swiftly and brutally, calling for their outright extermination in the wake of the slaughter of less than 200 settlers. This disproportionate response was due in part to Germany's desire for land, cattle and security, but it was also about avenging Germany's honour on the international stage.

The difficulty that Germans faced in quelling Herero discontent created further embarrassment for the country at a time when national prestige was measured in part by colonial conquest. A decisive victory over and strong message to the Herero was thus essential as a matter of German pride and stature." – (Ibid., p. 238).

Namibia also had a special place in the hearts of many Germans, national leaders and businessmen in Germany among others, and the settlers in that part of Africa. German South West Africa was not just another German colony like German East Africa or the other two German colonies on the continent: Cameroon and Togo.

The Germans wanted Namibia to be an integral part of Germany. It was intended to be a white man's land similar to what the British wanted to do in Kenya when they described their East African colony as "white man's country," and to what they did in Australia and New Zealand when they occupied and turned them into British possessions and founded white nations – which were predominantly British – on those lands at the expense of the indigenous people:

"Thus GSWA was not just any colony. Germany hoped it would become a 'new Germany,' a place that could accommodate the thousands of émigrés that Germany had been losing to the United States ad other countries because the Fatherland's territory and markets had become too small for its booming population.

However, to entice Germans to move to Southern Africa as early as 1882, the country's leadership had to promise them land, security and the opportunity to live as Germans lived in a place distant from Europe. Media reports and correspondence that characterised GSWA as Germany's last hope for settlement...created a greater need for these polices. To the extent that the Herero interfered with Germany's pursuit of its goal for a new cultural outpost in Africa – through resistance or sovereignty over valuable land, German forces and settlers felt they had to extinguish these people." – (Ibid.)

They proceeded to do so with a ruthlessness unprecedented in the history of the region, besides the massacres of the Khoi Khoi and the San – in varying numbers – which had been going in southern Africa, at the hands of the white settlers, since the 1600s.

The extermination of the Herero was systematic. And it was done purely in the interest of Germany as an imperial power without the slightest concern for the well-being of the indigenous people including those of other tribes, especially the Nama who, like the Herero, were also targeted for elimination because they rose up against colonial oppression and exploitation.

The genocide was carried out with pride by a nation which, like the other European powers, also saw itself as the embodiment of civilisation, obviously a civilisation that excluded Africans as members of an "inferior race," hence candidates for extermination. As Sarkin states with regard to the aims of the Herero genocide:

"The authoritarian nature of the German state did not drive Germany's genocide against the Herero. While it is true that, at the time, Germany fostered a militarised culture that facilitated the execution of the genocide, historical events indicate that this culture was not the driving force behind the state's policy to exterminate the Herero. Rather, the 1904 genocide bore the twin aims – one philosophical and one practical – of preserving German pride and acquiring land from the Herero....

The genocide had the philosophical goal of raising Germany's pride within its own state and Europe. The violent means by which German authorities snuffed out the Herero rebellion not only intended to demonstrate its force to the Herero, but to other nations and the German people themselves. The military response was yet another method by which Germany could demonstrate its unwillingness to yield colonial ground – politically or territorially....

General von Trotha...consciously viewed Herero massacres as a means by which to crush the tribe. While public executions of Herero had begun well before 1904, the genocide order systematised the practice and clearly linked it to Germany's land and power grab in the colony. The General's outrage at Herero resistance further inspired him to teach the rebellious tribe a lesson and secure Germany's authority as a colonial power in the eyes of its European neighbours.

Secondly, as Germany's targeting of the Herero made clear, the extermination, expulsion and enslavement of the tribe was a practical attempt to acquire land to appease the demands of the growing German settler population in GSWA. In an otherwise inhospitable terrain plagued by drought and mountains, the Herero nation possessed much of what little arable land was available in GSWA at the time.

Moreover,...limited land allocation by the German government to former soldiers did not satisfy settlers' demands. The clamouring of German settlers – who, beginning in 1903, were lured to GSWA with the promise of land and opportunity – for Herero land, at any cost fuelled the colonial and national administrations' violent anti-Herero campaigns....

The Herero were singled out for extermination by Germany because they inhabited the lion's share of arable land – to say nothing of cattle – from among Namibia's many ethnic groups.

However, German officials did not resort to violence immediately. They began with campaigns of trickery or deceit. For example, they changed the unit of measure agreed upon with their Herero trading partners or plied Herero chiefs with alcohol to secure land transfers. However, the Germans failed to grasp the indigenous concept of land tenure, which revolved around collective usufruct rather than individual title.

Thus, despite the contracts that Germans thought they had concluded with the Herero, the tribe never seriously entertained the idea that it had completely surrendered its sovereign territorial rights to the settlers. As a result, Germany employed more forceful means of land acquisition, such as military and bureaucratic control, followed by outright force between 1894 and 1915." – (Ibid., pp. 239 – 240).

The Herero faced other misfortunes. Conquest by the Germans was bad enough. They could not match Germany's military might. Then came natural catastrophes. Nature itself seemed to have conspired with their conquerors to make them suffer even more. Natural forces helped the Germans to not only seize even more land from the Herero but also livestock:

"Unfortunately, nature intervened in the Herero's quest to retain their land and between 1896 and 1899 the tribe was beset with an ecological blow that compelled it to cede some of its land rights. A rinderpest epidemic decimated much of the Herero's livestock, while having less impact upon the settlers' inoculated stocks.

With the Herero in a weak economic position, German settlers instituted several legislative ploys to divest the tribe of its remaining assets.

The colonists enacted draconian trespass and credit laws that the Herero could only repay in cattle for lack of currency. Not only did this dispossession leave the Herero economically depressed, but the absence of meat and milk compromised their diet and the loss of stock injured their sense of ethnic pride given that cattle were integral to

Herero culture.

As a result of these handicaps, the Herero were forced into the labour market and remained justifiably bitter against the Germans.

Thus, it was little surprise when the Herero rose up against the settlers in GSWA in 1904. Contrary to the wisdom of the time, the rebellion did not take Germany by surprise. Indeed, it had arguably designed the policies presaging the conflict to provoke precisely such a response.

As a result, the revolt presented the Kaiser with the opportunity – in the guise of admittedly brutal, though smaller-scale massacres of settlers by Herero rebels – to unveil his new settlement policy, which required the commission of genocide. The speed with which the Germans disposed the Herero – in less than a year – indicates that Germany had planned this policy extensively. It was not simply a response to a surprise Herero attack.

A third latent motivation behind the Herero genocide was Germany's racist ideology that placed the Aryan race above all others, a belief that would reappear decades later as a motivation behind the Holocaust. German propaganda at the time cast the Herero as an inferior race and at the same time characterised the tribe as launching a racist offensive against settlers via mutilation and indiscriminate murder.

This dualistic public relations campaign enabled the German state to muster support at home for its suppression of any Herero autonomy in GSWA.

While evidence suggests that the previously mentioned practical and philosophical concerns motivated the genocide, Germany's racist ideology certainly facilitated the execution of the order.

This ideology can be found in several of Von Trotha's statements,...evincing his hatred for the Herero people and his belief that they 'only respond' – i.e. vacate their land –

to brute force. Such statements serve as further evidence that Germany's actions at the turn of the twentieth century did not merely aim to quell a spontaneous indigenous insurgency but rather represented a premeditated, intentional extermination of the entire Herero tribe in the names of nationalism, land and racism.

Not even the isolated incidents of German humanity toward the Herero can blunt the historical record – in the form of newspaper accounts and government statements at the time – evidencing genocide.

Even Germany's Western counterparts – the very nations to whom Germany sought to demonstrate its strength – expressed their disapproval of the events unfolding in GSWA in 1905." – (Ibid., pp. 240 - 241).

Besides the striking parallels which have been drawn between the genocide against the Herero as well as the Nama and the extermination of the Jews in Nazi Germany, another disturbing reality is the historical roots of both holocausts, rooted in the teachings of some German and other European intellectuals and philosophers who tried to justify the superiority of the white race over other races; a point underscored – also at the Nuremberg trials – in a book by David Olusoga and Casper Erichsen, *The Kaiser's Holocaust: Germany's Forgotten Genocide and the Colonial Roots of Nazism*:

"This is the great post-war myth: the comforting fantasy that the Nazis were a new order of monsters and that their crimes were without precursor or precedent. They were not.

Much of Nazi ideology and many of the crimes committed in its name were part of a longer trend within European history. Nazism was both a culmination and a distortion of decades of German and European history and philosophy. It was, in part, the final homecoming of theories and practices that Europeans had developed and perfected in far-flung corners of the world during the last phase of imperial conquest.

There is nothing within that historical subsoil that made the ultimate flowering of Nazism inevitable, but there is much that makes it understandable. At Nuremberg, however, all such historical precedent was plunged into darkness. 'The greatest history seminar ever' did not look back far enough into history.

The Nuremberg Trials took as their start date the year in which a new age of barbarism had seemed to overwhelm Europe – 1914. This was year zero for the prosecuting nations, all of whom agreed that World War I had been the calamity that set Europe on course for the greater tragedies of World War II. The generation who had mutilated their own continent had, in the process, been disfigured politically and ideologically. The national enmities and the trauma of mass, mechanised killing had sown seeds for the savagery that lay at the heart of Nazism. At Nuremberg, everything before Somme, Verdun and Ypres was regarded as mere detail, as it was presumed that Nazism as an ideology had emerged fully formed from the chaos and resentment following Germany's defeat in 1918.

In its narrow historical focus, if in no other way, the trial of Hermann Göring was typical. When questioning began, on the morning of 13 March, Göring was asked for a 'short account of his life up to the outbreak of the First World War.' The president of the court repeatedly stressed the need for brevity. It was only when Göring's account reached 1914 that he was encouraged to elaborate and detailed questioning began. Over the course of the 218-day trial, Hermann Göring, the lead defendant, delivered only four sentences about his life before World War I and the role of his family in Germany's longer history.

Had the Nuremberg prosecutors looked further into Göring's past, and his nation's, they would have discovered another story of death camps and racial genocide. They would have seen that the ideas of many of the philosophers, scientists and soldiers whose theories inspired Hitler had underpinned an earlier, forgotten holocaust. Perhaps they might have recognised a continuity in German history and understood that Nazism was anything but unique. They might also have grasped the importance of the few sentences Göring uttered at his cross-examination, in which he described his family background and the world before 1914 that had formed him and his generation.

Göring, for his own reasons, was determined to use his last stand in the dock at Nuremberg as an opportunity to place the Third Reich within the mainstream of world history. One strand of his defence strategy was to claim that Nazism and the principles on which it had been founded were not unique but merely Germanic incarnations of the same forces with which the prosecuting powers had built up their own empires and expanded their own power.

....Göring directly compared the crimes he was defending in court with those perpetrated in the empires of the victor nations. The British Empire, he claimed, had 'not been built up with due regard for principles of humanity,' while America and 'hacked its way to a rich Lebensraum by revolution, massacre and war.'

Göring's attempts to compare the crimes of the Third Reich to the genocides and massacres of the age of empire could easily be dismissed as a desperate defence tactic. But behind the bluster, arrogance and amorality of a man who was patently unable to confront his own crimes, there is an uncomfortable truth.

When Göring was asked to speak briefly about his life before 1914, he outlined what he called 'a few points which are significant with relation to my later development.' He told the court of his father, who had been the 'first Governor of South-West Africa,' pointing out that in that capacity the elder Göring had 'connections at that time with two British statesmen, Cecil Rhodes and the elder Chamberlain.'

Hermann Göring's father, Dr Heinrich Göring, had indeed been a key factor in his son's 'later development.' In 1885 he had been appointed by Chancellor Bismarck to help establish the German colony of South-West Africa, today the southern African nation of Namibia. Dr Göring's role was one of slow negotiations with the indigenous African peoples, with no garrison and little funding. Fifteen years later, an official Nazi biographer of Hermann Göring shamelessly attempted to glamorise the elder Göring's record as an empire-builder. It describes how 'Young [Hermann] Göring listened, his eyes sparkling with excitement, to his father's stories about his adventures in bygone days. The inquisitive and imaginative lad was...thrilled by his accounts of his pioneer work as a Reichs Commissar for South-West Africa, of his journeys through the Kalahari Desert and his fights with Maharero, the black king of Okahandja.'

In truth, Heinrich Göring had no fights with any of the 'black kings' of South-West Africa. For three years he travelled across the southern deserts with a wagon full of so-called 'protection treaties,' desperately attempting to dupe or cajole the leaders of the local African peoples into signing away rights to their land. When his promises of protection were exposed as empty, he was recognised as a fraud and summarily expelled.

What inspired the elder Göring to volunteer for service in Africa was that, like many Germans in the late nineteenth century, he could foresee a time in which the land of that continent might become living space into which the German race could expand. It was imagined that Germany's colonial subjects – the black Africans of her new-found empire – would become the cheap labour of the German farmers. Those tribes unable or unwilling to accept their diminished status would face the industrial weapons that Göring knew would one day appear in the

South-West. Those Africans who stood in the way of the German race simply had no future. Like his son fifty years later, Dr Heinrich Göring understood that weaker peoples of the earth were destined to fall prey to the stronger, and rightly so." – (David Olusoga and Casper W. Erichsen, *The Kaiser's Holocaust: Germany's Forgotten Genocide and the Colonial Roots of Nazism*, London, UK: Faber and Faber Ltd., 2010, pp. 3 –4, 5 – 7).

The foundations for genocide had already been laid. It was only a matter of time before those beliefs and ideas would be given concrete expression:

"These beliefs were hardly controversial in certain political circles in the late nineteenth-century Europe....
Colonial genocide has always been a drawn-out process of massacres, famines, enslavement and hidden liquidations. A form of warfare without glory or glamour, it has never been the stuff of memoirs. The wars that built the British and French empires, that kept the rubber flowing in the Belgian Congo, that cleared the Pampas of Argentina and the Great Plains of the US, have similarly been overshadowed by an alternative and more glamorous history of colonialism, focusing on great battles and notable heroic figures.
The empires of Germany's Second and Third Reichs died soon after birth. The former took with it hundreds of thousands of lives; the latter, millions. Both were inspired by a nationalist and racial fantasy that began in the late nineteenth century. What was forgotten at Nuremberg and has been forgotten ever since is that the imperial ambitions and many of the crimes committed by the Third Reich have a precedent in German history. The nightmare that was visited upon the people of Eastern Europe in the 1940s was unique in its scale and in the industrialisation of the killing. The fusion of racism and Fordism was a Nazi innovation. Yet in many other respects, Germany had been

here before.

Five thousand miles from Nuremberg lies the tiny Namibian town of Lüderitz. Trapped between the freezing waters of the South Atlantic and the endless dune fields of the Namib Desert, it is without doubt one of the strangest places on earth.

The sea of sand dunes stops literally on the edge of town; they seem encamped, as if waiting for permission to enter. In the mornings, when the desert is screened behind a thick curtain of sea mist, Lüderitz looks completely un-tropical. It resembles an overgrown Arctic research station or a defunct whaling settlement, perhaps in the Falkland Islands or Greenland. Even on a good day the town looks half dead.

Most of the buildings are brightly painted in reds, oranges and yellows, and are randomly scattered over the half-dozen or so hills that surround the wide and blustery bay. The vivid colours of the buildings contrast with the sea-weathered rocks of the hills, which resemble wrinkled and dusty elephant hide. Recently the main avenues have been tarmacked, but the back alleys remain rough and pitted dirt tracks. Everywhere piles of dust and sand linger on street corners. A visitor arriving by ship would see nothing to indicate they were in Africa. On landing, their confusion would be compounded by a white population speaking German and hundreds of black Africans speaking the Afrikaans of the Boers.

Today most visitors to Lüderitz arrive by road. The B4 highway, an arrow-straight ribbon of black tarmac, shoots across the Namib Desert following the line of the old narrow-gauge railway that once connected the southern settlements of what was then German South-West Africa to Lüderitz Bay and from there to the great shipping lanes of Imperial Germany.

Each night, out beyond the town limits, the sand dunes inch their way onto the tarmac of the B4, in their nightly attempt to suffocate the town. Each morning a huge yellow excavation machine thunders out of town to clear the highway. The desert itself seems determined to seal Lüderitz off from the outside world. Like the forests of the Congo as witnessed by Joseph Conrad, the dunes of the Namib seem to be waiting with 'ominous patience...for the passing away of a fantastic invasion.'

In 1905 this tiny settlement was chosen as the site of a new experiment in warfare. Until perhaps only 30 years ago, Lüderitz's oldest residents had their own memories of what happened here in the first years of the twentieth century; they said nothing. Today it remains a secret. The tourist information office on Bismarck Strasse has nothing to say on the subject, none of the guidebooks to Namibia mention it and most of the history books they recommend as further reading are similarly mute. Yet what happened in Lüderitz between 1905 and 1907 makes it one of the pivotal sites in the history of the twentieth century.

The experiment took place on Shark Island, a squat, mean-looking ridge of rock that lies just across the bay, in full view of the whole town. It was in its way a resounding success, bringing to life a new device: a military innovation that went on to become an emblem of the century and take more lives than the atom bomb. For here, on the southern edge of Africa, the death camp was invented." – (Ibid., pp. 7, 8 – 10).

It went on to have an impact far beyond Africa. And its impact still resonates today in many countries round the globe, especially in remembrance of the Jewish holocaust, but tragically not of the genocide that was perpetrated against the Herero and the Nama in what is now Namibia because it is buried in history; not even acknowledged as a footnote to the history of imperial might, let alone of mankind:

"Today Shark Island is the municipal camping site for the town of Lüderitz. A new restaurant overlooking the island offers excellent South African wines and South Atlantic seafood. Diners are encouraged to sit out on the balcony and enjoy views of an island upon which, a century ago, three and a half thousand Africans were systematically liquidated. Just a couple of hundred yards away, beneath the waters of Lüderitz Bay, divers have reported Shark Island to be surrounded by a ring of human bones and rusted steel manacles. The human beings who were made to wear those chains and whose remains lie beneath the waves have been almost erased from Namibian and world history. The names of their tribes – the Herero, Witbooi Nama, Bethanie Nama – mean nothing to most people outside of Namibia." – (Ibid., pp. 10 – 11).

There are other secrets as well, and buried memories, which are unearthed and revived only once in a while:

"Shark Island is not Namibia's only secret. There is a mass grave under the sidings of the railway station in the Namibian capital Windhoek, and another on the outskirts of the seaside holiday town of Swakopmund. The national museum itself is housed in a German fort which was built on the site of another concentration camp.
But for most, Namibia is seen as a quaint backwater, a relic of Germany's short-lived foray into colonialism, and a microcosm of late nineteenth-century Germany that has somehow survived intact into the twenty-first. In the gift shops tourists buy postcards and picture books that depict this lost idyll. Streets are named after military commanders from aristocratic families. In the shopping malls one can buy replica hats of the *Schutztruppe*, the German colonial army. They come emblazoned with the red, white and black insignia of Germany's Second Reich – the age of the Kaisers. The German imperial flag, with its severe black eagle, is also for sale, alongside local history books that skirt over the wars that were fought

under that banner – wars that almost wiped out two of Namibia's indigenous peoples.

What Germany's armies and civilian administrators did in Namibia is today a lost history, but the Nazis knew it well. When the *Schutztruppe* attempted to exterminate the Herero and Nama peoples of Namibia a century ago, Hitler was a schoolboy of fifteen. In 1904, he lived in a continent that was electrified by the stories of German heroism and African barbarism emanating from what was then German South-West Africa.

Eighteen years after the Herero-Nama genocide, Hitler became closely associated with a veteran of the conflict. In 1922 he was recruited into an ultra-right wing militia in Munich that was indirectly under the command of the charismatic General Franz von Epp, who had been a lieutenant during Germany's wars against the Herero and Nama. As both a young colonial soldier and, later, a leading member of the Nazi party, von Epp was a fervent believer in the *Lebensraum* theory (the theory of living space), and spent his life propagating the notion that the German people needed to expand their living space at the expense of lower races, whether in Africa or Eastern Europe.

It would be an exaggeration to claim that Hitler was von Epp's protégé, but in the chaos of post-World War I Munich, von Epp, perhaps more than any figure other than Hitler himself, made the Nazi party possible.

It was through von Epp, in various convoluted ways, that Hitler met many of the men who were to become the elite of the party: von Epp's deputy was Ernst Röhm, the founder of the Nazi storm troopers.

Via the party's connections to von Epp and other old soldiers of Germany's African colonies, Röhm and Hitler were able to procure a consignment of surplus colonial *Schutztruppe* uniforms. Designed for warfare on the golden savannah of Africa, the shirts were desert brown in colour: the Nazi street thugs who wore them became known as Brown Shirts.

Today von Epp is viewed as a minor player in the history of Nazism. When the party came to power in 1933, his role was to campaign for the return of the colonies lost at Versailles for which he had fought as a young man. But by 1939 von Epp had become a marginal figure, excluded from Hitler's inner circle and eclipsed by younger men. His critical role in the development of the party as a political force has been overlooked. Yet in his writings before the war, Hitler recognised the role von Epp had played. In countless pictures and party propaganda films, von Epp and Hitler stand side by side.

In the last pictures taken of him, von Epp sits next to Hermann Göring. Both have been stripped of their uniforms and decorations as they await trial under American custody at Mondorf-les-Bains. The old general looks gaunt, slumped back in his chair squinting at the photographer. A generation older than many of his fellow inmates, von Epp died in custody just weeks after those pictures were taken.

Had he lived to stand trial alongside Göring, might von Epp's testimony have led the prosecutors to see the continuities between the genocide he had taken part in as a young infantry lieutenant and the acts of the Third Reich?

Today the memory of Germany's empire has become detached from European history. Nineteenth-century colonialism has long been viewed as a specialist subject, a historical annexe in which events were played out in near-complete isolation from Europe. Yet in colonial history, ideas, methods and individuals always move in both directions.

Hitler's 1941 statement that he would treat the Slavs 'like a colonial people' has lost its resonance, but for the Führer it was a phrase full of meaning, a shorthand readily understood by a generation of Nazis who were boys when the Kaiser sent his armies to Africa to destroy native rebels who had placed themselves in the path of Germany's racial destiny." – (Ibid., pp. 11 – 13).

Some Germans – young and old – in contemporary times have acknowledged the sins of their forefathers, with some of them even acknowledging collective guilt by their nation of which they an an integral part, thus forever linking them to its past including the terrible injustices it perpetrated against non-whites such as the Herero and the Nama in the name of white supremacy. But there are those who do not even want to use the word "genocide" to describe what happened in German South-West Africa when the Herero and the Nama were almost exterminated. They include government officials in spite of their admission that what the German rulers and soldiers did to the indigenous people of South-West Africa was wrong. As Jeremy Sarkin states in his book, *Colonial Genocide and Reparations Claims in the 21st Century: The Socio-Legal Context of Claims under International Law by the Herero against Germany for Genocide in Namibia, 1904 – 1908*:

"In 2004, the centenary of the Herero genocide was commemorated with various ceremonies in Namibia, including conferences and anniversaries to observe specific events that had occurred exactly 100 years ago....The Namibian event...included the German government....

Two complementary groups or committees decided to hold commemorative events throughout the year. One, The Coordinating Committee for the Commemoration of the Ovaherero Genocide, 100 Years After, was established as a community-based, non-political organization. Two events were held in January 2004 to commemorate the official beginning of the war: one in Windhoek and one in Okahandja – Waterberg – where the battle of the Hamakari took place.

The Namibian government did not officially take part

in the January commemorations, apparently because of the differences among the two committees, but individuals, ministers, and high-ranking government officials did attend one or the other function. At the later events, various government officials participated more fully and even delivered addresses.

The controversial nature of the commemorations gave rise to a perception that President Nujoma did not want to be part of these events and had declined several invitations to attend and participate. However, at times, President Nujoma has seemingly been sensitive to the war and the atmosphere it has caused.

In August 2003, when a German Scout group, the *Deutsche Pfadfinder Bund*, wanted to commemorate the war – as they had done annually – by touring the burial ground of German soldiers, President Nujoma prohibited it, arguing that the event was 'provocation of the highest order.' Minister Ngarikutuke Tjiriange also stated that the commemoration would have seen 'a breakdown of peace, law, and order in the country.'

At the Okahandja event in 2004, Germany's ambassador to Namibia and Chief Riruako spoke, both conveying messages of peace, reconciliation, and development. After these commemoration events, the two committees vowed to work toward a single agenda, dispelling perceptions that the two were at odds. Subsequently, later events, i.e., the anniversary of the battle of Waterberg in August 2004 and the commemoration of the issuing of the extermination order in October 2004, involved both committees.

Hence, the Namibian genocide was commemorated with a number of events in 2004. One of these was a conference at the University of Namibia, themed 'Decontaminating the Namibian Past.' It aimed to reduce the misrepresentations and ignorance that exist about the Herero, achieve greater tolerance among the various communities in Namibia, and 'promote empathy in

Namibia's historical discourses.' One panel of the 2004 University of Namibia conference focused on Damara history." – (Jeremy Sarkin, *Colonial Genocide and Reparations Claims in the 21st Century: The Socio-Legal Context of Claims under International Law by the Herero against Germany for Genocide in Namibia, 1904 – 1908*, Westport, Connecticut, USA: Greenwood Publishing Group, 2009, pp. 56, 57 – 58).

Yet acknowledgement of guilt by Germany has not gone far enough despite the government's professed commitment to reconciliation because of its refusal to pay compensation for the extermination of the Herero and the Nama and even to admit it was genocide; at a conference in Germany, the government did not even want to use the word "genocide," although its representative did in Namibia, grudgingly. As Sarkin states:

"Not all the conferences and events of the centenary year have been unreservedly positive. One conference that caused heated debate and controversy in both Germany and Namibia was a symposium held in Bremen in November 2004 to discuss the reconciliation process between the German Government and the Herero.
Among the delegates were the German Minister of Economic Development and Cooperation, Heidemarie Wieczorek-Zeul, who had offered the German apology three months before, and Namibia's minister of Information and Broadcasting, Nangolo Mumba. This conference did not promote the reconciliation process, as the Herero leadership did not feel it was a useful or legitimate attempt to address their concerns. On the contrary, they perceived it to be retarding the efforts to establish dialogue.
The Paramount Chief emphasized that reconciliation had to happen between the German Government and the Herero, and voiced his concern that 'reconciliation cannot

be the exercise of an academic conference' and that he detected attempts to divide the Hereros. He urged delegates to 'Stop adding insult to injury by encouraging division amongst our people. Any continuation of such evil designs will be viewed by all Ovahereros as a second round of genocide being perpetrated against our people. We shall resist that with all legitimate means at our disposal.'

Chief Riruako listed the conditions for reconciliation as being (1) a genuine apology by the Government of the Federal Republic of Germany (FRG); (2) acceptance of that apology by the descendants of the victims of the war of extermination against the Ovaherero; (3) willingness by the FRG government to engage the leadership of the Ovaherero in looking for practical and meaningful ways to make good for the physical, material, emotional, and psychological damage done to the Ovaherero by the German colonial authorities.

According to newspaper reports, Minister Wieczorek-Zeul was visibly upset by this response and commented: 'I heard very well what the Chief said, and I think that some o his remarks are detrimental to the process of reconciliation. It is unacceptable to use the word genocide in this context.'" – (Ibid., p. 58).

The refusal by the colonial powers to admit wrongdoing and call it exactly what is – massacres, extermination, genocide and so on – is very much an integral part of imperial history in order to justify conquest of the members of "inferior races," thus upholding white supremacy; so is the changing of local names to replace them with European ones from the land of the conquerors, which is tantamount to erasing the history of the indigenous people of the places whose names have been changed. The places with the new European names start a life of their own as if nothing had existed before. Their history is buried.

The imperial powers have been notorious for refusing to acknowledge guilt and offer compensation because they contend they did nothing wrong, or whatever they did to the indigenous people was very much a part of their mission to civilise them even if something went wrong in pursuit of that "noble" mission. As South African prime minister, Hendrik Verwoerd, bluntly stated:

"We are the people who brought civilisation to Africa."

It was in response to British prime minister, Harold Macmillan, who stated in the South African Parliament in February 1960 that the "wind of change" was blowing through Africa, with Africans demanding independence and nothing was going to stop that.

The British government itself never admitted that what Britain did to the Kikuyu in Kenya during Mau Mau in the 1950s was wrong. And it refused to pay compensation to the victims of the atrocities – tens of thousands of them, at least 100,000, many of whom perished in concentration camps – until it was sued. And there are a lot of people in Britain who still contend that their country does not owe the victims anything – they do not deserve any compensation; a sentiment shared by those in the corridors of power. As Tim Stanley stated in his article, "The British Must not Rewrite the History of the Mau Mau Revolt," in *The Telegraph*, London, 6 June 2013:

"Our role as the colonial power in the 1950s uprising in Kenya was shameful, but not deserving of compensation.

The Government has announced that Kenyans abused by British colonial forces during the Mau Mau uprising of the 1950s will receive compensation totalling £20 million, and that it regrets the 'suffering and injustice.' Be of no doubt: these people went through terrible things.

Wambuga Wa Nyingi, a former detainee at the bloody camp Hola, who says he was not a Mau Mau fighter, claims that he was 'battered on the back of my head and around my neck repeatedly with a club.' His unconscious body was mistaken for a corpse and dumped in a room with 11 murdered men. Mr Nyingi slept among the dead for two days before he was discovered.

But before we express regret or say sorry for anything, we have to make sure that we entirely understand what we're talking about. In the case of the Mau Mau uprising, only one side of the story tends to be told – a story that serves a particular political purpose. It's the tale of an evil imperial power that used internment and torture to keep hold of a beautiful African colony that only ever wanted to be free. It is a fantasy version of history.

The Mau Mau was a terrorist organisation, dominated by Kenya's major ethnic grouping, the Kikuyu. Kikuyu extremists were furious about what they saw as the theft of their land by white settlers, so they launched a war from the jungle against the colonial authorities. Crucially, like many terrorist groups they enforced discipline by declaring that anyone who was not with them was against them – which meant they also declared war on the vast majority of moderate Africans who did not share their demands. Something that began as a nationalist uprising quickly turned into an ethnic civil war.

Arguably the most famous victims of the Mau Mau were the white settler Ruck family, who lived in the Rift Valley just north of Nairobi. In January 1953, Mau Mau fighters stormed their remote farm house, and hacked to death Roger and Esmee Ruck and their six-year-old son, Michael. The images of bloodied teddy bears and broken toy trains strewn across Michael's bedroom floor inflamed British opinion. But the murder of a white settler family was actually very rare during the uprising: the Mau Mau preferred to kill Africans. In total, they murdered at least 1,800 fellow Kikuyus and Africans from other tribes, compared with just 200 British soldiers and 32 European settlers. African women and children were frequent targets.

One story that communicates the full horror of this war is the Lari massacre of March 1953. Lari was an area populated by Kikuyu who had refused to take the Mau Mau oath and so were regarded as traitors. The Mau Mau descended upon the community like something from hell. Some were slashed to death, some burned alive in their huts; many were maimed for life. Pregnant women were disembowelled, children were murdered. The massacre claimed 120 lives and bitter memories of the event still divide the Lari area today. It is one of many reasons why post-independence Kenya refused to recognise Mau Mau claims on ancestral lands and banned it as an organisation."

Even when Britain conceded – only after being sued – that she committed injustices against the Kikuyu during Mau Mau, she did not fully acknowledge her guilt. As Mike Pflanz, reporting from Nairobi, Kenya, stated in his article, "Mau Mau: Britain 'sincerely regrets' Colonial-era Abuses," in *The Telegraph*, London, 6 June 2013:

"Britain announced compensation for thousands of Mau Mau veterans, saying that it 'sincerely regretted' years of 'suffering and injustice' carried out under its imperial rule of Kenya, but stopped short of a full apology.

The brutal suppression of an independence rebellion led to torture, internment without trial and excessive numbers of executions, William Hague, the Foreign Secretary, said in a statement to Parliament.

He confirmed that more than 5,200 claimants would share compensation from the Government of £13.9 million, but said that the out-of-court settlement did not mean Britain was legally liable for the abuses, although he said the settlement was about a 'process of reconciliation.'

'I would like to make clear now and for the first time ... that we understand the pain and grievance felt by those who were involved,' Mr Hague said. 'The British Government recognises that Kenyans were subject to torture and other forms of ill treatment at the hands of the colonial administration. [We] sincerely regret that these abuses took place.'

Each of the 5,228 individuals will receive roughly £2,600 in compensation, the equivalent of educating one child for seven years, or of buying a second-hand car. Britain will also help to pay for a new memorial in Nairobi to what Mr Hague called 'victims of torture and ill-treatment during the colonial era.'

'The money is not the point, it was the apology that we have been asking for all this time,' said Paul Kimotho, 75, who was imprisoned and lost all but five of his teeth during beatings under interrogation by British officers. 'Now we Mau Mau and the British people can be brothers again and move forward in a spirit of development and friendship.'

More than 200 of the claimants gathered in an upmarket hotel in Nairobi to hear Christian Turner, Britain's High Commissioner to Kenya, read sections of Mr Hague's speech.

Women ululated and elderly men clapped and struggled to their feet for short shuffling dances as the deal was announced.

'Today's celebration is a true testimony to the fact that all those who commit serious human rights abuses violations, regardless of their standing...in society, or their might as nations, must be held to account,' said Atsango Chesoni, director of the Kenya Human Rights Commission.

A British personal injury law firm, Leigh Day, brought a test case to the High Court in London.

Judges rejected the Foreign Office's argument that the alleged crimes took place so long ago that a fair trial would be impossible.

'I take my hat off to Mr Hague for having the courage to make today's statement…albeit he was looking down the barrel of the gun in terms of a court process which he had a strong chance of losing,' Martyn Day, the firm's founder, said.

The Government will pay his firm £6 million in costs.

'This was a case that took four years, involved teams of up to 30 lawyers, and required the help of experts across the world,' said Dan Leader, Leigh Day's representative in Nairobi."

In neighbouring German East Africa (Deutsch-Ostafrika), my home country which was renamed Tanganyika and later Tanzania, Germany never acknowledged responsibility for the deaths of at least 200,000 – probably up to 300,000 or more – people who perished during the Maji Maji war of resistance against brutal German rule between 1905 and 1907, coincidentally or not, during the same period the genocide against the Herero and the Nama took place in German South-West Africa (Deutsch-Südwestafrika).

There are those who say about half a million people died during Maji Maji. And the grievances were similar – it was as if the German rulers in both German East Africa and German South-West Africa had a meeting and agreed to use extremely brutal tactics against the natives around the same time:

"The Herero and Nama uprising was followed by the Maji Maji Rebellion between 1905 and 1907 against German colonial rule in East Africa. The Maji Maji grievances would include the forced labor of African individuals to grow cotton for export, high taxation, and the killing of large segments of the population. This and more, led to open rebellion in July of 1905.

The Maji Maji fighter had overwhelming numbers, and used guerrilla tactics to their advantage. It took two years for German machine guns and cannons, along with the systematic destruction of villages, wells, fields, and food stores, to extinguish the last members of the rebellion. In the end, it is believed that between 200,000 and 500,000 African soldiers and civilians lost their lives in the conflict; the resulting famine would kill thousands more."
– (Asoka Esuruoso and Philipp Khabo Koepsell, eds., *Arriving in the Future: Stories of Home and Exile*, Berlin, Germany: epubli GmbH, 2014, p. 21).

Compensation to the survivors of the atrocities and to the families of those who died during Maji Maji was out of the question. As an imperial power, Germany felt that what she did in her colony of Deutsch-Ostafrika was the right thing to do in fulfillment of her mission of ruling and exploiting the natives, regardless of how many of them died during the conflict.

There are cases similar to that in other parts of Africa wherever imperial rule was imposed on the indigenous people by the conquerors from Europe in order to exploit them. Their lives meant nothing to the colonial rulers.

In the case of Namibia, it was Germany itself which almost ruled out reconciliation by refusing even to use the word "genocide" – let alone admit that it took place and was perpetrated against the Herero and the Nama by German soldiers. As Sarkin states:

"Key issues which remain stumbling blocks for both sides include the use of the word 'genocide' and whether reconciliation is possible in the absence of a program of reparations.

An additional tension that emerged from the Bremen conference is that the involvement of others resulted in the perception that the Herero are being told what to do.

Critically, the Herero were not officially consulted in the process of setting up the conference, nor were they involved in determining the agenda or program. Such omissions can only cause further resentment and anger.

Another issue is the failure of exhibitions and events reflecting on the histories of those countries that had colonies to include reflections of their colonial endeavors. In 2000, Smith noted that a new German History Exhibition in Berlin did not even mention the Herero Genocide at all....

Even in Namibia, the only memorials that exist are for the Germans who died in the Herero War. Remarkably, there are no memorials to honor the Herero who died during that war. Even though Namibia is now independent, the statues to the former German colonialists still remain. According to Gewald and Silvester, the most photographed statue in Namibia is *Der Reiter*, a statue unveiled on Kaiser Wilhelm II's birthday on January 27, 1914, memorializing the 1,633 Germans who died in the Herero War.

The statues are only part of the colonial legacy still visible in contemporary Namibia. Places, streets, etc. still bear the names of conquerors from colonial history. Many of the huge farms are still occupied by German farmers, whose farms carry German names – although some of these farms have English, Afrikaans, or even local names. One example of the renaming is that of the Windhoek main road, which has been changed from *Kaiserstrasse* – after Kaiser Wilhelm II – to Independence Avenue.

In certain cases names have been changed, but often only to accommodate other leaders requiring acknowledgment. With many colonial names remaining, the issue of names is significant. Despite numerous proposals to change various names, the sticking point has often been which language to use for new names, given the multitude of languages in use in Namibia.

Most names in Herero areas have not been changed

from those in use before independence. While proposals have been submitted to revive traditional Herero names in Herero areas, the Namibian Parliament rejected them in mid-2005, arguing that it would be at variance with reconciliation and would be perceived as such by white members of the community. One minister argued that the name Otjomuise for Windhoek was a name that 'nobody knows how to pronounce.' The Herero responded that the same applied to Ouagadougou, the capital of Burkina Faso, to which Namibian ministers often travel.

As mentioned before, the statues of some leaders are also controversial. The statue of the Herero chief Hosea Kutako outside the Parliament buildings in Windhoek was wrapped in plastic bags and under armed guard for many years on government orders. Only recently was the plastic removed.

Even today, the status of some traditional leaders is highly politicized, and only some leaders are formally recognized. The perception lingers that recognition is in large part contingent on links to and support of the ruling party." – (Ibid., pp. 58 – 60).

Even when the German government apologised for the atrocities which the German colonial rulers and soldiers committed against the Herero, the Nama and other groups such as the Damara, it did so only reluctantly, did not give a full apology – only expressed 'regret' – and *still* refused to pay compensation. According to a report by BBC News, "Germany Regrets Namibia 'Genocide,'" 12 January 2004:

"Germany has expressed its 'regret' for the killing of thousands of Namibia's ethnic Hereros during the colonial era.

Between 35,000 and 105,000 people were killed after the Hereros rebelled against German rule in 1904.

But Germany's ambassador to Namibia ruled out paying compensation, as the Hereros have demanded in a law suit.

Correspondents say Wolfgang Massing's statement, at a ceremony to commemorate the massacres, is the closest Germany has come to an apology.

History could not be undone, he said but 'we can give back to the victims and their descendants the dignity and honour of which they were robbed.'

'I also wish to express how deeply we regret this unfortunate past,' he said at a commemoration of the 12 January, 1904 uprising in Okahandja, the Hereros' former capital 70 kilometres north of the capital, Windhoek.

He said it would be unfair to Namibia's other groups to only compensate the Hereros.

Wells poisoned

But Herero Paramount Chief Kuaima Riruako insisted that compensation must be paid.

'The wounds of the past must be healed. Our reparation claim must only be seen as an effort to regain our dignity and help us restore what was wrongfully taken away from us,' he said. 'I once again invite the German government to accept the genocide of my people and engage in a dialogue with the Herero to iron out issues of mutual interest.'

After the Hereros rebelled, the German military commander, General von Trotha, ordered the Hereros to leave Namibia or be killed.

Germany's military commander vowed to wipe out the Herero.

'I, the great general of the German troops, send this letter to the Herero people... All Hereros must leave this land... Any Herero found within the German borders with or without a gun, with or without cattle, will be shot. I shall no longer receive any women or children; I will drive them back to their people. I will shoot them. This is my decision for the Herero people.'

Hereros were massacred with machine guns, their wells

poisoned and then driven into the desert to die."

Although Germany still refuses to compensate the Hereros and other Namibians who were the victims of genocide in South-West Africa, it is the same country which agreed to compensate Jews for the holocaust under the Nazis. Namibians are fully aware of the contradiction and the hypocrisy in this matter.

And while the extermination of the Herero and members of other tribes in South-West Africa is acknowledged as the first genocide in the 20th century, its victims are hardly remembered by the rest of the world except in scholarship – which is itself limited to a few specialists or to those who are interested in the subject, all a minority, nonetheless, in the international community.

The Herero and the Nama were exterminated simply because they resisted injustice in their own homeland which had been taken from them by invaders from Europe who claimed they had the right to create a living space for themselves at the expense of the indigenous people; a claim that was used to justify imperialism including massacres and other horrendous tragedies the "natives" were subjected to, as if the conquerors had divine mandate to rule, subjugate, oppress and kill Africans because, as members of an "inferior race," they did not deserve to live. As Adam Jones states in his book, *Genocide: A Comprehensive Introduction*:

"Drawn by opportunities for cattle ranching, some 5,000 Germans had flooded into the territory (South-West Africa) by 1903. Colonists' deception, suasion, and violent coercion pushed the native population into an ever-narrower portion of its traditional landholdings. In 1904, the Hereros rose up against the Germans. Herero chief Samuel Maherero led his fighters against military outposts, killing about 120 Germans. This resistance to colonial domination infuriated the German leader Kaiser

Wilhelm II, who responded by dispatching a hardliner, Lt.-General Lothar von Trotha, to 'German South-West Africa.'

Von Trotha was firmly convinced that Africans 'are all alike. They only respond to force. It was and is my policy to use force with terrorism and even brutality. I shall annihilate the revolting tribes with rivers of blood and rivers of gold. Only after a complete uprooting will something emerge.'

After defeating the Hereros at the Battle of Hamakari in August 1904, the German Army chased survivors into the bone-dry wastes of the Kalahari desert. Von Trotha then issued his notorious 'annihilation order' – *Vernichtungsbefehl*....The order remained in place for several months, until a domestic outcry led the German Chancellor to rescind it.

A contemporary account describes Hereros emerging from the Kalahari 'starved to skeletons with hollow eyes, powerless and hopeless.' They were then allowed to move from the frying-pan to the fire: concentration camps. 'A continuing desire to destroy the Hereros played a part in the German maintenance of such lethal camp conditions,' writes Benjamin Madley; he notes elsewhere that 'according to official German figures, of 15,000 Hereros and 2,200 Namas incarcerated in camps, some 7,700 or 45 percent perished.'

Following the cessation of the Herero war, another tribal nation, the Nama, also rose up in revolt against German rule and was similarly crushed, with approximately half the population killed. Many scholars accordingly refer to the Namibian events as the genocide of the Hereros and Namas."– (Adam Jones, *Genocide: A Comprehensive Introduction*, Routledge, Oxon, UK, 2006, p. 80).

He goes on to state:

"An advantage of a comparative and global-historical approach to genocide is that it allows us to perceive important connections between campaigns of mass killing and group destruction that are widely separated in time and space. Scholarship on the genocide against the Hereros provides an excellent example. It is increasingly acknowledged not only that this was the first genocide of the twentieth century, but that it paved the way, in important respects, for the prototypical mass slaughter of that century – the Jewish Holocaust. As summarized by Madley:

'The Herero genocide was a crucial antecedent to Nazi mass murder. It created the German word *Konzentrationslager* – concentration camp – and the twentieth century's first death camp. Like Nazi mass murder, the Namibian genocides were premised upon ideas like *Lebensraum* – living space, annihilation – *Vernichtungskrieg*, and German racial supremacy. Individual Nazis were also linked to colonial Namibia. Hermann Goering, who built the first Nazi concentration camps, was the son of the first governor of colonial Namibia. Eugen Fischer, who influenced Hitler and ran the institute that supported Joseph Mengele's medical 'research' at Auschwitz, conducted racial studies in the colony. And Ritter von Epp, godfather of the Nazi party and Nazi governor of Bavaria from 1933 – 1945, led German troops against the Herero during the genocide.'

Following the independence of Namibia in 1990,...survivors' descendants called on Germany to apologize for the Herero genocide, and provide reparations. Why, asked Herero leaders, was Germany willing to pay tens of billions of dollars to Jewish survivors of Nazi genocide, but not even acknowledge crimes against the Hereros?

Following strategies developed by Jewish advocates,

the Hereros filed suit in the United States for US$4 billion in compensation – half from the German government, half from German companies that were alleged to have profited from the occupation of Herero lands.

In August 2004 – the centenary of the Herero uprising – the German development-aid minister, Heidemarie Wieczorek-Zeul, attended a ceremony at Okakarara in the region of Otjozondjupa, where the conflict had formally ended back in 1906. The minister issued a formal apology that included the 'G-word':

'We Germans accept our historic and moral responsibility and the guilt incurred by Germans at that time....The atrocities committed at that time would have been termed genocide.'

She also promised German development aid as an oblique form of recompense." – (Ibid., p. 81).

The apology rings hollow when Germany still refuses to pay reparations to the Herero, and when it is offered grudgingly, even if the German cabinet member used the word "genocide" in her apology. She was not explicit in her apology. She did not say – "It *was* genocide." Subtle distinctions were made in her apology in an attempt to insulate Germany and the perpetrators of the genocide from being blamed for the atrocities:

"In 2004, one hundred years after the genocide, Germany's Development Aid Minister Heidemarie Wieczorek-Zeul issued an official apology for the atrocities committed by General Von Trotha, hereby subtly distancing Von Trotha's actions from official government involvement.

Despite this apology, the German government refused to speak of the events as 'having been genocide,' favoring the ambiguous statement of what 'would today be termed genocide.'

Germany has ruled out any form of financial

compensation for the victims' descendants." – (Asoka Esuruoso and Philipp Khabo Koepsell, eds., *Arriving in the Future: Stories of Home and Exile*, Berlin, Germany: epubli GmbH, 2014, p. 21).

Heidemarie Wieczorek-Zeul also implied that development aid to Namibia was enough as a form of compensation for the extermination of the Herero and the Nama; which are two different things. Development aid is not reparations.

African Americans in the United States have faced the same kind of opposition to their demand for reparations as descendants of the victims of slavery. And they continue to suffer because of the lingering effects of slavery compounded by the persistence of racism which affects blacks more than anybody else.

Some Americans, especially conservatives, have even argued that African Americans have already received and continue to receive reparations in the form of welfare assistance since a disproportionately large number of them are on welfare, unlike whites; an argument which is irrelevant to the debate on reparations since welfare assistance is available to anyone who is in need, regardless of race, and not just to African Americans. Millions of white Americans and others have received and continue to receive welfare assistance, yet their ancestors were not enslaved like the ancestors of African Americans were.

To equate development assistance with payment of reparations by Germany to the victims of genocide in German South-West Africa when other countries get the same kind of assistance from the same country is to imply that countries which get this kind of economic aid are also getting reparations from Germany even though they were not colonised by Germany and did not experience genocide at the hands of the German colonial rulers like the people of German South-West Africa did.

The tragic history of Namibia about the genocide

against the Herero and the Nama is one of the best examples of the callous nature of imperialism which has wreaked havoc among the indigenous people round the globe at the hands of their European conquerors for centuries.

The insensitive and predatory nature of imperialism was also demonstrated when European powers met in Berlin in February 1885 to decide how they should divide Africa among themselves – as if Africans did not even exist; and they were not invited for obvious reasons. There was not a single African representative at that conference. Africans meant absolutely nothing to them in terms of human rights, except as beasts of burden.

It was Africans who carried European explorers and travellers on their backs when crossing rivers, and on their shoulders, walking barefoot for miles and miles, when they went to Africa to claim vast tracts of land and establish spheres of influence for their mother countries. The areas and territories they claimed later became colonies.

It was also Africans who carried colonial administrators in hammocks as the new rulers went around enforcing colonial orders. It was they who cleared the bushes, built the roads and railways, worked deep in the mines to dig up gold, diamonds and other minerals, and who grew and harvested crops for the benefit of Europeans while getting nothing in return. All that took place in their own homeland for the benefit of their conquerors from Europe. It was their land and their resources – but it was as if none of that belonged to them. Many of them were also killed for nothing.

The genocide in German South-West Africa in which about 85 per cent of the Hereros and 50 per cent of the Namas perished; the deaths of up to 300,000 people in German East Africa during the Maji Maji war of resistance against the brutalities of German colonial rule; the atrocities and deaths of up to 10 million Congolese in the

Congo Free State under King Leopold II of Belgium, as well other innumerable brutalities and lost lives elsewhere on the continent, were all the product of the Scramble for Africa by the imperial powers whose devastating impact is still felt today and from which Africa may never fully recover.

More than two hundred years ago, Immanuel Kant, a leading German philosopher expressed his disapproval of the mistreatment of non-whites by their European conquerors, although he was a racist himself and had very low regard for black people.

A product of Europe that was in an advanced stage of material civilisation, and of his time, his racist views were typical of other Europeans, probably the majority of them, during that period. As I state in one of my books, *Africa is in A Mess: What Went Wrong and What Should be Done*:

"It is the West which still poses the biggest threat to our independence despite its professed commitment to the principles of racial and human equality. It is also the citadel of arrogance because it conquered the world.

Tragically, among all the people in the world, we Africans, black Africans, are the most despised. And much of this denigration of Africa has its roots in the West, although Westerners did not invent racism. It is a universal phenomenon. But the attitude of many Westerners towards Africans and people of African descent is not very good; nor is that of Asians and others. It is patently racist, and condescending at best.

James Baldwin's remarks about the attitude of many white Americans towards black Americans, descendants of Africa, is appropriate in this context in terms of analogy. As he stated in his essay, "Fifth Avenue, Uptown":

'Negroes want to be treated like men: a perfectly straightforward statement containing seven words. People who have mastered Kant, Hegel, Shakespeare, Marx,

Freud and the Bible find this statement impenetrable.'

It has been that way since Europeans conquered Africa. Success by black Africans in all fields of human endeavour has not changed this attitude. It has become second nature to many whites; with the advancement of the West being cited as proof of their racial superiority even if many of them don't say so publicly. We may be poor and far less developed in terms of material success, and we know when we are being despised and insulted.

The West has, indeed, achieved a lot in terms of material civilisation unmatched anywhere else in the world. And there is a lot that we have learned from Europeans probably even more so than we did when we were under colonial tutelage. And we continue to learn a lot from the West.

But there is nothing intrinsically virtuous, or intrinsically evil, about the West. I have lived in the West for many years and I have seen both. It has its virtues and vices just like any other part of mankind.

One of the worst things that came out of the West, which was a product of Western material civilisation, was greed which led to imperial ambitions and ultimately the conquest of Africa and other parts of the world. As Immanuel Kant, one of the leading Western philosophers who is also acknowledged by many as one of the world's greatest thinkers, stated in one his works *Eternal Peace and Other Essays*:

'If we compare the barbarian instances of inhospitality...with the inhuman behavior of the civilized, and especially the commercial states of our continent, the injustice practiced by them even in their first contact with foreign lands and peoples fills us with horror; the mere visiting of such peoples being regarded by them as equivalent to a conquest....

The Negro lands,..., the Cape of Good Hope, etc., on

being discovered, were treated as countries that belonged to nobody; for the aboriginal inhabitants were reckoned as nothing....And all this has been done by nations who make a great ado about their piety, and who, while drinking up iniquity like water, would have themselves regarded as the very elect of orthodox faith.'

Yet he did not bat an eye in denigrating Africa. He was an unreconstructed racist who also bluntly stated:

'The Negroes of Africa have received from nature no intelligence that rises above the foolish. The difference between the two races (black and white) is thus a substantial one: it appears to be just as great in respect of the faculties of the mind as in color.'

So, the argument that black people are genetically – hence intellectually – inferior to members of other races is nothing new. It is a stereotype rooted in Western intellectual tradition and has been given "credibility" by some of the most eminent thinkers of the Western world.

Besides Kant, other prominent Western philosophers who have ridiculed the African mind include Georg Hegel, David Hume, and Baron de Montesquieu.

Some of them did not even consider us to be full human beings. As Montesquieu stated in *The Spirit of the Laws*:

'These creatures are all over black, and with such a flat nose, that they can scarcely be pitied.

It is hardly to be believed that God, who is a wise Being, should place a soul, especially a good soul, in such a black, ugly body.

The Negroes prefer a glass necklace to that gold which polite nations so highly value: can there be greater proof of their wanting common sense? It is impossible for us to suppose these creatures to be men.'

Another great Western mind, David Hume, used his intellectual power to make this equally superstitious statement:

'I am apt to suspect the Negroes...to be naturally inferior to whites. There never was any civilized nation of any other complexion than white, nor even any individual eminent in action or speculation. No ingenious manufactures among them, no arts, no sciences....
Such a uniform and constant difference could not happen, in so many countries and ages, if nature had not made an original distinction betwixt these breeds of men.'

Hume was, of course, also an atheist and gave some of the strongest "proofs" on the "non-existence" of God. And he remains an icon in the pantheon of Western thinkers.

Equally irrational was Hegel whose great mind also led him to say:

'Africa...is no historical part of the world; it has no movement or development to exhibit.'

It is a sentiment echoed more than 100 years later in contemporary times by many people including one of the most prominent British historians, Arnold Toynbee, who died in 1975 when I was a student at Wayne State University where one of my professors extolled the virtues of Western civilization and the achievements of the West that provided such a sharp contrast with those of Africa that it was as if our continent belonged to another planet.

It was an empirical fact, and I was acutely aware of the difference in terms of material civilization and technological advancement. After all, there I was, from Africa, at one of the great centres of learning in the Western world to be taught by Westerners simply because we did not and still don't have enough schools in our countries. It makes us look bad, very bad. As Toynbee bluntly stated:

'The black races alone have not contributed positively to any civilization.'

No less condescending in his attitude towards us was that great humanitarian, physician, philosopher and theologian, Dr. Albert Schweitzer, who worked and died for us, the so-called members of the lesser breed. His work at the mission hospital he established in Lambarene, Gabon, in Equatorial Africa under French rule, is what legends are made of. He also wrote and spoke extensively about the works of Jesus and St. Paul and about the Bible in general as a true Christian who believed in the brotherhood of men and in the equality of all people here on Earth and before God.

Yet he made one of the most racist and paternalistic statements about blacks ever made by anybody when, without the slightest doubt in his mind, he stated:

'The Negro is a child, and with children nothing can be done without the use of authority. We must, therefore, so arrange the circumstances of daily life that my natural authority can find expression.

With regard to the Negroes, then, I have coined the formula: 'I am your brother, it is true, but your elder brother."

The implication is obvious. Whites have divine mandate to rule blacks. And younger brothers never catch up with their elder brothers, chronologically speaking; hence in terms of wisdom as well. The older are wiser.

That was the general attitude among Europeans before and after the conquest of Africa. The conquest of our continent only solidified this attitude, our defeat at the hands of our conquerors, because of our inferior technology, being cited as indisputable proof of our inferiority to them.

That was the technological theory of imperialism. They had guns. We had bows and arrows. And when we met on the battlefield, we were no match for them." – (Godfrey Mwakikagile, *Africa is in a Mess: What Went Wrong and What Should be Done*, New Africa Press, Dar es Salaam, Tanzania, 2006, pp. 133 – 137; Godfrey Mwakikagile, *Post-colonial Africa: A General Study*, New Africa Press, Dar es Salaam, Tanzania, 2014.

See also James Baldwin, "Fifth Avenue, Uptown"; Immanuel Kant, *Eternal Peace and Other Essays*, Boston: Houghton Mifflin, 1914, p. 68; Kant in Will Durant, *The Story of Philosophy*, New York: Pocket Books, 1974, p. 284. See also Godfrey Mwakikagile, *Africa and the West*, Huntington, New York: Nova Science Publishers, Inc., 2000, p. 218; Walter Rodney, *How Europe Underdeveloped Africa*, Dar es Salaam, Tanzania: Tanzania Publishing House, 1973; Kant, *Observations on the Feeling of the Beautiful and Sublime*, translated by John Goldthwait, Berkeley: University of California Press, 1960, pp. 111 - 113; Dinesh D'Souza, *The End of Racism: Principles for A Multicultural Society*, New York: Free press, 1995, p. 28. See also D'Souza, ibid., pp. 442, and 468; Baron de Montesquieu, *The Spirit of the Laws, Vol. 1*, translated by Thomas Nugent, Cincinnati, Ohio: Robert Clarke & Co., 1973, pp. 274 – 275; David Hume, "Of National Character," in D. Hume, *Essays: Moral, Political and Literary, Vol. 1*, edited by T.H. Green and T. Grose, London: Longman's Green and Co., 1975, p. 252; Hegel, *The Philosophy of History*, New York: Dover Publications, 1956, pp. 95 – 99; Arnold Toynbee, quoted by Felix Okoye, *The American Image of Africa: Myth and Reality*, Buffalo, New York: Black Academy Press, 1971, p. 7; Albert Schweitzer, *The Primeval Forest*, New York: Pyramid Books, 1974, p. 99).

That is what happened to the Herero. They were no match for the Germans on the battlefield. Their fate was sealed.

Their extermination is one of the saddest chapters in the history of imperial conquest. And unlike some of the conflicts between the indigenous people and the European colonisers in different parts of Africa, the war by the Germans against the Herero was initiated, planned and approved by the national leaders themselves in Germany. And it was waged with their full support. As Jeremy Sarkin states in his book, *Germany's Genocide of the Herero: Kaiser Wilhelm II, His General, His Settlers, His Soldiers*:

"Contrary to conventional wisdom, the Herero genocide was not the by-product of a rogue German general whose behaviour his Berlin superiors left unchecked in GSWA. On the contrary, in waging a campaign of murder, dispossession and enslavement against the Herero, Von Trotha was carrying out the express orders of the Kaiser himself.

This is a clarification of great import as the Kaiser's control over the genocide order would result in the responsibility of the German state for the Herero genocide and forms the basis for criminal liability and reparations from Germany to the Herero.

Evidence – including Von Trotha's statements of obedience to the Kaiser – demonstrates that the spirit of the extermination order originated in Berlin and was not the diabolical rampage of a single deluded officer in the field.

Furthermore, on a purely circumstantial basis, the Kaiser's aggressive rhetoric against the Chinese during the Boxer rebellion, as well as that pertaining to the Herero in general, illustrates that the genocide order was in keeping with the Kaiser's character. History has shown the Kaiser to be anything other than a magnanimous keeper of the colonies. On the contrary, he viewed Germany's territories as subhuman...." - (Jeremy Sarkin, *Germany's Genocide of the Herero: Kaiser Wilhelm II, His General, His Settlers, His Soldiers*, op.cit., p. 241).

In a very tragic way, the extermination of the Herero paved the way and laid the foundation for the establishment of the German colony of South-West Africa that later became the independent nation of Namibia.

Right from the beginning, the Germans used force to control the indigenous people who did not want to be ruled by their imperial conquerors. They resisted. The colonial rulers brought soldiers from Germany to subdue and subjugate them. Also, right from the beginning, the colonial rulers seriously considered putting the Herero, whose land and cattle they had forcible taken, in reserves which would have been tantamount to confining them in concentration camps. They finally did that when they rounded up the genocide survivors and put them in those camps. The victims included women and children.

The colonial rulers even argued that blacks were not entitled to human rights, and international protection, because they were subhuman; thus justifying the mistreatment and extermination of the Herero and the Nama.

After World War I, Germany lost all her colonial territories. South-West Africa was taken by South Africa. The biggest part of German East Africa, Tanganyika, was taken by Britain. Ruanda and Urundi, the smallest territories in German East Africa, became Belgian colonies.

The extermination of the Herero and the Nama was only the beginning of a litany of injustices against the indigenous people of Namibia, compounded by the refusal of the South African white minority rulers to relinquish control of the territory as mandated by the United Nations years later. They even wanted to make it an integral part of

South Africa.

Therefore, the end of German rule in South-West Africa as a result of Germany's defeat in World War I did not bring much relief to the indigenous people. They simply changed masters, both oppressive and racist.

When South Africa assumed control of the territory, the new colonial rulers committed atrocities against the indigenous people which were not very much different from those which had been perpetrated by the Germans. They were also the same kind of brutalities which were being committed against Africans by the white rulers within the Union of South Africa itself.

George Padmore, a renowned Pan-Africanist from Trinidad who later became a citizen of Ghana and served as an adviser on African affairs to Ghana's first president, Dr. Kwame Nkrumah, and who died and was buried in Ghana, stated the following about some of those atrocities in his book, *Pan-Africanism or Communism? The Coming Struggle for Africa*:

"The South African Government made it clear that blacks must not expect to get justice from the whites in the Union.

In 1922, General Smuts, one of the very founders of the League of Nations and the main architect of the Mandates system, approved the bombing of the Bondelswarts, a defenceless tribe in South-West Africa, the former German colony which the League of Nations had entrusted to the Government of South Africa as a mandated territory.

The history of this massacre may be summed up as follows:

'The Bondel Hottentots were a poverty-stricken tribe living in a reserve in the southern part of the territory.

They saw no advantage in working for local white farmers, who being ill-off themselves could neither feed, clothe nor pay them.

A law, passed according to the Administrator's

statement, in order to force the natives to work, imposed a prohibitive tax on the hunting dogs upon whose quarry the Hottentots managed to live.

They were already on the worst possible terms with the local police, and open friction occurred when a native notable, one Abraham Morris, returned in good faith but without authorization from the Cape Colony, and was summoned to be arrested.

The Hottentots refused to surrender Morris and apparently believing that the threats of the police meant the white men intended to destroy them went into laager on a rock-covered hill at a place called Guruchas.

By this time, the 'Native war' scare was running hard through the country; the white population was terrified.

The local police and the magistrate made some efforts to communicate with the Bondels, who declared that they did not mean to fight, but refused to surrender Morris and the leaders unless an amnesty was promised.

Mr. Hofmeyer, the Administrator of the territory, arrived, collected volunteers from the whites, and sent for aeroplanes from the nearest aerodrome.

His forces surrounded the hill where the Bondels were encamped with their women and children. The hill was bombed by aeroplanes from three o'clock till dark.

In the night a party of the Hottentots who were completely demoralised by this, to them, new and appalling form of attack, escaped from the camp. They were afterwards caught and completely defeated.

The surviving women and children were taken away from Guruchas and fed from the captured stock of their tribe. After some time when the fighting was over they were allowed to return to their reserve.

Abraham Morris was killed. Those of the leaders left alive were charged with high treason, and imprisoned, though the chief of them, Jacobus Christian, was released in 1924.'

What General Smuts started in 1922 under the League

of Nations, the British Colonial Secretary, Mr. Oliver Lyttelton (now Lord Chandos), was still carrying on in 1954 against the Kikuyu adherents of Mau Mau in Kenya.

It is this sort of legalized terrorism perpetrated in Africa in the name of 'law and order' that the Pan-African Congress was established to expose and combat." – (George Padmore, *Pan-Africanism or Communism? The Coming Struggle for Africa*, Dennis Dobson, London, 1956, pp. 135 – 136; Freda White, *Mandates*, J. Cape, London, 1926, pp. 136 – 137).

The League of Nations did nothing to help them despite its professed ideals of human equality. And with South-West Africa under the tight grip of South Africa, the people of the former German colony had no choice but to start fighting for independence.

Part Three:
The Struggle for Independence

THE people of Namibia started to demand their rights, including the right to self-determination, right from the beginning when they were conquered by imperial Germany.

In fact, they never stopped fighting even when they were being conquered. They resisted and fought back.

But it was not until years later that the struggle for independence as a well-coordinated campaign on a sustained and nationwide basis began in earnest with the founding of the South West African People's Organisation (SWAPO). SWAPO became the most effective political organisation in the country. It was also one of the most successful liberation movements in the history of Africa.

The struggle was directed against apartheid South Africa which ruled the former Germany colony as another province of the apartheid state, although the territory never became an integral part of South Africa in the legal sense. But the apartheid regime's jurisdiction over the former German colony amounted to virtual annexation.

Apartheid laws were enforced in South-West Africa

after the National Party came to power in South Africa in 1948 and formally introduced apartheid. As Dunia P. Zongwe states concerning the introduction of apartheid laws in South-West Africa:

"Like South Africa, Namibia's past is marked by the 'deep scars' of apartheid. Under the C Mandate of the League of Nations, which entrusted South Africa with the administration of South West Africa/Namibia on behalf of the British Crown, South Africa was allowed to extend its judicial system over South West Africa/Namibia, which it did until Namibia's independence. Inexorably, the extension of South Africa's legal system to Namibia was co-extensive with the introduction of apartheid laws and policies in Namibia in 1948.
The apartheid policy meant in the first place that Blacks had to be separated from people of another colour in constitutional, political, social and other respects; and in the second place that Blacks were ethnically divided into different nations. The idea gradually developed of establishing each nation in its own 'homeland.' Until the country's independence from South Africa on 21 March 1990, inequality had persisted for a long time." – (Dunia P. Zongwe, "Equality has no mother but sisters: The preference for comparative law over international law in the equality jurisprudence in Namibia," in Magnus Killander, ed., *International Law and Domestic Human Rights Litigation in Africa*, Pretoria University Law Press, Pretoria, South Africa, 2010, pp. 127 – 128).

The consolidation of power by the South African apartheid regime in Namibia played a major role in the growth of the independence movement in the former German colony. It also served as a catalyst in the mobilisation of forces for the independence struggle by the African nationalists who were determined to free the country from white minority rule.

The nationalist movement was also fuelled by the apartheid regime's refusal to relinquish control of Namibia in defiance of a United Nations resolution which clearly stated that South Africa had no legal mandate to rule the former German colony. In 1966, the UN told the South African apartheid regime to withdraw from Namibia and let the country attain sovereign status. The apartheid regime refused to do so, contending that the UN had no mandate over the territory.

In 1968, the United Nations (UN) and the Organisation of African Unity (OAU) formally announced that South-West Africa was from then on known as Namibia. Apartheid South Africa refused to acknowledge that and continued to call the territory – South-West Africa.

The hegemonic control the apartheid regime had over Namibia for decades had far-reaching consequences even long after the country won independence. In addition to enduring inequality among the races during the apartheid era and even after Namibia won independence, lingering effects of apartheid in the former German colony include continued separation of ethnic and racial groups, reinforced by a racial hierarchy that was institutionalised during colonial rule by South Africa. As Maria Mboono Nghidinwa states in her book, *Women Journalists in Namibia's Struggle, 1985 – 1990*:

"To this day, separate ethnic, linguistic and ethnic identity (sic) is prevalent in Namibian society mainly because of South Africa's previous policy of separate development. The policy not only meant separate development of 'races,' but also the separate development of ethnic groups, meaning that people were forced to live in designated areas called 'homelands' or reserves in rural Namibia.

Furthermore, this policy ensured that there would be separate reserves for Basters, Caprivians, Damaras, Hereros, Kavangos, Namas and for the Ovambo ethnic groups. Similar division was extended to those who lived in urban areas, such that they were divided into separate locations according to their ethnic groups. And, of course, the white population occupied the more upscale areas of these urban areas.

Similar to the German colonial era, which included the genocide committed against the Hereros and many Nama people in 1904, South African apartheid caused indiscriminate cruelty, human suffering, and oppression on a staggering scale by the military and police forces.

It was very difficult for South Africa to release its hold on Namibia, primarily due to the latter's rich mineral resources, including diamonds." – (Maria Mboono Nghidinwa, *Women Journalists in Namibia's Struggle, 1985 – 1990*, Basler Afrika Bibliographien, Namibia Resource Center & Southern Africa Library, Klosterberg, Switzerland, 2008, p. 13).

Another reason the South African apartheid regime did not want to relinquish control of Namibia was security. Like the other countries bordering South Africa in the north still under white minority rule, Namibia served as a buffer against the freedom fighters who wanted to penetrate South Africa from their bases in the independent African countries. That is why the apartheid regime also supported the white minority rulers in Rhodesia, now Zimbabwe, and the Portuguese colonial rulers in Mozambique. And because of South Africa's refusal and unwillingness to withdraw from Namibia, the African nationalists felt that the only way they could liberate their country was by armed struggle.

The origin of SWAPO can be traced back to the 1950s as a regional movement of Ovambo migrant workers in South Africa. It was regional in character because of its ethnic dimension: the migrants workers who formed the organisation came from Ovamboland in South-West Africa. The emphasis was on helping Ovambo workers.

Yet by the very nature of the struggle – for the rights of the Ovambo migrant workers – the movement had nationalist elements embracing the whole country, hence other ethnic groups. The rights of the Ovambo migrant workers were inseparable from the rights of other Namibians.

The organisation which fought for the rights of the Ovambo was known as the Ovamboland People's Congress (OPC). It was formed in Cape Town, South Africa, in 1957 and was patterned after South Africa's African National Congress (ANC). It drew its membership from northern South-West Africa but later evolved into the Ovamboland People's Organisation (OPO).

The Ovamboland People's Organisation was formed in Namibia in 1958. Although predominantly Ovambo, it welcomed other South West Africans to join the struggle against white minority rule across the country.

Also critical to the formation and evolution of SWAPO as a nationalist movement was the role of chiefs and traditional institutions of authority in terms of mobilisation at the grassroots level in the rural areas and as custodians of African values and traditions – hence the dignity of the African and his way of life – vital to fuelling the nationalist struggle against alien rulers. It was the chiefs who even sent the first petition to the United Nations demanding freedom and equality for black Namibians. It was also traditional rulers who laid the foundation for the establishment of the nationalist movement among the people of different ethnic groups and backgrounds across the country.

The struggle against apartheid in neighbrouring South Africa also inspired Namibians to mobilise forces in their struggle against their own racial oppressors.

One of the first developments took place within South Africa itself where Namibian students formed their own organisation which later became the nucleus of the South West Africa National Union (SWANU). SWANU became one of the nationalist movements struggling for independence in Namibia.

The role played by migrants workers in the formation of the Namibian nationalist movement can not be underestimated:

"While Kaxumba was mobilising people in northern Namibia, a parallel development by other Namibians working in Cape Town took place. *Tate* Andimba yaToivo recalled:

'One day in 1954, as we picked up the newspaper in Cape Town, we noticed a photopgraph of Mburumba Kerina. He was speaking at the UN in New York and telling the whole world about the sufferings of the Namibian people under apartheid. This article was published with Kerina's address. We copied it down and started writing to him.

In 1957, Namibians working in Cape Town formed an organisation called the Ovamboland People's Congress [OPC], and with Kerina's advice, we also wrote petitions to the UN directly and through him. We requested the UN to terminate the South African administration over Namibia, and to place Namibia under the Trusteeship Council, and to do away with the contract labour system.

The police detected our activities, and in 1958 I was deported from Cape Town. I went up north and started working together with Kaxumba and others. We continued with our political work, mobilising the people, particularly the contract workers in mines and factories.

Kaxumba and I were banned from joining *akaholo* and and from leaving Owambo to go to the south. They said that we had a bad influence on other workers. We intensified our political work by holding meetings and listening to public complaints.

The political movements were formed out of meetings and discussions of real issues and problems faced by the workers and the community at large. *Nghuwoyepongo*, which means, Voice of an Orphan, was formed when people realised that their *omalenga* went along along with the colonial government, they turned their backs on them, and no longer looked after their problems. *Nghuwoyepongo* was an underground pressure group that pressurised traditional leaders and the UN to terminate the mandate.

In 1958, another political organisation called the Ovamboland People's Organisation was formed inside Namibia; it merged *Nghuwoyepongo* and the Ovamboland People's Congress.

In 1959, after the forced removal of our people from the Old Location to Katutura, the repression increased and there was a police order to kill Sam Nujoma. With the help of Chief Hosea Kutako, Nujoma escaped into exile through Botswana and managed to reach the United Nations in New York. He sent a message from New York asking us to form an umbrella organisation that represented all the people of Namibia.

The lobbying began for OPO, SWANU [South West Africa National Union] and CANU [Caprivi African National Union] to join hands and amalgamate into one umbrella organisation. Some people from these organisations came together to form the South West Africa People's Organisation [SWAPO] in 1960. Kaxumba was a driving force. And, all these political activities led to Kaxumba's arrest and banishment into the unknown forest by the police.'" – (Andimba Toivo yaToivo in Ellen Ndeshi Namhila, *Kaxumba KaNdola: Man and Myth, The Biography of A Barefoot Soldier,* Basler Afrika Bibliographien, Basel, Switzerland, 2002, pp. 36 – 37).

SWAPO was formed on 19 April 1960 under the leadership of Andimba Toivo yaToivo. Within five years of its founding, it became the dominant political organisation in the struggle for the independence of Namibia; its stature enhanced by international recognition, including recognition by the United Nations in 1972 as the sole representative of the Namibian people in their quest for freedom and independence.

Another group which later merged with SWAPO was the Namibia African People's Democratic Organisation (NAPDO) formed in 1970. It joined SWAPO in 1976.

Agitation for independence by the nationalist leaders was complemented by armed resistance. Just six years after SWAPO was formed, forces of the apartheid regime clashed with SWAPO units on 26 August 1966, an incident that marked the beginning of what came to be known in South Africa as the Border War.

But its history is deeper than that. The conflict was rooted in the conquest of German South-West Africa by South Africa during World War I. The conquest led to the occupation of South-West Africa by South Africa. The territory was under South African military rule from 1915 to 1920 when the League of Nations designated it as a mandate to be ruled by South Africa; an occupation South Africa refused to end until the white minority government was forced to do so decades later.

Therefore, the Namibian people did not seek a military solution right away as means to achieve their independence. SWAPO took up arms and started to wage guerrilla war as a last resort.

It was the refusal by apartheid South Africa to relinquish control of South West Africa which forced SWAPO to resort to guerrilla warfare.

SWAPO formed the South West African Liberation Army (SWALA) – renamed the People's Liberation Army of Namibia (PLAN) – in 1962 to liberate the territory. But it was South Africa which started the war. Its forces attacked units of the People's Liberation Army of Namibia at Omugulugwombashe in northern Namibia on 26 August 1966, thus initiating military conflict between the two sides which lasted until the late 1980s during the Namibian war of independence.

SWAPO guerrilla fighters first entered Namibia in September 1965 and then in March 1966. But no major confrontation between the two sides took place until August 1966.

SWAPO first wanted to establish training camps inside Namibia to train its fighters. One of those camps was established at Omugulugwombashe in June 1966 under the leadership of John ya Otto Nankudhu. He received military training in the Soviet Union. After finishing his training in 1964, he returned to Africa and established the first SWAPO guerrilla training camp at Kongwa, central Tanzania, in the same year. He was one of the first six guerrilla fighters who entered Namibia in 1966 to recruit and train freedom fighters.

After the attack on SWAPO's training camp at Omugulugwombashe by South African forces, the freedom fighters prepared for a counterattack.

On 29 September 1966, Nankudhu, who had survived the South African military strike at Omugulugwombashe, led SWAPO fighters in an attack on Oshikango, a village in northern Namibia on the border with Angola. On the night of 14 December 1966, SWAPO launched its first attack inside Namibia when its fighters invaded a farm at Maroelaboom after cutting telephone lines between the farm and the police station at Maroelaboom.

Throughout the seventies and eighties, SWAPO continued to infiltrate Namibia and wage guerrilla warfare against the South African forces in order to force the apartheid regime to relinquish control of the territory and declare independence.

Although SWAPO fighters did not defeat the South African security forces on the battlefield, they exerted enough pressure on the apartheid regime for it to rethink its strategy of trying to defeat the freedom fighters instead of negotiating with them to bring an end to the conflict. SWAPO succeeded in forcing South Africa to start negotiating with the nationalist leaders and to make meaningful concessions when negotiations for Namibian independence started in earnest in the late 1980s. The concessions finally led to independence for Namibia on 21 March 1990.

Right from the beginning, SWAPO's credibility as the legitimate representative of the Namibian people even before Namibia won independence was enhanced by its history as an inclusive, broad-based organisation. It was a product of different groups. Other groups joined SWAPO to form the nationalist movement which eventually won independence for Namibia.

Like all the other liberation movements in Africa, SWAPO also used the international arena to pursue its goals. The most effective forum was the United Nations. The UN also had the legal mandate to demand South Africa's withdrawal from the territory and to guide it towards independence. As Cleophas Johannes Tsokoyadi, a Zimbabwean diplomat who represented his country at the United Nations and held other diplomatic posts, states in his book, *Namibia's Independence Struggle: The Role of the United Nations*:

"While Namibia suffered under the yoke of colonialism like many other post-colonial countries, it provided the United Nations with an opportunity to fulfil the organisation's purposes and principles which include the right of each nation – large and small – to national self-determination. If the Berlin Conference on the Partition of Africa can be said to have 'legitimised' colonialism, the mandate and trusteeship systems de-legitimised it.

Namibia gave the United Nations a forum to confront the practical issues of racism, racial discrimination, *apartheid* and human rights.

The dynamics of 'settler colonialism' and 'kith and kin' played an important part in prolonging Namibia's struggle for independence and also helped to condemn Namibia to a hard and long armed liberation struggle. *Apartheid* South

Africa's intransigence and the support that Pretoria received from the former colonial powers were directly related to South Africa's status as a former 'settler colony'....

The question of Namibia was so long drawn-out that there seems to have developed confusion as to who were the parties to the conflict. Under the trusteeship system, South Africa merely administered Namibia on behalf of the United Nations. Legally speaking, the dispute was between South Africa and the United Nations, as reinforced by Security Council and General Assembly resolutions as well as by the International Court of Justice advisory opinions. The UN therefore, had the historical, moral and legal responsibility to bring Namibia to independence.

In supporting the people of Namibia in their struggle for independence, the Organisation of African Unity, through the sub-regional Frontline States, demonstrated their commitment to the total liberation of Africa. This Pan-Africanism was an important factor in sustaining the morale and hope of the people of Namibia. Anti-colonial solidarity was a major push behind the formation of the Non-Aligned Movement in 1961. The Movement lived up to its principles in its support for the people of Namibia."
– (Cleophas Johannes Tsokoyadi, *Namibia's Independence Struggle: The Role of the United* Nations, Xlibris, 2011).

In its struggle to liberate Namibia from the colonial apartheid regime, SWAPO did not rely exclusively on internal resources; nor was that its strategy. SWAPO leaders knew there was an imperative need to seek external support, financial, diplomatic, and material, in order to wage a successful campaign against the apartheid regime in power in Namibia. And it was very successful in mobilising external resources for the struggle. As Lauren Dobell states in her book, *Swapo's Struggle for Namibia, 1960 – 1991: War by Other Means*:

"Against a repressive South African state, Swapo would pit resources drawn from within and without the movement. And indeed the movement's leadership proved exceptionally adept at exploiting its external assets – encompassing the financial, material, moral, organisational, institutional, and, most critically, diplomatic resources placed at Swapo's disposal by what has been termed 'a world waiting and wanting to lay the table.'[13]

It made much less of the internal resources available to it – in particular the commitment, courage and potential militancy of its rank and file.

The external resources commanded by Swapo grew steadily throughout the war, in scope and quantity, to the point where it enjoyed financial support per capita unequalled by any other southern African liberation movement. These impressive resources were intertwined, and their configuration at any one time had a great deal to do with the way in which Swapo understood the reality it confronted, and adjusted its practice and rhetoric accordingly.

Swapo's leadership chose to pursue the diplomatic route in its struggle to liberate Namibia. This, it will be argued, had fateful consequences for the movement's political strategy, and crucial implications for its military strategy.

Swapo's armed struggle – bluntly characterised in the early 1980s as possibly the most inept in the Third World[4] – was waged mainly for propaganda purposes, while the organisation and mobilization of popular resistance at home was neglected by the leadership in exile, as it pursued recognition by the international community of Swapo's status as the 'sole and authentic representative of the Namibian people,'[5] and for the independence of Namibia – in that order. Swapo's focus on this international strategy would ensconce the hegemony of the exiled leadership over Swapo's hamstrung internal 'wing' – a fact critical to understanding the Namibian liberation struggle and the shaping of Swapo's development thinking." – (Lauren Dobell, *Swapo's Struggle for Namibia, 1960 – 1991: War by Other Means*, Basel, Switzerland: P. Schlettwein Publishing, 1998, pp. 19 – 20. See also, cited by Lauren Dobell, 3. Erika Thiro-Beukes, Attie Beukes and Hewat Beukes, *Namibia: A Struggle Betrayed*, Rehoboth: Akasia Drukkery, 1986, p. 10; cited by L. Dobell, 4. *The Star*, Johannesburg, South Africa, "No end in sight to this festering war," 29 August 1983; cited by L. Dobell, 5. Swapo was recognized by the United Nations General Assembly as "the authentic representative of the Namibian people" in Resolution 3111 adopted on 12 December 1973. Three years later, on 20 December 1976, UNGA Resolution 31/146 amended the title to "sole and authentic.")

Most of the material support SWAPO sought came from outside Africa. But the success of its military strategy was largely determined by the support it got from African countries close to Namibia which served as operational and rear bases for its freedom fighters in waging the armed struggle against the apartheid forces.

One of those countries, close to Namibia, was Zambia. It was the first to win independence in the southern African region, in October 1964, and found itself on the frontline during the liberation struggle against white minority regimes in the region; not only because it provided support to the freedom fighters but also because of its geographical proximity to the combat zone.

However, its role in the liberation of Namibia has also raised some questions about its strategy, even its commitment, to help liberate that country.

What may not be taken into account in the criticism of Zambia is the difficult position the country found itself in during the wars of liberation in the entire southern African region. Its military weakness and close proximity to the citadel of white supremacy, apartheid South Africa, made the country highly vulnerable to attack by the apartheid forces, forcing it to make some decisions and even concessions it may not have made had it been in a safer and stronger position during that critical period, thus compromising its role as a frontline state in the liberation struggle.

Zambia was also economically dependent on white-ruled southern Africa – Rhodesia, South Africa and Mozambique – for access to the sea until years later when the Tanzania-Zambia railway was built by the Chinese (1970 – 1976) to enable the country to export and import its goods through Tanzania.

President Julius Nyerere of Tanzania acknowledged Zambia's difficult position and vulnerability at the hands of the white minority regimes in southern Africa when he addressed the Tanzanian National Assembly (parliament) in Dar es Salaam on 14 December 1965 to explain why Tanzania broke diplomatic relations with Britain, and why it was imperative for other African countries to honour their pledge to do so following Britain's unwillingness and refusal to use force to oust the Rhodesian white minority regime which illegally declared independence on 11 November 1965. Tanzania was the first country to sever ties with Britain. As he stated:

"Finally, on 20 November (1965) Britain accepted a Security Council resolution which included this phrase: 'Calls upon all states...to do their utmost in order to break all economic relations with Southern Rhodesia, including an embargo on oil and petroleum products'....

The reaction of the country which claims responsibility for Rhodesia has rather been different. On 23 November (British Prime Minister) Mr. Wilson spoke to the house of Commons, saying, 'We are going to study all aspects of trade and oil...we are not going in for a trade embargo or oil embargo alone.' And in explanation of this he said that there are many difficulties and 'there is the position of Zambia to be considered'!

That Zambia had supported the resolution appeared irrelevant to the British Prime Minister, who clearly thought he knew the business of that independent African state better than Kaunda. On 1 December, however, Mr. Wilson again said, 'We are not contemplating an oil embargo immediately.'

What is Africa expected to think of this mockery of a UN resolution which was already – at Britain's insistence – less than a firm, binding declaration of determination to defeat Smith?

On 1 December, however, Mr. Wilson announced new and much sterner economic measures against Rhodesia. Ninety-five per cent of Rhodesia's exports to Britain were then blocked, and financial measures taken which could have had a fairly quick and fairly severe effect on the economy of that colony. But Mr. Smith (prime minister) of Rhodesia was yesterday reported to have said that these have come too late to affect Rhodesia's economy.

I do not believe that he is bluffing. He has had weeks in which to prepare for these measures. But the timing is not my only criticism. I have argued that economic sanctions against Rhodesia will not work as long as South Africa is allowed to trade freely with the rebel colony. And it is Britain which has blocked obligatory sanctions under Chapter 7 of the UN Charter.

Commitment to Zambia

This brings me to my basic criticism of the British approach. It is a half-hearted approach, but one which leaves Zambia to pay a heavy price.

If effective and obligatory economic measures are instituted, and if alone they can bring down the Smith regime reasonably quickly and allow a new start to be made on the road to independence on the basis of majority rule, then on that basis I should be willing to support them: ON ONE CONDITION. That condition is that Zambia is not left alone to take the consequences of this procedure.

No African state is more concerned than Zambia that the Smith regime shall be defeated. No African President is more concerned that this shall be done without bloodshed and without unleashing a racial or ideological war. We in Tanzania join him in both these ambitions. But the power supplies of the Zambian copperbelt are in rebel hands; the power station of the Kariba Dam has been occupied by troops of the rebel regime. Is Dr. Kaunda expected to sit quiet while increasing economic pressure on the rebels makes them more and more desperate, until they finally use their power to interfere with his power supply? What happens to his own economy, and his own peace meantime?

In November, a week after UDI (Unilateral Declaration of Independence by the white minority in Rhodesia), Dr. Kaunda called for British troops to guard the Kariba Dam. A British representative was sent to Lusaka to discuss the request. Later the British Commonwealth Secretary was sent to Lusaka. The reason? That Britain was only prepared to send troops on conditions – and the conditions amounted to the defence of Rhodesia against attack quite as much as the defence of Zambia against attack from the rebels.

Dr. Kaunda accepted a Royal Air Force contingent because it was essential that his own country have some answer to the Southern Rhodesian and South African planes on his border. But, in the face of tremendous pressure, he has refused to accept ground forces under the conditions which Britain is imposing.

But the fact remains that the British Government has been more willing to use Zambia's difficulties as an excuse for inaction, than it has been to use them as a reason for action....

We continue to be ready to allow the transit of any goods or personnel, from any place, needed by Zambia to protect her interests and pursue the fight against Smith at the same time.

No one can drive a wedge between Zambia and Tanzania: neither can anyone hide behind Zambia's needs when they are trying to evade their responsibilities....

Africa has reason for its action, reasons for saying that the British Government has not shown serious determination either to get rid of those in Southern Rhodesia who have usurped British power, or to replace them with representatives of the people....

I have further shown that in so far as Britain has taken action which will, in the long term, cause difficulties for the Smith regime, she has failed to safeguard the interests of that independent African state which stands in hourly threat from that regime. She has failed to live up to the responsibilities she has claimed, and she has failed to protect – or allow others to protect – an independent state which is threatened because of her failure to immediately overthrow the rebel regime." – (Julius K. Nyerere, in his speech "The Honour of Africa," the National Assembly, 15 December 1965, *Freedom and Socialism: A Selection from Writings and Speeches, 1965 – 1967*, Dar es Salaam, Tanzania: Oxford University Press, 1968, pp.124 – 126. See also:

'For several years President Nyerere had been actively concerned with the situation in Rhodesia, and had been working through diplomatic channels to try and get from the British Government of the day a commitment to the principle of majority rule before independence.

In June 1965, the President had disassociated himself from that part of the Commonwealth Conference Communique which referred to Rhodesia because the British Government had refused to make this commitment even privately.

Following the unilateral declaration of independence by the Smith regime in Rhodesia, a Ministerial Meeting of the Organization of African Unity was held in Addis Ababa and, on 2 December 1965, passed a resolution calling upon all African states to break diplomatic relations with Britain if concrete steps to bring down the Smith regime had not been taken before 15 December.

President Nyerere addressed the National Assembly on Tuesday, 14 December 1965, at 5 p.m. on this subject, and the following day diplomatic relations between the two countries were brought to an end.'" – (Ibid., p. 125).

It is therefore important to understand Zambia's position during the liberation struggle in the context of southern Africa and what kind of problems the country faced in helping the freedom fighters in the region.

Even the man who led Swapo and who became the first president of independent Namibia, Sam Nujoma, had his credibility questioned, according to a report, "History Battle: Zambia's dubious role in Namibia's freedom fight," in *The Daily Press*, 15 March 2013:

"The difficult past of Zambia's ambiguous role in Namibia's and Angola's freedom fight is haunting current President, thus Foreign Minister, Rupiah Banda. The 1970s anti-communist Zambian regime is said to have killed Namibian freedom fighters in agreement with apartheid South Africa and Sam Nujoma. Historians confirm the allegations.

'There is no such a thing and the allegations are totally false,' President Banda responded to the allegations from Namibia's National Society for Human Rights (NSHR), that he and former President Kenneth Kaunda had entered into a *détente* with South Africa and Henry Kissinger's USA, leading to the disappearance of Namibian fighters.

'And you know my conscience will not allow me to be a leader even here if I was involved in any disappearance of anybody anywhere in the world. I will not be President of this country and I will be prepared to resign even today. There was no such a thing,' President Banda insisted.

What are the accusations that make a Zambian President offer his resignation if found true? They are explosive enough to cast a dark shadow over Zambia's and Namibia's history and their current leaderships. And historians speaking to *afrol News* confirm there is much truth to the allegations.

NSHR Director Phil ya Nangoloh started the debate in anticipation of President Banda's official visit to Namibia, demanding an explanation for what happened to dozens of SWAPO freedom fighters that disappeared in Zambia during a 1976 purge against the left wing of the freedom movement, which is now Namibia's ruling party.

Himself a SWAPO fighter in those days, the outspoken human rights activist outlines how SWAPO leader Sam Nujoma – Namibia's first President – and Zambian President Kaunda together with his FM Banda plotted to disarm SWAPO fighters then based in Zambia who were in opposition to Mr Nujoma's anti-communist stance.

According to Mr Nangoloh, an anti-communist *détente* between the US, apartheid South Africa and Zambia was in the making in 1974. The alliance was to stop the advance of Marxist movements in the region; in particular Angola's MPLA and partly Mozambique's Frelimo, but also Zimbabwe's ZANU led by Robert Mugabe and Zambia-based factions of SWAPO, both seen as radical and pro-communist.

As part of this détente, 'SWAPO's armed wing, the People's Liberation Army of Namibia (PLAN) – like Zimbabwe African National Union (ZANU) forces in Rhodesia – had to be disarmed and be barred from using Zambia as a springboard to attack South African forces in Namibia's Caprivi Strip,' Mr Nangoloh says.

During September 1975, Zambia formally ordered PLAN fighters to cease all military activities on Zambian soil. In April 1976, Namibia's PLAN fighters in south-western Zambia were "violently disarmed by Zambian troops," he adds.

Mr Nangoloh claims PLAN fighters in Zambia were thereafter taken to 'the notorious Mboroma concentration camp near Kabwe' in Zambia, where several were killed. At a later location, the Nyango camp, between 40 and 60 'radical' or 'rebel' PLAN commanders 'started disappearing without a trace individually and or in small groups,' he further claims.

The majority of PLAN fighters however were later sent for 'rehabilitation' to Mr Nujoma's new main bases in Angola. Also here, many 'disappeared' or were killed at Mr Nujoma's orders.

Mr Nangoloh's allegations have spurred strong reactions in Zambia, not only from President Banda. According to official history writing in Zambia, the frontline nation played an important role in the independence struggle of Southern Africa. Zambia hosted a large number of freedom movements, was a safe haven for oppressed neighbours and showed great hospitality at a great political and economic price.

This 'official history' of Zambia undoubtedly is true, and Zambians can for the most take pride in their nation's important part in Southern Africa's liberation history.

But also Mr Nangoloh's accounts are mostly to be believed, historians hold. They are parallel truths driven by a very difficult situation for Zambia in the 1970s, which however has been poorly documented and described so far.

Indications of President Kaunda's double play can be found in standard history textbooks, such as Oliver and Atmore's trendsetting *Africa since 1800*. Here, both Zambia's key role as a frontline state hosting foreign freedom movements and President Kaunda's 'bizarre meeting' with South African Prime Minister John Vorster in a train coach straddling the Zambian-Rhodesian border in August 1975 are described.

Also, President Kaunda's tense relations with Mr Mugabe's ZANU and Angola's MPLA are well-documented and referred to in common textbooks. ZANU fighters were arrested in Zambia, having to evacuate to Mozambique and Tanzania. Mr Mugabe in a 1976 interview even called the Zambian government 'an enemy of our revolution.' President Kaunda only had a relaxed relation to the South African communists (SACP), who formed the core of the ANC's armed wing Umkhonto we Sizwe.

But the depth of President Kaunda's involvement in fighting freedom movements he deemed Marxist or pro-communist have only been poorly studied. This also includes Zambia's role in the Namibian freedom struggle and SWAPO leader Nujoma's role in the regional play. As Cape Town history professor emeritus Christopher Saunders writes in a 2007 essay, there are 'worrying trends' in current Namibian history writing concerning 'patriotic history' as supported by the ruling SWAPO.

The rather well-documented executions of dissident SWAPO members at Mr Nujoma's orders lately have only been brought up by Mr Nangoloh and his NSHR in Namibia. Books on the issue by Mr and Ms Beukes (1986) and Ben Motinga (1989) were published in Namibia shortly before independence in 1990, but not after.

All other accounts have come from exiled Namibians or foreign historians. Siegfried Groth, a German pastor who had worked closely with SWAPO, in 1995 published his critical book *Namibia: The Wall of Silence* (Peter Hammer Verlag, Wupertal, Germany, 1995, 211 pages). 'When Groth's book appeared, the Namibian President, Sam Nujoma, appeared on state television to warn the nation against Groth's 'false history',' professor Saunders notes.

Paul Trewhela, a former South African political prisoner and exile, is among those having dug most deeply into these aspects of the Southern African liberation struggle. Mr Trewhela in a longer interview told *afrol News* that Mr Nangoloh's accounts are 'at least generally correct.'

President Banda was 'wilfully and knowingly not telling the truth. This has been the case with the SWAPO government throughout too,' he added.

'In the decades following independence, Zambia was in a very difficult situation,' Mr Trewhela however defends the Kaunda government. Zambia, as a landlocked country at the time had hostile white minority governments to its west, south and east, including Portuguese-ruled Angola and Mozambique, apartheid states South Africa and Rhodesia and South African-occupied South West Africa (Namibia).

Zambia's economic routes to the coast were very vulnerable. 'In the mid-1970s, President Kaunda was also very suspicious of Soviet interests in Africa,' Mr Trewhela confirms. There was an enormous pressure placed on Zambia by Western and South African interests to resist Soviet penetration, in Angola in particular, once the Portuguese colonial empire collapsed in 1974.

'This took the form of requiring, and securing, Zambian state participation in measures to prevent the Marxist MPLA from gaining control of Angola following the departure of the Portuguese forces. The Zambian state in turn required, and secured, collaboration in this from the SWAPO leadership, then based in Zambia,' Mr Trewhela explains.

Several international, non-Namibian historians confirm this. The Canadian historian Lauren Dobell writes in a 1995 book that 'SWAPO had been a minor but captive player' in the Kissinger detente strategy of the mid-1970s. Also heavyweight historians Stephen Ellis and Tsepo Sechaba in a 1992 book say SWAPO had 'compromised dangerously with the Vorster-Kaunda-Kissinger plan to invade Angola' in order to get President Kaunda's support to move headquarters from Tanzania to Zambia.

Zambia and SWAPO thus initially sided with pro-Western UNITA in the Angolan civil war. At one moment, 'units of the SWAPO military were ordered into battle in Angola on the same side as UNITA and the South African army, against the MPLA and its Cuban allies,' Mr Trewhela says, around the same time as SWAPO was fighting the South African army in Namibia.

Mr Nujoma's anti-communism move 'in turn provoked rebellion from SWAPO troops and the SWAPO Youth League, which was suppressed by force by the Zambian state and by SWAPO leaders,' Mr Trewhela adds. But, all of this was 'subsequently denied when both the Zambian state and the SWAPO leaders adapted to the victory of the MPLA in Angola, brought about by the defeat of the South African Defence Force by Cuban troops and weapons.'

Only after this victory did SWAPO move to Angola, after the ANC's Oliver Tambo had managed to persuade the MPLA to forgive Mr Nujoma. At first, 'the Angolans were angry over SWAPO's manoeuvres against the MPLA, and were unwilling to grant the organisation bases in Angola,' historians Ellis and Sechaba write. After ANC persuasion, 'SWAPO was duly granted bases in Angola, and in course of time it adopted Marxist rhetoric in line with that of its hosts.'

But meanwhile, Mr Nujoma and President Kaunda still were facing rebellious fighters and critical SWAPO cadres in Zambia. Historian Susan Brown writes that, in September 1975, 'the Zambian government ordered SWAPO to cease all military activities from Zambian soil. SWAPO was also ordered to vacate its farm outside Lusaka, where about 500 people were based, by the end of September. SWAPO sources were reported as claiming that Zambia had, in addition, intercepted all arms supplies to SWAPO.'

In 1975, the purges started. Historian Lauren Dobell writes: 'In the early hours of 21 April 1976, the Zambian army and police arrested 27 SWAPO members in Lusaka, of whom eleven ... considered to be leading the rebellion, were singled out and taken to Nampundwe Camp, where they were detained for two months before being transferred to prisons in Tanzania. Between 1,600 and 2,000 dissident fighters were also rounded up in the Western Province and taken to Mboroma Camp, near Kabwe.'

Pastor Groth, who spoke to many of those detained in Mboroma, says most fighters were given an option to rejoin SWAPO, now based in Angola: 'The majority of these prisoners came to the tough decision to return to SWAPO. Some 600 out of this group were taken from Mboroma to a re-education process at the SWAPO farm in Nyango; others to Angola. Little is known about the destiny of the returnees.'

Mr Trewhela holds that 'the disarming of PLAN fighters by the Zambian army in 1976 has been abundantly confirmed. The lack of adequate accounting for missing former PLAN fighters arrested in Zambia at this time is also confirmed.'

He adds that the SWAPO purges of the 1970s were mainly in Zambia. 'Its purges of the 1980s then took place at its subsequent bases in southern Angola, where a Marxist one-party state assured much greater scope than in Zambia for the Nujoma leadership to murder and imprison SWAPO members at will.'

While the disappearance of SWAPO fighters in Zambian and Angolan exile is little discussed in Namibia, non-SWAPO historians mostly agree that many Namibians – probably hundreds – died at the hands of their own leadership during the freedom struggle. There also seems to be agreement that several SWAPO – but also ZANU and MPLA – fighters were killed by Zambian authorities or troops.

Mr Trewhela told *afrol News* he basically agrees with the accounts of Mr Nangoloh, only disagreeing with some details. 'Probably nobody has been more dogged and courageous in pursuit of the truth in the region than Phil ya Nangoloh, who has been threatened on many occasions,' says the South African specialist writer.

'In general, though, my belief is that Zambia does have a case to answer concerning the welfare and lives of Namibian nationals held as prisoners under its own state authority in the mid-1970s, and that the full history of the detente scenario in Southern Africa should be brought to light,' Mr Trewhela concludes.

'Clarification of the reality of this period in the history of Southern Africa from 35 years ago is an urgent necessity for the region as a whole, above all for Namibia, where there has been no Truth and Reconciliation Commission. It would be a huge step if the truth about as many instances as possible could be quietly and comprehensively established, without fear or favour,' he adds."

In spite of the "dubious" role Zambia may have played in the liberation of Namibia, as some critics contend, there is no question that President Kenneth Kaunda and his government, as well as the people of Zambia, played a critical role in the liberation of all the countries which were still under white minority rule during that period. It was the only country in southern Africa, besides Tanzania a little farther north, which provided operational bases for the freedom fighters who were waging war against the white racist regimes in southern Africa – in Zimbabwe, Angola, Namibia and South Africa. Without Zambia providing such logistical and material support, and facilitating the incursions by the freedom fighters into the white-ruled territories, the liberation struggle would not have proceeded the way it did, and may have taken longer to achieve it goal of liberation.

The countries which helped SWAPO by providing material support for the liberation struggle included the People's Republic of China, the Soviet Union, Cuba,

Yugoslavia, Tanzania, Zambia, Algeria, Libya, and Bulgaria. They also, especially Tanzania and Zambia, provided diplomatic support in the international arena where they kept the Namibian struggle in the spotlight.

Even the white minority regimes in southern Africa acknowledged the vital role Zambia and Tanzania were playing in the conflict between the freedom fighters – whom they called "terrorists" or "terrs" – and the white rulers in the region. As Colin Legum and John Drysdale stated in *Africa Contemporary Record*:

"The Rhodesia rebel Minister of Law and Order, Mr. Lardner Burke, extending the state of emergency at the beginning of 1968, said that the number of 'terrorists' waiting in Zambia and Tanzania to cross the Rhodesian border continued to mount. The South African Deputy-Minister of Police, Mr. S.L. Muller, said Tanzania posed 'the greatest potential threat to the Republic.'

He claimed there were '40 camps in Tanzania for the training of terrorists and all the offices of subversive organisations.' In Zambia, he said, there were '19 training and transit camps.'

A new external service of Radio Tanzania was inaugurated in 1968 to assist in 'propagating the ideological principles of the liberation movements'....

The armed guerillas first entered South Africa's horizon in South West Africa in 1966 under the guidance of the S.W. People's Organisation (SWAPO), led by Mr. Sam Nujoma; and in 1967 in Rhodesia when the ANC (of South Africa) linked forces with ZAPU.

By 1968 the potential threat of escalating guerilla attacks became elevated to a top priority of the South Africa regime, in stark contrast to its claims in 1948 that its policies (of apartheid) would increase the country's state of security. Late in 1967 the Government appointed an expert in counter-insurgency, Lieutenant-General C.A. Fraser, as General Officer Commanding Joint Combat

Forces.

This threat was taken a stage further on April 24 (1968) by Commandant-General S.A. Melville, former head of the S.A. Defence Force, who said that South Africa already had sufficient justification and provocation for retaliation against countries which 'harboured' and encouraged terrorists whose only intention was to penetrate South Africa or South West Africa he supported the Minister of Defence's view that such countries should receive a 'sudden hard knock.'

On April 25, the Deputy Minister of Police, Mr. S.L. Muller, informed parliament on information about fresh groups of 'terrorists' gathering in Zambia....

On May 17, Mr. Vorster (the prime minister), speaking at the National Party's 'twenty years of Nationalist rule festival,' said slowly but surely an army would be built up in certain Central African States for an eventual 'now or never' attack on South Africa....These people have put it very clearly that they will abandon their plans only if South Africa is prepared to hand over to the Blacks'....

Two days before, on May 15, at a summit meeting of 14 Central and East African leaders in Dar es Salaam (Tanzania), full support was promised to the guerilla movements fighting in Southern Africa....

On June 11, the Portuguese authorities announced they had smashed an attempt by the PAC (Pan Africanist Congress) to establish a new route to South Africa through Mozambique. They claimed that four guerillas had been killed in a fight near Vila Pery, only 50 miles from the Rhodesian frontier.

In July, SWAPO claimed its guerillas had struck some deadly blows at S.A. Strategic points including the airfield at Katima Mulilo in the Caprivi Strip along the Botswana/South West Africa frontier. At first the S.A. Authorities denied reports of any guerilla activities in the Caprivi Strip; but later they confirmed the existence of considerable activity.

On August 8, the Commandant-General of the S.A. Defence Force General Hiemstra, replying to a question whether guerilla fighting in Rhodesia could develop into a full-scale war as in Vietnam, said: 'Most certainly yes'....

In October, S.A.'s Commissioner of Police, Major-General J.P. Gouws, admitting guerilla activities in the Caprivi Strip, said that guerrillas after failing to penetrate by the use of force, were now concentrating on slipping into the country to recruit local support for planned insurgency. The most important 'terrorist activity' had occurred at Katima Mulilo. 'Terrorists' were moving from village to village in an attempt to recruit local chiefs....It was impossible to keep intact 5,000 miles of South African border and 'some terrorists may have avoided security forces and be working much further inland'....

The Minister of Interior, Mr. L. Muller, denied SWAPO reports that 63 Africans had been 'publicly slaughtered' after attacks in the Caprivi Strip on October 13. But intelligence officers said there were signs of fresh attacks from 'across the Rhodesian frontier soon.' They claimed that the guerilla attacks would be spearheaded by about 2,000 Africans who had left the country 'under the pretence of studying abroad.'

this warning was repeated by the Minister of Police and Interior, Mr. Muller, on October 13. So far from the danger of guerilla attacks having receded, he warned, 'in actual fact the forces against South Africa were now stronger than ever before.' The major activity, he continued, was taking place at Katima Mulilo where groups were moving from town to town and attempting to influence chiefs to co-operate with them." – (Colin Legum and John Drysdale, eds., *Africa Contemporary Record: Annual Survey and Documents 1968 – 1969*, London: Africa Research Limited, 1969, pp. 220, 290 – 291, and 292 – 293).

The countries which were accused of harbouring and

training "terrorists" were Tanzania and Zambia; an accusation which also showed the important role the two countries were playing in the liberation struggle in the entire region of southern Africa still under white minority rule which included Namibia.

Namibian freedom fighters under the umbrella of SWAPO may not have inflicted heavy damage on the South African forces during the liberation struggle; but they did have spectacular success in the international arena where their diplomatic offensive against the apartheid regime was supported by the United Nations itself and individual countries on such a significant scale that without such support, the liberation organisation would not have been as effective as it was in its quest for Namibian independence. The United Nations established the UN Fund for Namibia to which contributions were made by the UN member states.

Guerrilla warfare alone would not have helped SWAPO achieve that goal. As Richard Dale states in his book, *The Namibian War of Independence, 1966 – 1989: Diplomatic, Economic and Military Campaigns*:

"Once SWAPO committed itself to battle against the South African regime on 26 August 1966, it selected the customary weapon that militarily weak commonly use in a revolutionary war, namely, guerrilla warfare.

Charles Maechling, Jr., has distinguished between guerrilla war and revolutionary war, indicating that 'the injection of ideology into guerrilla operations transforms partisan warfare into revolutionary war.' The term partisan warfare, he noted, is a far older one than guerrilla warfare, which dates back only to the resistance to the French invasion of Spain at the time of Napoleon.

Although the central goal of such combat was political control of the population, rather than of the territory, the guerrilla forces faced a well-armed, technologically sophisticated foe sustained by the resources of an industrialized economy. Indeed its foe has been termed 'the apartheid war machine.' Conducting a guerrilla campaign against the South African military and police forces was a daunting challenge to SWAPO, and one obvious way of diluting the strength of its military and police opponents was to diminish, if not terminate, the flow of internationally-based economic resources needed by the SADF (South African Defence Force) and the SAP (South African Police) operating in Namibia.

The task of mobilizing international support for applying militarily-related economic sanctions against South Africa was a challenging one for SWAPO and its diplomatic allies in the United Nations, although beginning in the 1970s it was able to point to two international achievements to marshal support for its position. First, it was able to point to its own legitimated position as the sole, authentic representative of the Namibian people, according to two United Nations General Assembly resolutions. In addition, the General Assembly granted it observer status in the General Assembly and in international conferences held under the aegis of the General Assembly. The United Nations Security Council, which had veto power over sanctions resolutions, granted no such privileges to SWAPO.

The second achievement concerned the Organization of African Unity (OAU), which functioned as a gatekeeper for national liberation groups. This organization was also an observer in the General Assembly upon an earlier recognition. By 1974, there was a nexus involving General Assembly-approved observers, the OAU, and national liberation movements. The OAU, through its Liberation Committee based in Dar es Salaam, Tanzania, provided a modicum of financial assistance to those liberation groups it recognized. However, SWAPO leaders were upset about the meager arms assistance that the OAU Liberation Committee provided." – (Richard Dale, *The Namibian War of Independence, 1966 – 1989: Diplomatic, Economic and Military Campaigns*: Jefferson, North Carolina, USA: McFarland & Company, Inc., Publishers, 2014, pp. 54 – 55).

He goes on to state:

"Although the OAU reflected the African nations' desire to maximize their influence in global affairs and to express their extreme displeasure with white minority regimes, not every nation contributed to the liberation fund, thus creating a free rider problem for the organization. Franz Ansprenger has provided data on the financial contributions to the Liberation Committee for the 1963 – 1973 period.

According to the personal recollection of the first Prime Minister of Namibia, Hage H. Geingob, the African diplomats eased the passageway for SWAPO representatives at the United Nations through their contact networks. Moreover, the United Nations, through its Council for Namibia, provided the necessary funding for SWAPO to have an office in New York. Lynn Berat added that the Council, in turn, represented SWAPO in several international organizations as a non-voting observer.

SWAPO drew compound interest from its OAU recognition as the sole representative of the Namibian people. The OAU granted exclusive recognition to SWAPO in 1965. Moreover, SWAPO could point to the delegitimation of the South African presence in Namibia by both the International Court of Justice – in an advisory opinion – and the United Nations Security Council.

Given the nature of the South African economic interests and investments of the Western permanent membership of the Security Council *vis-à-vis* the General Assembly, it was an easier task to persuade the non-Western members of the General Assembly – who tended to have fewer vested interests in South Africa – to undermine the economic underpinnings of the South

African military and and police establishment." – (Ibid., p. 55).

Dale further states:

"Even though I refer to the South African military and police establishment, it needs to be emphasized that this establishment functioned in both South Africa and Namibia, whereas SWAPO engaged both South African police and army units in Namibia – and Angola – rather than in South Africa. Thus, PLAN (People's Liberation Army of Namibia) had mainly one theater of operations, whereas the SADF/SAP continuously functioned in two theaters – and projected its presence to a range of Southern African nations, including Angola and Zambia. Consequently, it made no strategic or tactical sense for SWAPO to treat the SADF/SAP as two distinct units, one in Namibia and the other in metropolitan South Africa, and to impose sanctions merely on the forces stationed in, or assigned to, Namibia.

Force rotation was an essential attribute of the SADF/SAP *modus operandi*. The case, therefore, had to be made against the entire military and police forces, resident and non-resident, which, in turn, would allow for a widening of the international campaign to include African nationalist groups in South Africa." – (Ibid.).

Among all international forums, the campaign against South Africa was most effective at the United Nations. It was the focal point of international opinion and therefore the right place for SWAPO to concentrate its efforts to win support for its case against the apartheid regime.

The United Nations also played a very important role as a source of financial support for SWAPO in its campaign against South Africa to isolate and force the apartheid regime to relinquish control of Namibia and grant the country independence. Some of the funds were also used to support SWAPO programmes which were not military in nature. Military support came mostly from the Soviet Union and other Eastern-bloc countries including the People's Republic of China which was not a member of that bloc.

The role of the United Nations as a benefactor of SWAPO has also been underscored by Dale in his work on Namibia's struggle for independence on three fronts – diplomatic, economic and military – although there is some disagreement on the amount the liberation organisation received from the world body. As he states:

"One of the more significant aspects of the Namibian War of Independence is the financial backing of the two protagonists in what amounted, at least originally, to an asymmetrical conflict in which there was a marked imbalance in access to economic resources. Lauren Dobell claimed that, when examined from a *per capita* perspective, SWAPO received more 'financial, material, moral and diplomatic resources' than any other South African liberation movement. Yet she provided no numerical and comparative data to support this claim.

On the one hand, the United Nations served as a diplomatic forum for both the South African regime and the Namibian nationalists to seek and encourage supporters as well as to castigate each other and to undermine the supporters of their opponents. On the other hand, it became one of the financial patrons of SWAPO over the course of time. This reflected not only the growing ranks – and majority status – of African and Asian states within the United Nations, especially within the General Assembly but also the salience of anti-colonial rhetoric and actions to these new members.

Moreover, the top two leadership roles in the important Fourth – Trusteeship – Committee of the General Assembly – the chairmen and vice-chairmen – more often than not went to delegates from former colonies. This committee met more often than any other General Assembly committee, and it attracted top delegates from the anti-colonial states.

Furthermore, the plenary sessions of the General Assembly adopted the overwhelming majority of the Fourth Committee draft resolutions without making any changes.

As the era of decolonization advanced with the General Assembly, so too did the palpable UN support of SWAPO which had acquired a hegemonic position as well as observer status within the General Assembly. It had no important nationalist rivals.

The Pretoria regime found this incremental policy appalling, charging that the United Nations was no longer an impartial organization, and,...the South African authorities used their political leverage to terminate the financial support that the United Nations provided SWAPO during the run-up to Namibian independence in 1989.

This remonstrance did not mean, however, that the South Africans adopted a neutral financial stance in the 1989 Constituent Assembly elections (in Namibia). Far from it. They provided ample slush funds to anti-SWAPO political parties competing in that crucial election....

Just how much financial aid the United Nations provided SWAPO is a question that has not been definitively answered so far because the sources tended to be scattered, on the one hand, and because the data sometimes need to be disaggregated, on the other hand." – (Ibid., pp. 55 – 56).

SWAPO also received substantial amounts of financial assistance from individual countries and anti-apartheid organizations as well as other groups around the world. That was besides the amount collected under the UN auspices.

The anti-apartheid campaign was global and well-coordinated by some groups. There was hardly a country where there was no anti-apartheid organisation or activity. Although the organisations which carried on the campaign did so on their own initiative, SWAPO played an active role in many of their activities.

Even students in many countries mobilised forces to help SWAPO and other liberation movements in southern Africa. They organised campaigns against white minority rule, raised funds and coordinated their efforts with other groups who collectively constituted a network of activists round the globe.

Some of the most memorable events in the campaign against white-minority rule took place on Africa Liberation Day in the United States in the seventies when I was a student at Wayne State University in Detroit, Michigan. They were nationwide, every year on May 25th, which was also the day when the Organisation of African Unity (OAU) was officially formed in Addis Ababa, Ethiopia, in 1963.

Speakers who addressed the rallies included American civil rights leaders and other people such as Dr. Walter Rodney, the author of *How Europe Underdeveloped Africa*, who during that time taught at the University of Dar es Salaam in Tanzania but who travelled to the United States where he was invited to participate in the campaign against white minority rule in southern Africa. Representatives of the southern African liberation groups, including SWAPO, were some of the participants.

The global campaign against apartheid and other white minority regimes in southern Africa was one of the most effective weapons SWAPO used in its struggle for Namibian independence:

"SWAPO emissaries cultivated a wide array of financial patrons outside of the United Nations to defray the expenses of their organization, and most of these patrons were members of a global web of anti-apartheid interest groups that focused on Namibia and on South Africa – and usually on other white-ruled Southern African nations as well.

Nina Drolsum has termed these non-governmental groups (NGOs) solidarity organizations, while Mark Israel referred to some of the politically active expatriate South Africans in Britain 'international solidarity lobbyists.' Gretchen Bauer used the term 'solidarity literature' to cover the writings of these groups.

Their principal tasks were to mobilize subnational, national, and transnational support for the liberation movements and, conversely, against the South African and other Southern African minority-ruled regimes.

Characteristically, they demonstrated a strong strain of humanitarian concern, which was often theologically grounded, and did not countenance any direct military aid to SWAPO, preferring instead to allocate their resources to benign, non-violent pursuits. Within North America and Western Europe, the solidarity organizations tended to cluster at the center-left and left of the political spectrum."
– (Ibid., p. 57).

Religious groups were some of the strongest opponents of the apartheid regime and other white minority-ruled governments in southern Africa. One of the most prominent opponents of apartheid was Father Trevor Huddleston who, together with Julius Nyerere who was then the leader of the independence movement in Tanganyika before he led his country to independence, launched the Boycott Movement in London in June 1959 aimed at mobilising forces round the globe to boycott South Africa because of its racist policies.

On 26 June 1959, Julius Nyerere was the principal speaker – along with Father Trevor Huddleston – at a meeting in London, which launched the Boycott South Africa Movement. It was re-named the Anti-Apartheid Movement in 1960.

That was at a time when most African leaders were only concerned about the independence struggle and problems in their own countries. Tanganyika itself was then not yet independent. But Nyerere still felt that it was necessary for the people of Tanganyika and others to get involved in the struggle for the liberation of South Africa from apartheid. An injustice to one is an injustice to all because humanity is one. As he stated in his letter to the editor of *Africa-South*, October-December 1959:

"When I was a schoolboy, a friend of mine took me to the tailor one day and had me measured for a pair of shorts. We were great friends. His was mine and mine was his. He knew I needed a pair of shorts very badly. A few days later I got my pair of shorts, well made, fitting perfectly. I was proud of myself and proud of my friend. But it was not long before I discovered how my friend had obtained the money with which he had bought that pair of shorts for me. I returned it to him immediately. I could not disapprove of the manner in which the money had been obtained and still enjoy what the money had bought for me.

It is this same principle, which makes me now support the boycotting of South African goods. We in Africa hate the policies of the South African Government. We abhor the semi-slave conditions under which our brothers and sisters in South Africa live, work and produce the goods we buy. We pass resolutions against the hideous system and keep hoping that the United Nations and the governments of the whole world will one day put pressure on the South African Government to treat its non-European peoples as human beings.

But these resolutions and prayers to the United Nations are not enough in themselves. Governments and democratic organisations grind very slowly. Individuals do not have to. The question then is what an individual can do to influence the South African Government towards a human treatment of its non-white citizens.

Can we honestly condemn a system and at the same time employ it to produce goods, which we buy, and then enjoy with a clear conscience? Surely the customers of a business do more to keep it going than its shareholders. We who buy South African goods do more to support the system than the Nationalist Government or Nationalist industrialists.

Each one of us can remove his individual prop to the South African system by refusing to buy South African goods. There are millions of people in the world who support the South African Government in this way, and who can remove their support by the boycott. I feel it is only in this way that we can give meaning to our abhorrence of the system, and give encouragement to sympathetic governments of the world to act.

It is most fitting that Jamaica, that island which has solved its racial problems so well, should have taken the action it has in support of the boycott. It is equally fitting that the Trade Union Congress of Ghana should immediately have given its support. I was personally happy to participate in a meeting in London where the boycott was launched. Already the authors of apartheid are beginning to feel the sharp effect of the boycott. But they cannot feel it fully until every person in the whole world who disapproves of the South African system withdraws his support of it by withdrawing his contribution to its upkeep.

I must emphasise that the boycott is really *a withdrawing of support*, which each one of us gives to the racialists in South Africa by buying their goods. There is a very real sense in which we are part of the system we despise, because we patronise it, pay its running expenses.

We are not being called upon to make much of a sacrifice. We are not being called upon to go hungry and court imprisonment. That is the lot of our brothers and sisters inside South Africa. We are being asked to substitute other goods for South African goods, however much of a sacrifice this may mean to our suffering brethren in South Africa itself. We are not being called upon to support or not to support the oppressed in South Africa. We are being called upon to stop supporting those who oppress them.

The issue is as simple as that. Let every man and woman who disapproves of the South African system search his or her conscience, and decide to support or not to support the racialists of South Africa." – (ANC Documents, African National Congress (ANC), South Africa. See also *Voices*, Africa Resource Center, On the Boycott of South Africa, by Julius Nyerere, then president of the Tanganyika African National Union (TANU), in a letter to the editor of *Africa-South*, October–December 1959; reprinted in Godfrey Mwakikagile, *Nyerere and Africa: End of an Era*, Fifth Edition, Pretoria, South Africa: New Africa Press, 2010, pp. 550 – 552).

The campaign against the apartheid regime automatically included the white government of Namibia which was an integral part of the white minority government of South Africa. Therefore the Boycott Movement launched in London in 1959 against South Africa was inextricably linked with SWAPO's campaign and struggle for Namibian independence.

Together with the diplomatic offensive, mass rallies and economic campaigns against apartheid South Africa, the armed struggle still remained a vital component of the entire liberation strategy and was pursued with vigour by SWAPO with the support of African countries and other allies.

Yet, even Botswana, a country that was geographically in a very strategic position to serve as a conduit and as a rear base for the freedom fighters in southern Africa did not – and could not – do what a country like Tanzania, far away from apartheid South Africa, could do, for obvious reasons.

But in spite of its difficult position, Botswana was still able to help the freedom fighters the best way it could, thus incurring the wrath of the apartheid regime next-door which launched retaliatory strikes against the offices and other facilities of the freedom fighters who were based or who had sought sanctuary in Botswana. As Johann Alexander Müller states in his book, *The Inevitable Pipeline into Exile: Botswana's Role in the Namibia Liberation Struggle*:

"Without any doubt, Botswana was of strategic importance for both SWAPO and SWANU. This was not due to any active support the liberation movements received from Gaborone, but was rather a result of the inevitability of using its territory for those wanting to leave Namibia. In consequence, both SWAPO and SWANU established structures in Botswana, which were not only useful for simple transit, but also for the facilitation of communication and logistics.

Nevertheless, the general policy in the Bechuanaland Protectorate and Botswana not to allow military activity on its territory was a heavy burden. For SWANU, this policy was one of the factors that made all its military efforts fail. For SWAPO it meant that a strategic retreat into Botswana was to be avoided.

Besides, the option of establishing a military training camp in Botswana was hardly considered. Neither was infiltration into eastern Namibia ever considered by SWAPO. It remains highly speculative whether this would have proved efficient, taking into account that SWAPO was certainly more popular in the northern regions, where it eventually infiltrated its cadres, than in the Herero areas in eastern Namibia." – (Johann Alexander Müller, *The Inevitable Pipeline into Exile: Botswana's Role in the Namibia Liberation Struggle*, Basel, Switzerland: Basler Afrika Bibliographien, 2012, p. 218).

He goes on to state:

"Botswana managed to develop her own position throughout the years of the liberation struggle without having to constantly fear South African retaliation and without being seen as a vassal of Pretoria as, for example, Malawi was continuously being accused of.

Recollecting Vincent Khapoya's five factors in determining the level of support the liberation movements could receive from a certain African country, we have to assert that out of the five criteria the geographical position was the most crucial factor. This position resulted in Botswana's geopolitical dependence on South Africa and hence had a considerable impact on the way Botswana handled the liberation movements. It is clear though that Khapoya's factors lack the means to explain the activities of the Namibian liberation movements on the territory of Botswana as they only refer to the national level whereas, as we have seen particularly in the case of the Ovaherero in Botswana, informal structures played a very important role as well....

Over the years, Botswana increased her independence from outside influences – ...despite occasional border violations from South Africa and Rhodesia – when making decisions with regard to the liberation struggle in the neighbouring territories and thus gained what Jackson would have termed 'positive sovereignty' – the competence to exercise leadership in her territory." – (Ibid., pp. 220 – 221).

In spite of Botswana's support for the freedom fighters, there were circumstances beyond her control which made it very difficult if not impossible in some cases for her to fulfill her obligations to the liberation struggle. As Johann Müller explains:

"The assumption that Botswana's path towards more independent decision-making, with regard to the handling of the liberation movements, would be facilitated by developments in Angola, Mozambique and Zimbabwe undoubtedly proved to be true. In general, the number of refugees from these territories decreased dramatically with their independence. Furthermore, the opening up of the Angolan option for SWAPO members on their way into exile and the diminishing pressure from the eastern flank with the independence of Zimbabwe removed a great burden from Botswana.

Yet, this did not automatically result in more liberal conditions for the remaining freedom fighters. For SWAPO members, the importance of Namibia's eastern neighbour had declined, but SWANU members continued to face hardships in Botswana for reasons...beyond the control of the Botswana government.

There was never the slightest doubt that Botswana would not, at any stage of the liberation struggle in the neighbouring countries, soften her policies on the activities of the liberation movements. On the contrary, the clause to abstain from both military activities and politics on the territory of Botswana was universally accepted by government and opposition parties, as well as liberation movements.

Needless to say, the 'no violence' policy could not be given up mainly owing to South African pressure. In this respect, the eventual establishment of an army in 1977 was a confession that certain investments in issues of 'high politics' had to be made to guarantee the well-being of the country – although the BDF (Botswana Defence Force) was mainly a reaction to Rhodesian insurgencies at the time and not necessarily to South African intimidation." – (Ibid., pp. 221 – 222).

Botswana may not have provided military support to Namibian freedom fighters. But it facilitated the liberation struggle in other ways.

Although SWAPO leaders felt that international pressure through diplomatic channels, especially the United Nations, was a more practical and effective way to end South Africa's occupation of Namibia and enable the country to win independence, they did not rule out armed struggle as a complementary strategy to exert more pressure on the apartheid regime in order to force it to relinquish control of what had become a *de facto* province of South Africa even though it was still recognised as a separate country known as South-West Africa.

South Africa was determined to hang on to the territory, thus ruling out any negotiations with SWAPO, at least during that time. Attempts had even been made by the apartheid regime to negotiate with SWAPO but *only if* it could manipulate the process and ensure its continued to dominate Namibia. According to the International Institute for Strategic Studies (IISS):

"As South Africa faced both a growing insurgency and increasing pressure in the UN to grant Namibia independence, Prime Minister Vorster launched a bold initiative to pre-empt both SWAPO and the UN.

In September 1975, he invited moderate leaders of Namibia's 11 official ethnic groups to meet and draft a constitution for the territory, after which they were to establish an interim government to lead Namibia to independence. By preparing the territory for independence and allowing its black population a say in its affairs, Vorster hoped to ward off UN sanctions, while assuring Pretoria's control over the pace and direction of the independence process.

The draft constitution presented in March 1977 entrenched ethnicity as the organizing principle of the political system, and called for South Africa to control defence, foreign affairs and other matters until independence, which was scheduled for December 1978.

The Western powers, fearing that South Africa might implement the constitution unilaterally, organized a diplomatic *démarche* in Pretoria.

In April 1977 senior ambassadors from the United Kingdom, Canada, France, the Federal Republic of Germany (FRG) and the United States – the Western members of the UN Security Council – opened intensive private discussions with Vorster and political leaders in Namibia. By the end of the year, this so-called Contact Group, acting independently of the UN but with its approval, achieved astonishing results.

After warning Vorster that the Western powers could not support the interim constitution and that he could no longer count on Western vetoes to stave off sanctions, they persuaded him to nullify his constitutional initiative, to agree to end apartheid in Namibia and to hold free elections in which SWAPO could participate. He further agree to appoint a South African Administrator-General (A-G) to run the territory and prepare it for elections to a Constituent Assembly, as called for in UN Security Council Resolution 385." – (The International Institute for Strategic Studies (IISS), *Africa Volume II, Adelphi Papers*, London, new York: Oxford University Press, 2006, p. 229).

Without external pressure, the apartheid regime was not prepared to make any concessions on its own. While it is true that SWAPO did not pose a serious military threat to the regime in Namibia, its commitment to armed struggle played a role in encouraging external powers to encourage broad-based talks and pursue a negotiated settlement of the problem involving all the parties concerned:

"The Contact Group then began a long series of intermittent negotiations involving separate talks with South Africa, Namibia's internal political groups, the UN, the Front-line States and SWAPO.

Some agreement was reached on the conditions for the run-up to independence, for example, reduction of SADF (South African Defence Force) numbers and the confinement of SWAPO and the SADF to base; and the appointment of a United Nations Special Representative (UNSR) to oversee a cease-fire. In April 1978 a general framework for a settlement was accepted by South Africa 'in principle' and was adopted by the UN Security Council in September 1978 as UNSC Resolution 435." – (Ibid).

South Africa accepted a "general framework for a settlement" only under pressure, and only "in principle"; not out of genuine commitment to resolution of the problem. There were hardliners in the South African government who were not interested at all in resolving the matter. They were determined to maintain and perpetuate apartheid rule in Namibia. Together with many whites in South Africa, if not the majority, they had a fortress mentality and viewed black majority rule in any of the neighbouring countries as the coming of Armageddon for which they had to be prepared to sacrifice their lives in defence of a white nation and civilisation:

"By early 1978,...it was evident that the Namibian policy was causing serious discord in Vorster's cabinet, and that he was not prepared to negotiate seriously over the future of the territory.

South African relations with the West had deteriorated markedly following the Soweto uprising of 1976 and Western demands for fundamental change in Pretoria's race policies.

A *contretemps* with the West in 1977 over evidence of an impending South African nuclear test had further soured relations.

Vorster thus felt that a conciliatory stance on Namibia would be unlikely to bring any softening in Western policy towards South Africa. Moreover, the ailing Vorster was preparing to step down as Prime Minister, while his hawkish Defence Minister, P.W. Botha, was exerting an increasing influence on foreign policy." – (Ibid., pp. 229 – 230).

Apartheid leaders were not really concerned that Western powers who were their allies would punish South Africa for violating UN resolutions or any of the agreements they had made with other countries or parties. It was Western powers who had refused to impose economic sanctions on South Africa to force the regime to abandon its racist policies. It was the same Western powers who continued to sell arms and military hardware to South Africa in defiance of UN resolutions against such sales. It was also the same Western powers who continued to trade with South Africa, knowing full well such economic ties would continue to strengthen, not weaken, apartheid.

Through the years, South African leaders also knew they had powerful friends in the West who were lobbying and campaigning on their behalf in Western countries and in international forums. Some of them were in government and in legislative chambers including the British parliament and the United States Congress. They included powerful leaders such as British Prime Minister Margaret Thatcher, American President Ronald Reagan, United States Senator Jesse Helms and others, especially conservatives.

When the hawkish defence minister, P. W. Botha, succeeded Vorster as prime minister, the apartheid regime became even more intransigent. As events were to show years later, it was under Botha when South Africa became most violent in terms of suppressing its opponents – including hundreds of students who were killed by security forces in Soweto for opposing apartheid – and attacking and killing South African freedom fighters and political dissidents living in exile in neighbouring countries.

Nelson Mandela wrote in his book, *Long Walk to Freedom*, how he prepared to meet Botha for the first time and how he stopped half-way in Botha's office, just as Botha did, before they shook hands. Nicknamed "the Great Crocodile", Botha was known for his fiery temper and for pointing and wagging his finger at people when he was angry or reprimanding them. As Mandela stated:

"On July 4, I was visited by General Willemse, who informed me that I was being taken to see President Botha the following day....

I was tense about meeting Mr. Botha. He was known as die Groot Krokodil – the Great Crocodile – and I had heard many accounts of his ferocious temper. He seemed to me to be the very model of the old-fashioned, stiff-necked, stubborn Afrikaner who did not so much discuss matters with black leaders as dictate to them. His recent stroke had apparently only exacerbated this tendency.

I resolved that if he acted in that finger-wagging fashion with me I would have to inform him that I found such behavior unacceptable, and I would then stand up and adjourn the meeting." – (Nelson Mandela, *Long Walk to Freedom: The Autobiography of Nelson Mandela*, New York: Little, Brown, 1993, p. 97).

Yet it was also under Botha that South Africa witnessed the beginning of the end of apartheid and also the beginning of the end of South African rule over Namibia. As the struggle against apartheid intensified, South Africa became even more isolated internationally. The new prime minister was fully aware of that. He also knew he could not arm-twist world powers if they were determined to pursue a negotiated settlement of the Namibian problem and eventually of South Africa itself with regard to apartheid.

But Botha also had his own strategy. While not antagonising Western powers which were trying to help resolve conflict, he made sure that he did not fully commit himself to any negotiated settlement of the Namibian question. Yet by doing so, he antagonised SWAPO, the only group which was acknowledged and accepted by the United Nations and the Organisation of African Unity as the sole and genuine representative of the Namibian people; he also angered the leaders of the frontline states – Tanzania, Zambia, Mozambique, Angola and Botswana – who led the struggle, among African countries, against white minority rule on the continent:

"In October 1978, Botha succeeded Vorster to the premiership. Although he was a hardliner regarding Namibia, he knew that outright repudiation of the Contact Group's mediation would further isolate South Africa and would end the Western powers' invaluable Security Council vetoes on its behalf. Botha therefore opted for a policy of calculated ambiguity towards the Namibian talks.

In what Brian Urquhart, former UN Under Secretary-General for Special Political Affairs, later characterized as a 'Penelope's Web exercise,' South Africa managed to give the appearance of co-operating with the Contact Group and moving the negotiations forward, while in fact avoiding firm commitments and blocking progress. Such tactics were extremely effective as Pretoria clearly had the most to lose from the proposed settlement, and was further in a strong bargaining position *vis-à-vis* SWAPO and the Contact Group.

Robert Mugabe's sweeping victory in Zimbabwe's independence elections in early 1980 sent shock waves through the South African leadership, which had backed the moderate Bishop Abel Muzorewa. Immediate and bleak parallels were drawn with the Namibian situation. Mugabe's success, along with growing hopes that a

Republican election victory in the US would ease Western pressure on Pretoria, ruled out any South African concessions in the talks in 1980.

South African intransigence led to a hardening of attitudes on the part of SWAPO and the Front-line States, which called for sanctions and an intensified guerrilla warfare. They were supported by the USSR, which had opposed the Western-led peace effort from the start. Indeed, Oleg Troyanovsky, the USSR's Permanent Representative to the UN, repeatedly accused the Contact Group of conspiring with Pretoria to block a settlement and substituting promises for action.

While thus warning the Front-line States and SWAPO against putting their trust in the peace initiative, the USSR bowed to pressure from the African states not to veto continued UN support for the initiative, because despite their misgivings, the African leaders saw it as the best hope for achieving a settlement." – (The International Institute for Strategic Studies (IISS), *Africa Volume II, Adelphi Papers*, op.cit., p. 230).

Despite the odds against SWAPO because of South Africa's formidable military machine, the freedom fighters remained undaunted. And although they also engaged in conventional warfare, the guerrilla tactics they used against the apartheid forces enabled them to sustain their military campaign because they were an elusive target even in counter-insurgency operations launched by the South Africans and the South-West African security forces which were an integral part of the South African army.

SWAPO fighters were nowhere close to FRELIMO and MPLA fighters in Mozambique and Angola, respectively, in terms of organisation, mobilisation, training, combat experience and ability to wage war, let alone capture territory and establish administrative zones under their rule the way FRELIMO and the MPLA did during the struggle for independence. But in spite of all that, SWAPO was still a factor to contend with, in its own context, because of its determination to carry on the campaign even if it was unable to inflict heavy damage on the South African armed forces.

SWAPO freedom fighters also had an additional advantage from the late seventies in terms operation and logistics: a relatively secure rear base in Angola after that country won independence from Portugal in 1975, especially when fighting intensified in the region during that period because of the involvement of several actors and armies – internal and external – in the conflict:

"The diplomatic manoeuvring between 1977 – 1980 was accompanied by a rise on bush warfare by all parties. SWAPO, operating from its new sanctuary in Angola, staged several raids into Ovamboland in 1977, and the SADF estimated that several hundred SWAPO operatives remained active inside Namibia at the year's end. In 1977 South Africa began training ethnic Namibian units to track down guerrillas.

The war against SWAPO began in earnest in March 1979, with a combined air- and land-attack by the SADF which destroyed more than a dozen SWAPO camps in Angola and Zambia. SWAPO attacks continued, however, prompting Botha to call up 8,000 reservists, raising the SADF troop presence in Namibia to around 30,000.

By 1980, the 32 Battalion, composed of former FNLA guerrillas, was operating virtually full time inside Angola, where it established a buffer zone 20 – 30 miles deep to intercept SWAPO infiltrators *en route* to Namibia.

Botha's objective, however, was not only to contain SWAPO, but to destroy it as a credible guerrilla force in order to diminish its appeal inside Namibia and to weaken its claim to international support. Deep penetration raids inside Angola were therefore stepped up." – (Ibid.).

Although the independence of Angola was a blessing

for SWAPO, since it enabled the liberation movement to establish operational bases in that country with the full support of the Angolan government, it also led to the expansion of the war in the region when South Africa sent its troops into Angola to destroy SWAPO training camps and other facilities and also to overthrow the Angolan MPLA government which supported SWAPO.

South Africa also used UNITA forces, rivals of the MPLA, which were active in southern Angola to help the apartheid regime find SWAPO camps and destroy their communications facilities. Although UNITA was opposed to the MPLA government and waged its own war against it in order to overthrow it, it was at the same time fighting a proxy war for South Africa which also wanted the MPLA out of power. As a result of that, UNITA got a lot of support from South Africa for helping the apartheid regime wage war against its two enemies: the MPLA government and SWAPO inside Angola.

UNITA fighters were trained at South African military bases in Namibia and received weapons and fuel from the same bases to wage war in Angola against the MPLA and SWAPO.

The situation got worse in the early 1980s when South Africa expanded its military operations in Angola in order to destroy SWAPO.

The decision to intensify the conflict also drew inspiration from an external power, not just from within South Africa itself where security concerns were high on the agenda of Botha's government.

A conservative American, Ronald Reagan, had just won the presidential election in November 1980 and the apartheid regime now had a friend in the White House in Washington. The American secretary of state during that time, Alexander Haig, had, although indirectly or by intimation, made it clear in 1981 that the United States would not exert pressure on the apartheid regime to withdraw from Namibia or to change its policies because the two countries shared values which were worth preserving. The implication was obvious: let South Africa continue with its apartheid policies; protect South Africa as a Western ally and an embodiment of Western civilisation on the African continent despite her racist policies.

President Reagan himself said at a press conference in Washington, D.C., in 1985 and in a radio interview in the same year that there was no more racial segregation in South Africa; and that the problem which Americans once had no longer existed in South Africa. It was full endorsement of South Africa's racist policies. Reagan already a reputation as an opponent of civil rights legislation in the United States since the sixties which outlawed racial segregation and discrimination and was intended to guarantee racial equality for blacks. He was considered by many people to be a racist.

I remember watching and listening to Bob Schieffer of CBS News when he asked Reagan again at the same press conference in Washington, D.C., if there really was no more apartheid in South Africa. Somebody else had asked the president the same question earlier based on some statements he made before saying the kind of segregation that existed sometime ago in the United States no longer existed in South Africa.

Reporters at the press conference could not believe what he had just said. He was defending apartheid. He retracted his statement later. Still questions lingered, regarding his commitment to racial equality, as people wondered – why would he make such a statement in the first place? Didn't he really know that apartheid existed in South Africa and that black people and other non-whites were victims of racial discrimination in that country?

It was that kind of attitude that emboldened P. W. Botha to be more aggressive in his pursuit of SWAPO and in his invasion of Angola because he knew he had a friend in the White House who was not going to apply pressure on him to change or moderate his policies:

"The Botha government, emboldened by the more sympathetic policy of the Reagan administration, had launched a series of military actions in 1981 – 2 that raised the level of conflict from a Bush war with SWAPO to conventional conflict with Angola.

South African concerns centred on measures taken by the Angolans to defend their southern border against armed incursions by the SADF, including the emplacement of surface-to-air missile complexes and a buildup of heavy weapons, all supplied by the USSR.

Thus, in August 1981, South African jets attacked Angolan radar and missile sites, while SADF armoured columns crossed the border in an eight-day campaign against Angola's regular army, the People's Armed Forces for the Liberation of Angola (FAPLA).

The South African assault led to heavy fighting between the SADF and FAPLA, and resulted in South African capture of tanks, rockets and other weapons, as well as 29 Angolan soldiers.

Further incursions in 1981 and 1982 took the SADF deep inside Angola, where they skirmished with Cuban forces for the first time since 1975.

In December 1983, South Africa carried out another major incursion, codenamed *Operation Askari*, which lasted for five weeks. The declared objective was to pre-empt alleged SWAPO preparations for a large-scale penetration of Namibia. SADF officials had previously been voicing concern, however, over a chain of Cuban defence positions allegedly placed 100 miles north of the border. Thus while the South African Air Force (SAAF) attacked SWAPO bases 180 miles north of the border, ground forces drove 125 miles into Angola, where they engaged both Angolan and Cuban troops. Once again, the SADF returned with large amounts of captured Soviet weapons.

That incursion led to a meeting of Cuban, Angolan and Soviet representatives in Moscow in early January 1984, following which the USSR announced a new military aid agreement with Angola. Moscow had planned a massive reinforcement of Angolan defence capabilities against future South African incursions. During the next 18 months, the USSR supplied FAPLA with large quantities of arms, including such sophisticated weapons as T-62 tanks, Mi-24 assault helicopters and advanced surface-to-air missiles.

Soviet officials also maintained a tough diplomatic line, renewing charges that the Western powers and South Africa were conspiring to crush SWAPO, and the negotiations should be called off. Angola and the Front-line leaders disagreed. They welcomed a surprise South African announcement on 31 January 1984, made under US pressure, that its forces were preparing to disengage from Angola. Two weeks later, the details of a cease-fire were announced in Lusaka, following talks between Angola, South Africa and the US.

The Lusaka Accord established an Angolan-South African Joint Monitoring Commission (JMC) to patrol the border and deal with cease-fire violations. South African forces were to leave Angola within a month, and neither SWAPO nor Cuban troops were to enter the cease-fire zone." – (Ibid., pp. 232 – 233).

The presence of Cuban and South African troops in Angola had created a difficult situation for SWAPO. For them to launch military strikes from Angola across the Angolan-Namibian border, they had to be prepared to face South African troops which were already in Angola and working with UNITA to neutralise SWAPO guerrillas. If South Africans were to stay in Angola, Cubans were also going to stay in Angola. In order for the Cubans to withdraw from Angola, South Africans had to pull out as well. It was a linkage which frustrated SWAPO leaders who were at war with South Africa in order to win independence for their country. They even asked for more weapons, including tanks, from the Soviet Union although they were mainly waging guerrilla warfare against the South Africans, but complemented with conventional military operations.

The Soviets agreed to provide SWAPO with advanced weapons in anticipation of a major conflict with the South African armed forces in Namibia, in spite of SWAPO's limited capability to wage such a war. Guerrilla warfare was the best means for them to fight the apartheid forces. As Piero Gleijeses states in his book, *Visions of Freedom: Havana, Washington, Pretoria, and the Struggle for Southern Africa, 1976 – 1991*:

"In 1980...the Soviet Union sent tanks and armored vehicles via Angola to SWAPO. The Cubans thought it made no sense, and neither did the Angolans. ' We didn't understand why they sent tanks and armored vehicles to SWAPO because it seems to us that SWAPO has to wage guerrilla war,' President dos Santos told Castro.

Therefore, the Angolans decided not to give the equipment to SWAPO but to keep it for themselves. 'I must admit that...we worried that our decision might be misunderstood,' dos Santos confided to Castro. Indeed, it was an irritant in Soviet-Angolan relations. In 1982, Ustinov complained to Colomé: 'SWAPO has still not received the tanks we sent them. If they had them they would be able to fight against the South Africans." – (Piero Gleijeses, *Visions of Freedom: Havana, Washington, Pretoria, and the Struggle for Southern Africa, 1976 – 1991*, Chapel Hill, North Carolina, USA: The University of North Carolina Press, 2013, p. 353).

Although the Soviets were ready to provide SWAPO with the military hardware they wanted, including tanks, armoured vehicles and heavy artillery, as a possible counterweight to the military might the freedom fighters faced, they were also aware of the harsh realities on the ground. As Jonathan Steele states in his book, *Soviet Power: The Kremlin's Foreign Policy – Brezhnev to Chernenko*:

"For several years Moscow had given small amounts of arms to the Southwest Africa People's Organization (SWAPO) which was conducting a guerrilla war against South Africa's illegal occupation of Namibia. With Angola now secured as a sanctuary for SWAPO, an interventionist Kremlin might have been tempted to exploit the general international odium against South Africa by stepping up military supplies in the Namibian guerrilla war to the point where SWAPO could win a military victory.

Giving in to African pressure, Moscow made some increase in its aid and logistical support to SWAPO, but the Kremlin was well aware that the military balance was even less in favor of its clients than it was in the Arab-Israel dispute. It deliberately prevented any serious escalation of the war on the part of its allies. Over the next few years the decisive increase in the conflict came not from SWAPO's side but from South Africa, which repeatedly invaded Angola while Moscow watched passively." – (Jonathan Steele states, *Soviet Power: The Kremlin's Foreign Policy – Brezhnev to Chernenko*, New York: Simon & Schuster, 1983, p. 170).

Still, SWAPO guerrillas – short of South African withdrawal from Namibia, and independence for their country – were not ready to stop fighting despite the odds against them and even when the Cubans, the Angolans and the South Africans tried to reach a settlement to end hostilities.

Apartheid forces had to be driven out of Namibia by any means possible, including war. It is therefore easy to understand why the Lusaka Accord was not well-received by SWAPO:

"SWAPO agreed to respect the accord, but refused to declare a truce. Its guerrillas continued to move towards Namibia, either through or around the cease-fire zone, which did not cover the entire border.

SWAPO's intransigence at this time reflected both resentment at being excluded from an agreement that seriously affected its operations, and Soviet encouragement for its hardline stance. In a series of high-level meetings in Moscow in 1984, SWAPO and the USSR reaffirmed their joint commitment to SWAPO's continuation of the armed struggle.

The phased withdrawal of South African forces fell behind schedule as local SADF commanders complained of numerous cease-fire violations by SWAPO. By May 1985, as the last South African troops pulled out of Angola, the JMC, rife with dissension, was disbanded. In the 18 months of its existence, however, no clashes had occurred between the SADF and FAPLA." – (*Africa, Voume 2, Adelphi Papers*, op. cit., p. 233).

But the South Africans were not entirely out of Angola. They went back in, with mechanised units, heavy artillery and war planes, to help UNITA fighters who were about to be routed by the Angolan army (FAPLA – *Forças Armadas Populares de Libertação de Angola* – The People's Armed Forces for the Liberation of Angola). South African military officers conceded that had they not intervened, the Angolan army would have destroyed UNITA in southern Angola.

Fighting continued until the end of 1985 and beyond until the major clash which took place at Cuito Cuanavale between the South African/UNITA forces and the Angolan army supported by Cuban troops.

In November 1987, the UN Security Council asked the South Africans to withdraw from Angola. But they refused to do so. It was only when they knew more Cubans were coming that they changed their position:

"On 25 November, the UN Security Council voted unanimously to condemn Botha's 'illegal entry' into Angola, and demanded that Pretoria withdraw its forces unconditionally by 20 December. South Africa's Foreign Minister rejected the demand a few days later.

On 5 December, however, as Cuban reinforcements and new Soviet-supplied weapons were arriving in Angola, General Geldenhuys announced the start of a 'tactical withdrawal' of his troops from Angola, to be completed by Christmas.

The nature and extent of South Africa's initial withdrawal remain unclear. In light of the heavy fighting that ensued in January and February 1988, it seems that South Africa withdrew some units, while leaving its 82nd Mechanized Brigade deployed near Cuito Cuanavale, and sending in more artillery as the battle settled into siege warfare. Prior to this, the prospects for a battle between the Cubans and South Africans were heightened by Angola's announcement on 10 December that it had authorized the recently-reinforced Cuban brigade to patrol in southern Angola for the first time and to engage South African forces there." – (Ibid., p. 236).

The Namibian liberation war was inextricably linked with the conflict in Angola. Without Angola, SWAPO would not have had any operational bases to enable the freedom fighters to enter Namibia from the north. The outcome of the Angolan conflict would very much determine when and whether or not Namibia would get independence from apartheid South Africa.

The Angolan conflict included the famous military engagement at Cuito Cuanavale between the South African forces together with UNITA and the Angolan army backed up by the Cubans. It was a defining moment for the history of the region. As Professor Piero Gleijeses of Johns Hopkins University stated in his article, "Cuito Cuanavale Revisited," in the *Mail & Guardian*, Johannesburg, South Africa, 11 July 2007:

"This year marks the 20th anniversary of the opening of the battle of Cuito Cuanavale, in south-eastern Angola, which pitted the armed forces of apartheid South Africa against the Cuban army and Angolan forces.

General Magnus Malan writes in his memoirs that this campaign marked a great victory for the South African Defence Force (SADF). But Nelson Mandela could not disagree more: Cuito Cuanavale, he asserted, 'was the turning point for the liberation of our continent—and of my people—from the scourge of apartheid.'

Debate over the significance of Cuito Cuanavale has been intense, partly because the relevant South African documents remain classified. I have, however, been able to study files from the closed Cuban archives as well as many US documents. Despite the ideological divide that separates Havana and Washington, their records tell a remarkably similar story.

Let me review the facts briefly.

In July 1987, the Angolan army (Fapla) launched a major offensive in south-eastern Angola against Jonas Savimbi's forces. When the offensive started to succeed, the SADF, which controlled the lower reaches of south-western Angola, intervened in the south-east. By early November, the SADF had cornered elite Angolan units in Cuito Cuanavale and was poised to destroy them.

The United Nations Security Council demanded that the SADF unconditionally withdraw from Angola, but the Reagan administration ensured that this demand had no teeth. US Assistant Secretary for Africa Chester Crocker reassured Pretoria's ambassador:

'The resolution did not contain a call for

comprehensive sanctions, and did not provide for any assistance to Angola. That was no accident, but a consequence of our own efforts to keep the resolution within bounds.'[1]

This gave the SADF time to annihilate Fapla's best units.

By early 1988, South African military sources and Western diplomats were confident that the fall of Cuito was imminent. This would have dealt a devastating blow to the Angolan government.

But on November 15, 1987, Cuban President Fidel Castro had decided to send more troops and weapons to Angola—his best planes with his best pilots, his most sophisticated anti-aircraft weapons and his most modern tanks. Castro's goal was not merely to defend Cuito, it was to force the SADF out of Angola once and for all.

He later described this strategy to South African Communist Party leader Joe Slovo: Cuba would halt the South African onslaught and then attack from another direction, 'like a boxer who with his left hand blocks the blow and with his right—strikes.'[2]

Cuban planes and 1,500 Cuban solders reinforced the Angolans, and Cuito did not fall.

On March 23, 1988, the SADF launched its last major attack on the town. As Colonel Jan Breytenbach writes, the South African assault 'was brought to a grinding and definite halt' by the combined Cuban and Angolan forces.

Now Havana's right hand prepared to strike. Powerful Cuban columns were marching through south-western Angola toward the Namibian border. The documents telling us what the South African leaders thought about this threat are still classified. But we know what the SADF did: it gave ground.

US intelligence explained that the South Africans withdrew because they were impressed by the suddenness and scale of the Cuban advance and because they believed that a major battle 'involved serious risks.'[3]

As a child in Italy, I heard my father talk about the hope he and his friends had felt in December 1941, as they listened to radio reports of German troops vacating Rostov on the Don—the first time in two years of war that the German 'superman' had been forced to retreat. I remembered his words—and the profound sense of relief they conveyed—as I read South African and Namibian press reports from these months in early 1988.

On May 26, 1988, the chief of the SADF announced that 'heavily armed Cuban and Swapo [South West Africa People's Organisation] forces, integrated for the first time, have moved south within 60km of the Namibian border.' The South African administrator general in Namibia acknowledged on June 26 that Cuban MIG-23s were flying over Namibia, a dramatic reversal from earlier times when the skies had belonged to the SADF. He added that 'the presence of the Cubans had caused a flutter of anxiety' in South Africa.

Such sentiments were, however, not shared by black South Africans, who saw the retreat of the South African forces as a beacon of hope.

While Castro's troops advanced toward Namibia, Cubans, Angolans, South Africans and Americans were sparring at the negotiating table. Two issues were paramount: whether South Africa would finally accept implementation of UN Security Council Resolution 435, which prescribed Namibia's independence, and whether the parties could agree on a timetable for the withdrawal of the Cuban troops from Angola.

The South Africans arrived with high hopes: Foreign Minister Pik Botha expected that Resolution 435 would be modified; Defence Minister Malan and President PW Botha asserted that South Africa would withdraw from Angola only 'if Russia and its proxies did the same.' They did not mention withdrawing from Namibia.

On March 16, 1988, *Business Day* reported that

Pretoria was 'offering to withdraw into Namibia—not from Namibia—in return for the withdrawal of Cuban forces from Angola. The implication is that South Africa has no real intention of giving up the territory any time soon.'

But the Cubans had reversed the situation on the ground, and when Pik Botha voiced the South African demands, Jorge Risquet, who headed the Cuban delegation, fell on him like a ton of bricks: 'The time for your military adventures, for the acts of aggression that you have pursued with impunity, for your massacres of refugees ... is over.' South Africa, he said, was acting as though it was 'a victorious army, rather than what it really is: a defeated aggressor that is withdrawing ... South Africa must face the fact that it will not obtain at the negotiating table what it could not achieve on the battlefield.'[4]

As the talks ended, Crocker cabled Secretary of State George Shultz that they had taken place 'against the backdrop of increasing military tension surrounding the large build-up of heavily armed Cuban troops in south-west Angola in close proximity to the Namibian border ... The Cuban build-up in southwest Angola has created an unpredictable military dynamic.'[5]

The burning question was: Would the Cubans stop at the border? To answer this question, Crocker sought out Risquet: 'Does Cuba intend to halt its troops at the border between Namibia and Angola?' Risquet replied, 'If I told you that the troops will not stop, it would be a threat. If I told you that they will stop, I would be giving you a Meprobamato [a Cuban tranquilliser]. ... and I want to neither threaten nor reassure you ... What I can say is that the only way to guarantee [that our troops stop at the border] would be to reach an agreement [on Namibia's independence].'[6]

The next day, June 27, 1988, Cuban MIGs attacked SADF positions near the Calueque dam, 11km north of the Namibian border. The CIA reported that 'Cuba's successful use of air power and the apparent weakness of Pretoria's air defences' highlighted the fact that Havana had achieved air superiority in southern Angola and northern Namibia.

A few hours after the Cubans' successful strike, the SADF destroyed a nearby bridge over the Cunene river. They did so, the CIA surmised, 'to deny Cuban and Angolan ground forces easy passage to the Namibia border and to reduce the number of positions they must defend.'[7] Never had the danger of a Cuban advance into Namibia seemed more real.

The last South African soldiers left Angola on August 30, before the negotiators had even begun to discuss the timetable of the Cuban withdrawal from Angola.

Despite Washington's best efforts to stop it, Cuba changed the course of Southern African history. Even Crocker acknowledged Cuba's role when he cabled Shultz, on August 25, 1988:

"Reading the Cubans is yet another art form. They are prepared for both war and peace. We witness considerable tactical finesse and genuinely creative moves at the table. This occurs against the backdrop of Castro's grandiose bluster and his army's unprecedented projection of power on the ground.'[8]

The Cubans' battlefield prowess and negotiating skills were instrumental in forcing South Africa to accept Namibia's independence. Their successful defence of Cuito was the prelude for a campaign that forced the SADF out of Angola. This victory reverberated beyond Namibia.

Many authors—Malan is just the most recent example—have sought to rewrite this history, but the US and Cuban documents tell another story. It was expressed eloquently by Thenjiwe Mtintso, South Africa's ambassador to Cuba, in December 2005:

'Today South Africa has many newly found friends. Yesterday these friends referred to our leaders and our combatants as terrorists and hounded us from their countries while supporting apartheid ... These very friends today want us to denounce and isolate Cuba. Our answer is very simple: it is the blood of Cuban martyrs—and not of these friends—that runs deep in the African soil and nurtures the tree of freedom in our country.'

References:

N-1. SecState to American embassy, Pretoria, Dec. 5 1987, Freedom of Information Act (FOIA)

N-2. Transcripción sobre la reunión del Comandante en Jefe con la delegación de políticos de África del Sur (Comp. Slovo), 'Centro de Información de las Fuerzas Armadas Revolucionarias (CIFAR),' Havana

N-3. Abramowitz (Bureau of Intelligence and Research, US Department of State) to SecState, May 13 1988, FOIA

N-4. 'Actas das Conversações Quadripartidas entre a RPA, Cuba, Estados Unidos de América e a Africa do Sul realizadas no Cairo de 24-26.06.988,' Archives of the Central Committee of the Communist Party of Cuba, Havana

N-5. Crocker to SecState, June 26, 1988, FOIA

N-6. 'Entrevista de Risquet con Chester Crocker, 26/6/88,' ACC

N-7. CIA, 'South Africa-Angola-Cuba,' June 29, 1988, FOIA; CIA, 'South Africa-Angola-Namibia,' July 1, 1988, FOIA

N-8. Crocker to SecState, Aug. 25, 1988, FOIA."

The inability by South Africa to defeat the Angolan army and Cuban troops at Cuito Cuanavale amounted to a humiliating defeat for an army that had a reputation as the most formidable military machine on the continent.

Instead of conceding defeat, South African military officers and leaders tried to rationalise and justify the outcome by contending that their mission had only a limited objective and was not an attempt to crush the Angolan and Cuban forces. According to a report by the International Institute for Strategic Studies:

"Cuito Cuanavale is more than just another of southern Angola's devastated and abandoned towns. Its airfield, which can handle MiG fighters and large cargo planes, was one of the most southerly bases available to government forces. The town is also the site of an advanced radar installation – one of a chain across southern Angola to guard against South African air attack. Situated on the west bank of the Cuito River, Cuito Cuanavale is the gateway to Angola's remote south-east region. As such, it has been the staging-ground for successive FAPLA attacks against UNITA's main base at Jamba.

It is hardly surprising then that Cuito Cuanavale was the site of a four-month siege in 1987 – 8 by South African armour and artillery, and a dogged, dug-in defence by FAPLA.

Fighting continued on a large scale, with an estimated 4,000 SADF and SWATF troops, 8,000 UNITA and 10,000 FAPLA forces, the latter backed up by several thousand Cuban reinforcements who at first only assumed defensive positions around the town.

In mid-January, however, Castro – who by his own account took direct charge of the defence – ordered a Cuban attack on the South African forces which were threatening to annihilate three FAPLA brigades trapped east of the river. He compared their plight to the British forces stranded at Dunkirk, except that there were not 'even a few ships' to rescue the Angolans.

The attack, in which Castro claimed that seven Cuban tanks were destroyed, relieved the pressure on the

Angolans, who then dug in with their backs to the river and minefields protecting their front positions. The South Africans launched several unsuccessful attacks on the FAPLA forces in February and March 1988. Afterwards, the SADF limited its activity to long-range artillery bombardment until May, when it withdrew the last of its forces from the town.

SADF officials later asserted that their only objectives at Cuito Cuanavale had been to keep the airfield under fire and to render the town useless to FAPLA. If so, it took from February to May to accomplish – a long and costly effort *for so modest and impermanent a result* (italics added).

In fact, South African actions suggest that at least the original objective was to capture the town and permanently deny the use of its airstrip to FAPLA. According to US diplomats, the South Africans' success at the Lomba River had led them to believe that FAPLA could be dealt a decisive blow at Cuito Cuanavale, but their confidence was eroded by the loss of hard-to-replace aircraft and tanks and the stalwart Cuban-Angola defence. Western intelligence sources said privately that President Botha called off the attack after receiving an assessment of the SADF casualties it was likely to entail.

By May, South African attention had turned to southwestern Angola, where a bold deployment of Cuban troops towards the Namibian border was causing alarm in Pretoria." – (*Africa, Volume 2, Adelphi Papers*, op.cit., pp. 237 – 238).

What happened at Cuito Cuanavale – the biggest military engagement on African soil since World War II – had a profound impact on the chain of events which unfolded later and which ultimately led to the independence of Namibia.

Namibia's liberation was facilitated by the intervention of Cuban troops in Angola who were invited by the

Angolan government to help the Angolan army fight and push out South African forces which had invaded the country in an attempt to install a puppet government that would be friendly to the apartheid regime and establish a buffer zone to prevent freedom fighters from using Angola as a launching pad to attack Namibia and eventually South Africa itself.

Had South Africa not invaded Angola, there would have been no need for Cuban troops – tens of thousands of them (more than 40,000) – in Angola. The invasion was a blessing in disguise for Namibia.

Unable to defeat the Cubans, the apartheid regime had to make concessions and a commitment to resolve the Namibian problem.

It agreed to relinquish control of Namibia. It could no longer defy UN resolutions demanding its withdrawal from the territory. Otherwise the war would have spread to Namibia where the South Africans would have to fight the Cubans who were ready to cross the border; they were already flying MiG 23s over Namibia which the South Africans were unable to shoot down. Castro had already given orders to his troops in Angola to attack South African military bases in Namibia if the conflict escalated.

But in order for South Africa to relinquish control of Namibia, Cuban troops would had to leave Angola.

Had Cuban troops not gone to Angola, Namibia would not have won independence when it did. Even South Africa itself would not have ended apartheid when it did.

The South Africans would have remained defiant and would not have complied with UN resolutions demanding their withdrawal from Namibia. SWAPO guerrillas were not strong enough to defeat the apartheid forces in Namibia on their own.

The war by SWAPO to liberate Namibia lasted for almost 24 years from 1966 to 1990 at a cost of more than 20,000 lives.

The independence of Namibia signalled the end of

white minority rule on the continent. Only South Africa remained under white domination. But the white minority rulers of South Africa knew their days were also numbered.

Even the apartheid regime was represented at the Namibian independence celebrations by the South African president himself. According to a report from Windhoek, Namibia, by Christopher Wren, "Namibia Achieves Independence After 75 Years of Pretoria's Rule," in *The New York Times*, 21 March 1990:

"After 75 often restive years under South African control, Namibia was born today as the world's newest independent nation.

At a ceremony in Windhoek's sports stadium, the South African flag was lowered as many in the assembled crowd chanted 'Down! Down!' Then the new blue, red, green and gold flag of the republic of Namibia was hoisted, shortly after midnight and slightly behind schedule, to jubilant cheers.

'In the name of our people, I declare that Namibia is forever free, sovereign and independent,' said Sam Nujoma, the leader of the South-West Africa People's Organization, the main Namibian nationalist movement. Mr. Nujoma was then sworn in as the country's first President by the United Nations Secretary General, Javier Perez de Cuellar.

'As of today, we are masters of this pastoral land of our ancestors,' said Mr. Nujoma, whose guerrilla movement, popularly known as Swapo, fought a 23-year-long war against South African control. 'The destiny of this country is now in our own hands.'

South Africa's President, F. W. de Klerk, who came to hand over the territory personally, appeared solemn, in contrast to the broad smile displayed by Mr. Nujoma. Mr. de Klerk stood erect with his hand over his heart as the blue, white and orange flag of South Africa was taken down.

Mr. de Klerk declared that South Africa had lived up to its promise to give independence to the territory, which he and other South Africans long called South-West Africa. 'We extend a hand of friendship to our new neighbors,' Mr. de Klerk said in urging that the bitterness of the past be put aside. 'Good-neighborliness is in our mutual interest.'

As recently as two years ago, South Africa had more than 50,000 troops committed to the war against Swapo. The black nationalist guerrilla group has been transformed into a political party that now dominates the elected Namibian Government. In 23 years of fighting beginning in 1966, the South Africans suffered thousands of casualties in an effort to hold sway over the territory of 1.3 million, and the Namibians suffered casualties in the tens of thousands.

Mr. de Klerk's predecessors sought to justify their efforts to hold onto Namibia as necessary to stem the advancing tide of post-colonial black Governments, a pattern that the South Africans feared would threaten their system of apartheid, or institutionalized racial separation. Pretoria's decision to let go of the territory ended a long and difficult history.

'We Africans' Found Answer

Today, President de Klerk spoke of the political settlement paving the way to Namibia's independence as "the culmination of protracted negotiations in which we Africans found a solution to an African problem."

South Africa had claimed the right to remain in Namibia under its 1920 mandate from the League of Nations, and in 1946 considered annexing it as a fifth province.

Germany declared what is now Namibia as its protectorate in 1884 and as its colony in 1890. In 1915, South Africa seized the territory from Germany during

World War I and held onto it, initially under a mandate from the old League of Nations. Over the decades, it ignored repeated calls by individual countries and by the United Nations to free the territory.

Extensive diplomatic efforts were mounted to arrange Namibia's independence, with a near-miss in the late 1970's, when South Africa backed out of a United Nations Security Council plan for independence.

Finally in 1988, South Africa agreed to give up Namibia as part of a United States-brokered accord that also provided for the withdrawal of Cuban forces from Angola. Elections for an assembly that would write a constitution were held late last year.

Regional Diplomacy

The agreement to end the conflict also paved the way for new domestic policies being pursued by South Africa. Those policies have so far led to the release of Nelson Mandela and the legalization of the African National Congress.

At the Namibian independence ceremony late Tuesday night and early today, Mr. Nujoma hailed President de Klerk for 'active statesmanship and realism' in giving up Namibia.

'This, we hope, will continue to unfold in South Africa itself,' Mr. Nujoma said. He alluded to demands there for black majority rule and to the pending meeting next month between Mr. de Klerk and a delegation from the African National Congress led by Mr. Mandela.

Here in the capital, the arrival of independence for this arid and sparsely populated region was greeted with a pealing of church bells and a cacophony of automobile horns.

Evolution of Decolonization

In proclaiming its freedom to an explosion of cheers and fireworks, Namibia ended the long wait as Africa's last colony, joining the march to self-rule in black Africa that began with Ghana more than three decades ago.

Mr. Nujoma alluded to this when he described Namibia as 'a new star that has arisen on the horizon of Africa.'

An intermittent rain limited the size of the turnout but did not dampen the enthusiasm of the amiable crowds that filled the 17,000-seat stadium.

'It's a blessing from above on our new country,' a television commentator said of the rain, which is usually welcome in a dry country like Namibia.

Many Overseas Dignitaries

Foreign guests at the midnight ceremony included heads of state or senior cabinet ministers from more than 30 countries. Among them were President Kenneth D. Kaunda of Zambia, President Joaquim Chissano of Mozambique, President Hosni Mubarak of Egypt, and Col. Muammar el-Qaddafi of Libya. The United States was represented by Secretary of State James A. Baker 3rd, and the Soviet Union by Foreign Minister Eduard A. Shevardnadze.

Other visitors included Yasir Arafat, chairman of the Palestine Liberation Organization, and the Rev. Jesse Jackson.

Mr. Mandela, the senior figure in South Africa's liberation struggle, arrived late Tuesday as an honored guest. The crowd that welcomed him included a contingent of black South Africans waving the banners of the African National Congress.

'The whole world, especially Africa, rejoices with Namibia,' Mr. Perez de Cuellar said. 'What is a triumph for

Namibia is a triumph for Africa and indeed the principles that are enshrined in the Charter of the United Nations.'

U.N. Transition Role

The United Nations monitored Namibia's yearlong transition to independence under Resolution 435, enacted by the Security Council in 1978.

When the transition got under way last April 1, border fighting broke out as Swapo guerrillas crossing the border from Angola were attacked by South African security forces who left the bases to which they had been confined.

After fierce clashes, a cease-fire and withdrawal of the guerrillas was arranged. The transition process subsequently unfolded smoothly. In elections in November, 97 percent of registered voters turned out to cast their ballots for a 72–member assembly that drafted a constitution.

The South-West Africa People's Organization won 57 percent of the vote in November, but failed to obtain the two-thirds margin it sought, which would have allowed it to write its own constitution. Nonetheless, Swapo's political leadership in the war against South Africa now makes up the top echelon of the independent Government.

Wealth and Poverty

The new Government has inherited prosperous towns, good telecommunications, many fine roads, mineral wealth, game areas, great natural beauty and other aspects of an advanced society. However, it also confronts a high illiteracy rate and extensive poverty that will be difficult to end, given the new country's now-limited economic means. Moreover, the economy is closely tied to South Africa's, and Namibia's potential deep-sea port, Walvis Bay, remains a South African-controlled enclave cut into the Namibian coast.

Although the United Nations Transitional Assistance Group, which had as many as 8,000 soldiers, policemen and civilians here last year, will leave before the end of the month, Mr. Perez de Cuellar promised today that the role of the United Nations 'in assisting the Government and people of independent Namibia will not cease.'

The new nation has accepted an invitation to become the 50th member of the Commonwealth. It was considered eligible because of its links with South Africa, a former British colony not welcome in the Commonwealth because of its apartheid policies.

It is also expected to become the 52nd member of the Organization of African Unity and the 160th member of the United Nations.

Hifikepunye Pohamba, a Swapo official who will be the new Home Affairs Minister, told reporters that March 21 was chosen as the date for independence to express solidarity with South Africa's black majority in it struggle against apartheid. It is the 30th anniversary of the Sharpeville Massacre of 1960, in which South African police killed many township demonstrators.

The only country not invited to Namibia's birth ceremonies was Israel, because of its reported military links to South Africa and in deference to the Arab nations who sent representatives."

The independence of Namibia had a profound impact on neighbouring South Africa. It was the beginning of the end of white minority rule on the continent.

The citadel of white supremacy was no longer insulated from the nationalist tide that had swept across the continent ushering in the dawn of a new era of black majority rule. For decades, the apartheid regime has used its northern neighbours – Rhodesia, Mozambique, Angola – as buffer zones when they were under white minority rule to protect itself from nationalist insurgencies by South African freedom fighters who were determined to end white minority rule in their homeland. That was no longer the case.

With the independence of Namibia, the South African freedom fighters were now literary face-to-face with the apartheid rulers. It was a death knell for the apartheid regime. The bell had tolled in Namibia. It was now only a matter of time before the walls of this citadel of white supremacy would come tumbling down.

Almost exactly four years after Namibia won independence, apartheid formally ended in South Africa when Nelson Mandela was elected president in April 1994 in the country's first multi-racial democratic elections, ending centuries of white minority rule in that country. The end of apartheid in South Africa also marked the end of white minority rule on the continent.

Part Four:

The People of Namibia: Unity in Diversity Comparative Analysis

NAMIBIA does not have many ethnic groups or a large population as many other African countries do. But it has a number of groups which are profoundly different from each other; for example, the Baster, a product of mixed races; the Ovambo of Bantu stock; the San and the Khoikhoi, non-Bantu groups. Each group is unique its own ways.

It is this uniqueness of ethnic and cultural identity which has been one of the most effective tools in constructing a Namibian national identity in the post-apartheid era on the basis of unity in diversity when it can be a disruptive force if not carefully managed or if it is exploited by unscrupulous politicians for partisan interests and by other people in pursuit of whatever agenda they want to pursue at the expense of national unity.

The quest for unity in diversity has also entailed the adoption of a neutral language, English, as Namibia's official language. In the absence of an indigenous language that is accepted as the *lingua franca*, the government of Namibia felt that it had no other choice besides adopting English as the official language.

Although Oshivambo is spoken by about 50 per cent of the people of Namibia, it is an ethnic language clearly identified with the Ovambo ethnic group. Its adoption as the country's official language would have caused an uproar among non-Ovambos in the country and would never have been accepted as the national language unless all the other native languages were accorded the same status as happened in South Africa after the end of apartheid.

Namibia decided not to take that approach, giving all indigenous languages official status which would have amounted to what the government feared would be linguistic fragmentation of the country along ethnic lines (in a country that was already linguistically fragmented along those lines), and instead chose a language that was not identified with the white minority rulers, Afrikaners, in spite of the fact that Afrikaans is virtually Namibia's *lingua franca*.

Adoption of Afrikaans would have caused the same uproar it did in South Africa during the apartheid era when black students in Soweto refused to accept it as the medium of instruction and instead chose English, triggering the massacre of hundreds of black students by the security forces, an event that marked the beginning of the end of apartheid. As Harald Haarmann states – on Namibia's adoption of English as the official language – in *Handbook of Language and Ethnic Identity*:

"In neighboring Namibia, racial conflicts during the imposed apartheid rule were not as severe as in South Africa. This is one of the reasons why, in the newly independent state, the former colonial language, English, has been adopted as the one and only official language. There are more native speakers of German than of

English in Namibia. Nevertheless, it was felt that a neutral language such as English would provide the most favorable prospects for avoiding the cumbersome business of official multilingualism, with the participation of several European and indigenous African languages. Experts have noticed, however, that official monolingualism in Namibia is developing at the cost of local languages, which lack a tradition of standardization and its resulting language cultivation and maintenance." – (Harald Haarmann in Joshua A. Fishman, ed., *Handbook of Language and Ethnic Identity*, New York: Oxford University Press, 1999, p. 72).

Most African countries do not have an indigenous language which has been adopted as the official language; nor do they have an African language which is a product of many African languages, like Kiswahili (Swahili), and which is accepted as a *lingua franca* in East Africa.

Kiswahili is the national language of Tanzania and Kenya and is increasingly gaining acceptance in Uganda where the government has also made it one of the two official languages, together with English, although it is not widely spoken in that country as it is in Tanzania and to a smaller degree in Kenya where it is also an official language like English. Kiswahili also is the *lingua franca* of eastern Congo (Democratic Republic of Congo) and is widely spoken in Katanga Province.

Oshivambo, the most widely spoken indigenous language in Namibia because of the numerical preponderance of its indigenous speakers, the Ovambo, does not have that status in Namibia, like Kiswahili, to make it a credible candidate to become the country's national language. It is too ethnic.

By remarkable contrast, Kiswahili does not belong to any tribe; no tribe – besides the Swahili people, Waswahili – can claim it as its own indigenous language or its progenitor. That is one of the main reasons why it has been embraced and accepted by all the tribes in Tanzania as the national language. There is no single tribe in Tanzania that linguistically dominates the other tribes. Because Swahili belongs to no particular tribe, it belongs to all.

Kiswahili has given Tanzania a solid national identity, although at the expense of tribal languages. There are many young people in Tanzania who don't even know – let alone speak – their tribal languages. Even people from the same tribe, and from the same families, speak Swahili instead of their tribal language.

Even I can no longer speak my tribal language although I lived in Tanzania for the first 23 years of my life, although I still understand it well. But I have not forgotten Kiswahili. That is the language I used most of the time when I was growing up in Tanganyika, later Tanzania.

But, in spite of all that, tribal languages are not going to become extinct in Tanzania, although they have been supplanted by Kiswahili in most cases, a language that is also helping neighbouring Kenya to solidify its national identity.

Although Swahili has played a critical role in identity formation at the national level in Tanzania, a country where most of the people simply identify themselves as Tanzanians, the adoption of English as the official language of Namibia may raise some concerns among many people because of its impact on the children and on the future of the indigenous languages in that country; concerns which also justify the government's commitment to the creation of a modern Namibian nation on the basis of unity in diversity although it is resolutely opposed to what it fears would be "linguistic fragmentation" if native languages were elevated to official status at the national level; hence its choice of English as the only official language.

One of the Namibians who expressed some concerns about the adoption of English as the official – national –

language despite its advantages was Beven Liswani Kamwi, then a student at the University of Namibia studying for a master's degree in English, in an article, "Namibia: Pros and Cons of English as Official Language," 11 September 2012:

"My short paper seeks to critique the pros and cons of adopting English as Namibia's official language and medium of instruction and its implications. Before I start the discussion at hand, it is of utmost importance to provide a brief description of Namibia in relation to language policy.

Namibia is a country with approximately 2.1 million inhabitants, according to the 2011 population census statistics. Officially Namibia has thirteen languages of instruction in the first grades of schooling.

Out of these languages, three including English are European languages, while two, namely German and Afrikaans, are connected with the colonial history of Namibia. Interestingly, with such a low population figure, Namibia is home to many languages hence it was a daunting task to enact a neutral language policy to accommodate all parties in the country. This was also observed by one Maho in 1998. Maho remarked that Namibia is a vast country inhabited by few people, but it has many tongues.

Let it be borne in mind that Namibia is a multi-cultural, multi-ethnic and multi-lingual society, thus Namibia's approach to language policy and planning was based on the policy of unity in diversity.

At independence, the framers of the constitution decided to adopt English as the official language of Namibia, thus serving as a unifier among the many prevailing ethnic languages and cultural diversities in Namibia. From the linguistic and cultural perspective, one notices that with the introduction of English as an official language and medium of instruction in Namibia, many

Namibians are losing their cultures and competency in their mother tongues.

This is further worsened by the exposure to various media such as TV and radio that mostly conform to the use of English. This use of English appears to emanate from Namibia's language policy, which has adopted English to be the official language. Needless to say, the language policy in pre-independent Namibia did not seek to promote local languages and cultures but rather sought to marginalize them further since its policies were based on apartheid.

It is on this basis that at independence, a language policy was adopted with the aim to rectify the language disparities of the past. This gave birth to the declaration of English as an official language and some local languages. So the question which boggles the mind is, whether this language policy has really achieved its objectives in the period since its adoption? Admittedly, such question is open to diverse responses depending on one's detailed analysis of the issue.

My opinion on this is that, good as it may appear on paper, the language policy document leaves much to be desired in terms of accomplishments. Instead of promoting local languages and cultures, the language policy has made English dominant over them. Moreover, it is interesting to note that the Namibian language policy for education states that for pedagogical reasons, it is ideal for learners to study through their home languages and this obviously could also play an important role in local language promotion and cultural preservation.

In addition, the same language policy (1990) also outlines that the education system should promote the language and cultural identity of all learners through the use of the mother tongue as a medium of instruction at lower levels as well as teaching it throughout formal education. However, the practical reality on the ground is discouraging as the true reflection of the matter shows a number of shortcomings, amongst others, insufficient resources are available in local language development, insufficient teachers are qualified to teach the mother tongues, and general support from all the stakeholders for the development of African languages lags behind. We even observe a situation of unequal language development. In light of this, the dominant status of English is prevalent in many areas such as administration, education, courts, broadcasting and so on.

In contrast, the status of national languages is low as they are excluded from almost all official domains by the current language policy.

If this trend continues, then the use of national languages and the preservation of local cultures will not gain momentum. These local languages, which in my view are already minority languages in functional terms, will turn into marginalized languages in the future.

While it is an undeniable fact that English plays a key role both locally, regionally and internationally, this must not make us denigrate our national languages as they are the repositories of our cultures and define our existence as human beings. So, when we speak or use English, let us not forget the important roles that our mother tongues play in our lives." – (Beven Liswani Kamwi, "Namibia: Pros and Cons of English as Official Language," 11 September 2012, listserv.linguistlist.org/pipemail/lgpolicy-list/2012).

In addition to English being promoted at the expense of local languages, especially in the case of schoolchildren and older students, there is the question of its functional utility as a uniting factor in a country where the indigenous languages are so dominant across the nation even if it is only in the districts and regions where they are spoken.

Even if you succeed in uniting students from different tribes by enabling them to communicate in English, including adults from different tribes who already know the language, the majority of the people, especially in the rural areas, will remain the way they are: speakers of their native languages.

Also, Europe has played a role in determining and shaping Namibia's language policy, even if indirectly, not only because English is a European language, hence a product of Europe; the nation-state itself – Namibia and the rest across the African continent – is a product of Europe, inherited at independence; so are all institutions of authority in all the countries on the continent which were once ruled by European colonial powers, and even some of the policies adopted by African governments – they are influenced by European ideologies, and schools are patterned after the Western intellectual tradition. The institutions inherited from the departing colonial masters were never restructured to reflect African realities. And that includes schools.

After winning independence, African countries remained officially monolingual, using English, French or Portuguese, languages of the former colonial powers which were the official languages of those countries during colonial rule. Nothing else had changed much after the end of colonial rule, besides the skin colour of the rulers, white replaced by black in most cases.

The power structures remained the same, and all the other institutions, including schools, remained the same. The countries remained "united" as they were under colonial rule. What helped them to remain united were the institutions they inherited and kept intact after the colonial rulers left. Language – English, French or Portuguese – was one of the strongest bonds that kept them united. As Anke Beck states in "Language and nation in Namibia: The Fallacies of Modernization Theory," Martin Putz, ed., *Discrimination Through Languages in Africa?: Perspectives on the Namibian Experience*:

"Because of its neutral quality, English is believed

capable of overcoming ethnic rivalries in divided Namibia – a quality so much needed in a society where Bantu education and the concept of mother-tongue education at its basis were perceived to have deepened or even created gaps between the ethnic groups. This perception is also supported by more than 80% of Beck's respondents, who believe that English has the capacity to unite the Namibian people in the spirit of reconciliation.

But why, we may ask, should a language be able to overcome ethnic differences? Or, starting from the beginning, how, in the first place, would a language be able to *create* ethnic differences? Why does one need a 'neutral' language to unite a multilingual state? And why was that 'neutral' language, in the majority of cases, the language of 'the' or 'a' former colonizing country of the industrialized West?

In order to explain this phenomenon, however, we must refer back to the second half of the 19th century when European nation-states were in the making.

The roots of the irrefutable oneness of language and society is derived from Western social philosophy at the end of the eighteenth and the beginning of the nineteenth century.

As a reaction to the events of the French Revolution and the industrial revolution, a rethinking of the relationship of state and society became necessary. The consequence of these two turning points in history was the emancipation of the individual from the feudal community, together with aspirations for a new solidarity of state and people. The philosophical debate was carried on by focusing on the question of how to attain a societal homogeneity while 'persuading' the free individual (Kant) to integrate into the given norms of a united society....

Herder already points to the territoriality of language and nation, an idea which Modernization theory would revive in the 1960's.

....The 19th century model of the 'Kulturnation' was

initially revived and translated into the contemporary nation-building discussion of the 1960's by the Almond-Pye Commission of the American Research Council, which laid the foundations for what would become known as the 'Modernization School.'

It is important to note that this school of thinking and the concept of Herder's belief in the success of the 'Kulturnation' come from the same philosophical strands. Both believe that homogeneous language groups have the highest potential to 'prosper in peace.'

Since the pluriethnic and plurilingual character of most former colonized countries were regarded as detrimental to the nation-building activities of the state, it was regarded as vital to crush those identities which were thought to oppose the new state identity.

Subsequently, pluriethnic/plurilingual nations, striving to establish a common identity had to strive for a common language, too. Besides 'practical consideration' it was exactly this belief which encouraged the newly independent states to follow the 'one language–one nation' approach.

....Official rhetoric and propaganda about 'one nation–one language' finds ready-made resonance in the sentiments of national aspirations. Such rhetoric, however,...obscures the questionable and eurocentric, eurospecific assumptions on which they are based.

It is not my contention here that everything and anything which is Europe-biased is detrimental to the national interests of 'Third World' countries.

However, borrowing and implementing eurocentric ideas and theories in Namibia could have been based on a much more rigorous scrutiny of their applicability in Namibia. It seems that such a scrutiny was never undertaken." – (Anke Beck, "Language and nation in Namibia: The Fallacies of Modernization Theory," in Martin Putz, ed., *Discrimination Through Languages in Africa?: Perspectives on the Namibian Experience*, Berlin,

Germany: Mouton de Gruyter, 1995, pp. 212, 214 – 215, and 218).

Namibia's language policy has its advantages, especially in this global village where English is the most widely used language. It is a policy formulated with good intentions. But good intentions are not enough.

Monolingualism will probably remain an unattainable ideal in Namibia's context, as is the case with most African countries, because of the dominance of the indigenous languages which are the primary languages of the vast majority of the people.

Therefore, Namibia's adoption of English as the official language in a country where most people don't know and don't speak English does not make it a national language – simply because the government says so – the way Kiswahili is in Tanzania where, for all practical purposes, it *is* the national language. Almost every Tanzanian speaks Kiswahili.

That is a vital distinction between an official language and a national language; an indispensable tool in nation building and identity formation.

Almost 88 per cent of the people of Namibia speak African languages. English is spoken by less than 1 per cent of them. It may be official but it is *not* national. As Jenna Frydman states in "A Critical Analysis of Namibia's English-Only Language Policy":

"English (is spoken) by a mere 0.8% (Brock-Utne and Holmarsdottir 2001; Pütz 1995). Ironically, English, the first language of the smallest percentage of Namibia's population, is the official language of the country, used in all of its formal domains.....

As the apartheid system became increasingly more oppressive, SWAPO, the leading organization in Namibia's liberation movement, deemed it necessary to replace Afrikaans, the 'language of the oppressors,' and to establish a language policy in preparation for an independent Namibia.

The outcome of SWAPO's language planning for an independent Namibia was a policy of official monolingualism with English serving as the single official language....

The decision to establish English as the sole official language in Namibia was based on an ideology informed chiefly by the sociopolitical circumstances of the country. Oppressed and divided by South Africa's apartheid regime, Namibia sought liberation and unity. English, they believed, would be the vehicle to achieve these ideals.

If Afrikaans was the language of oppression, then English was the language of resistance and liberation. Imbued with this symbolism, English and its prospect as Namibia's official language gained widespread support among the masses, whose views by and large echoed those of the SWAPO government.

Despite the fact that only 0.8% of the population spoke English as a first language and only another 4% as a second language, surveys show that English was the favored language among Namibians (Pütz 1995). Even in Kaokoland, where 91.7% of the population claimed to not understand English at all, English was highly preferred as the official language (Maho 1998).

English came to the fore in Namibia as a language of resistance and liberation that would serve as a tool in the country's struggle for independence. After this ideology was promoted by the SWAPO government and embraced by its people, it evolved to also incorporate the pursuit of unity, which was deemed integral for a successful independent Namibia.

South Africa had long pursued a policy of ethnolinguistic fragmentation in Namibia to divide its people, so with imminent independence it became of utmost importance to unite the Namibian population into one nation. This, SWAPO believed, could only be achieved with English, a neutral and extra-ethnic language, as the official language. In the foreword to the UNIN document, director Hage Geingob (1981) stated clearly that 'the aim of introducing English is to introduce an official language that will steer the people away from lingo-tribal affiliations and differences and create conditions conducive to national unity in the realm of language.'

Thus, when the UNIN document *Towards a Namibian Language Policy: English as the official language* was published in 1981, English had already been decided upon as Namibia's official language, and primarily on ideological grounds." – (Jenna Frydman, "A Critical Analysis of Namibia's English-Only Language Policy," University of Illinois at Urbana-Champaign, Illinois, USA, 2011, pp. 182, 183).

The main reason English was chosen to be the official language was that it would foster unity among Namibians of all ethnic groups and races, and thus help to build a unified nation; unlike any of the other languages whose choice as the national language would have been resented by other groups and would have further divided the country.

English was also the language that had been used by SWAPO during the liberation struggle and had therefore already qualified as a unifying language at the national level.

In spite of its long history in a country that was once a German colony, and its status as the official language during German colonial rule and as one of the the two official languages together with Afrikaans during apartheid, German was not chosen to be the official language of Namibia.

Although it was not considered to be the language of the oppressor like Afrikaans since Germans were not in power during the apartheid era when the people of

Namibia were fighting for independence, the German language was tarnished by its association with brutal German rule when tens of thousands of members of the Herero and the Nama ethnic groups were exterminated in the early 1900s.

The post-colonial government did not explicitly state why German was not chosen to be Namibia's official language. But probably another reason why German was not chosen was that it does not have the international stature English has, even though it is important in Namibia as a commercial language.

Even French was considered; which is understandable because of its status as one of the two main international languages together with English, although no reasons were given why it became one of the contenders for official status as the Namibia's official language.

Given its Pan-Africanist inclinations, and considering its history as a movement committed to the liberation of the entire continent, it is also understandable why SWAPO stated that Pan-Africanism – its promotion and so on – was one of the criteria which had to be taken into account when choosing a national language. But, in pursuit of that goal, it is not clear why the government did not even consider adopting Swahili to be the official language of Namibia, especially when it is the only indigenous African language which has been accepted as one of the official languages of the African Union (AU) which replaced the Organisation of African Unity (OAU) in July 2002; and was already a contender for official status in the OAU even before Namibia won independence.

Kiswahili is the most widely used African language in terms of the number of countries where it is spoken. There are more countries in Africa which use Swahili than those which use any of the other African languages.

Some of the strongest proponents for the adoption of Kiswahili as the continent's official language include renowned writers such as Wole Soyinka of Nigeria and

Ayi Kwei Armah, a Ghanaian.

Even many SWAPO members and other freedom fighters from other countries in southern Africa – Zimbabwe, South Africa and Mozambique – who spent many years in Tanzania which was the headquarters of all the African liberation movements, know Kiswahili.

One of them was Joaquim Chissano, president of Mozambique, who addressed the African Union in Kiswahili in July 2004 to underscore the importance of adopting it as one of Africa's official languages. According to a report by Panapress (PANA) from the African Union's headquarters in Addis Ababa, Ethiopia, "Mozambique's Chissano Addresses Summit in Kiswahili," 7 July 2004:

"Outgoing African Union (AU) chairman Joaquim Chissano of Mozambique on Tuesday made history by partly using Kiswahili to address the continental body's third annual summit in Addis Ababa.

Kiswahili is widely spoken in East Africa, parts of central Africa and in certain Indian Ocean islands.

Chissano, who also retires from the Mozambican presidency later this year, read more than two thirds of his report and farewell speech in Kiswahili, thus becoming a pioneer in the utilisation of an African language during a continental summit.

The Bantu language with a slight influence of Arabic is commonly spoken in Kenya, Uganda, Tanzania, Somalia, Rwanda, Burundi, Malawi, Mozambique, Comoros and eastern DR Congo, among other countries.

Although AU documents are not yet translated into Kiswahili, Chissano described his initiative as 'a provocation.'

His Kenyan counterpart Mwai Kibaki also spoke in Kiswahili in his contribution to the general debate at the third AU summit.

Observers familiar with the debate on the introduction of African languages during discussions of the continental body were not surprised that Kiswahili became the first to be used.

The constitutive Charter of the now defunct Organisation of African Unity (OAU) hinted about their introduction, while Article 25 of the African Union's constitutive Act clearly stated their importance.

'The working languages of the Union and all its institutions, if possible, include African languages, as well as Arabic, English, French and Portuguese,' reads article 25 of the AU Act.

The AU charter clarifies the term 'if possible' contained in the OAU charter to mean when translation is guaranteed.

This was the case when two Kiswahili speakers addressed the summit on Tuesday.

The audience applauded the initiative in spite of a few moments of confusion.

The utilisation of Kiswahili was first endorsed by the Southern Africa Development Community (SADC) before being tabled for discussion last year during the second AU summit in Maputo, Mozambique, where it was formally recognised as one of the Union's working languages.

Other main African languages such as Hausa, Mandingo, Lingala and Fulani could also be used during AU meeting once simultaneous translation into the other working languages is possible."

According to another report, BBC, "Swahili Baffles African Leaders," 6 July 2004:

"A summit of African leaders was thrown into confusion when Mozambique's president addressed the meeting in an African language – Swahili.

Officials scrambled around looking for interpreters and President Joaquim Chissano offered to translate himself.

The African Union uses Arabic, French, English and Portuguese in its summits.

Mr Chissano said he made his farewell address as AU chairman in Swahili to further the AU pledge to promote African identity and languages.

Swahili is spoken by around 100 million people in East Africa and there are moves to add it to the list of official languages.

But Mr Chissano is not a native Swahili-speaker.

Reuters news agency reports that most African leaders and ambassadors were baffled, unable to understand what he was saying.

After his speech, Sudan's ambassador to Ethiopia announced that Nigeria's Olusegun Obasanjo had been elected as the next AU chairman, noting that his speech would be in 'another African language' – Arabic."

In the case of Namibia, only time will tell what role English plays in promoting unity and in helping the country to form a strong national identity.

Probably the biggest obstacle to promoting unity by using English is that the language is not understood by the vast majority of Namibians. You can *not* unite a country by leaving out the majority: the people who live in the rural areas, most of whom know nothing about English, let alone the language itself.

In a country without an indigenous common language which is spoken by everybody including those who never went to school, the way Kiswahili is spoken and understood by every Tanzanian, indigenous languages do have a role to play in uniting the country. And they are the only ones which can play that role because of their widespread use, although within their own areas.

A language can *not* be a unifying factor – at the national level – unless it is a language of the people, not just the elite, understood in the rural areas where the majority of the people live. English does not meet that criterion in any African country; nor does French or Portuguese.

It does not make much sense to say former colonies in Africa are English-speaking or French-speaking countries when the vast majority of the people in those countries – probably more than 80 per cent – don't even know English and French but instead speak their own native languages on daily basis.

A multilingual approach may therefore be a more realistic alternative in the quest for unity – and equality – even in Namibia as it is in South Africa. It guarantees communication on a much wider scale all the way down to the grassroots level. No-one is left out, and no-one feels marginalised by using somebody else's language, except his or her own, as English continues to be taught.

English should be taught together with local languages which can be an effective medium of instruction in schools. Children learn better in their own native language than they do in a foreign language.

Once students reach secondary school, they can then be taught all subjects in English after learning the language for a number of years as the was the case in Tanganyika, later Tanzania, before and after independence. I am a product of that school system.

I started learning English when I was in middle school in Tanganyika. That was in January 1961 when I was in Standard Five. I was eleven years old. It was also a boarding school and went up to Standard Eight. It had students and teachers from different parts of Tanganyika, which helped us to know and accept members of other tribes as fellow Tanganyikans, instead of seeing them as "foreigners" in our home district.

We were in class together; we stayed in the same dormitories; we ate and played together, without discrimination, enabling us to develop a strong sense of national identity at a very early age, although we did not, conceptually, know what national identity and other concepts such as nation-building meant. But we knew we were all Tanganyikans, later Tanzanians – after

Tanganyika united with Zanzibar in April 1964 to form Tanzania – an identity that transcended our ethnic identities.

We also had two American Peace Corps teachers who taught us English and other subjects including mathematics as much as our African teachers did.

Before then, when I was in primary school from Standard One to Standard Four, I was taught all subjects in Kiswahili.

When I went to secondary school in 1965 (Standard 9 – Standard 12 or Form One to Form Four), I was ready to be taught in English after learning the language for four years in middle school from 1961 to 1964. And when I finished secondary school in 1968 after completing Standard 12, I went to high school (Standard 13 – Standard 14 or Form Five to Form Six), ready to study advanced texts in English. I had already studied Shakespeare and other works of literature when I was in secondary school.

Secondary school education prepared us well for the future in terms of employment and higher education, although not every student excelled in English; in fact, only very few did. But most of the students knew the language very well after finishing secondary school.

It is also when students are in secondary school that they can have a better understanding of concepts such as national identity, nationhood, nation-building including national policies, and become aware of things from a broader national perspective.

They can also play a major role in building a truly united country if they attend school with members of other tribes and are sent to school in other districts and regions, away from their own, as one way of breaking down ethnic barriers and fighting tribalism; a policy which has been very effective in Tanzania since independence even though tribalism has never been a major problem in the country. It still helped us to build a truly united country where the people are proud of their national identity as Tanzanians instead of glorifying their tribes; which is in sharp contrast with most African countries, a phenomenon that has also been observed by many foreigners who have been to Tanzania.

It is impossible to build a truly united country if some groups are marginalised and if discrimination of any kind is condoned or ignored. A nation with a solid national identity must be inclusive, embracing all groups regardless of race, ethnicity, religion, origin, or social and economic status. As Ronald Aminzade states in his book, *Race, Nation, and Citizenship in Post-Colonial Africa: The Case of Tanzania*:

"It is clear that the process of developing rules governing membership in a national community – i.e., the terms of citizenship – always involves exclusive as well as inclusive dimensions. As Charles Tilly observed, nations are necessarily exclusive in that they are communities of individuals who claim to be united by certain characteristics that differentiate them from others. Nation-building, he writes, is a process based on 'the drawing and politicization of us-them boundaries, the exclusion of visible others, [and] the foundation of membership on not being something else.'[10] The building of a nation, in other words, requires the creation of 'others' who are outside the boundaries of the political community.[11]

Love of one's country is typically accompanied by fear or hostility toward those perceived to pose internal or external threats, and that hostility may be expressed in practices and policies that range from collective violence to territorial expulsion to public policies restricting access to land, property, jobs, education, legal protection, political participation, or social welfare.

Tanzania provides an important case for studying exclusionary processes in the construction of the nation given that observers frequently cite it as one of the few cases of *inclusive* civic nationalism in Africa. 'Few countries in the world can match Tanzania's record of inclusion,' writes Godfrey Mwakikagile. 'And it is not uncommon to hear people from other countries who have lived in Tanzania say, 'There is no racism and tribalism in Tanzania.'[12]

Whereas many other African nations have experienced violent ethnic conflicts, Tanzania witnessed a successful nation-building project in an ethnically diverse society. Neighboring Kenya has been repeatedly plagued by politicized ethnic violence, including a 2007 general election in which an estimated 1,000 people were killed and 600,000 displaced.

Tanzania has also been relatively immune from racial and xenophobic violence. Although Tanzania had a colonial history of racial formation similar to that of Kenya and Uganda, unlike its East African neighbors, Tanzania did not experience any anti-Asian race riots from 1965 to 1991.

Some Asian-Tanzanians attained high-ranking ministerial positions within the postcolonial government, which repeatedly issued appeals for racial harmony. After attaining independence, Tanganyika, as the territory was known both as a British colony and before its union with Zanzibar, welcomed foreigners from still-colonial African countries as heroes of the liberation struggle and allowed Western expatriates to play a prominent role in the nation's new public university." – (Ronald Aminzade, *Race, Nation, and Citizenship in Post-Colonial Africa: The Case of Tanzania*, New York: Cambridge University Press, 2013, p. 5. See also, cited by R. Aminzade, Charles Tilly, "Boundaries, Citizeship, and Exclusion," in *Identities, Boundaries, and Social Ties* [AU: editors?] Boulder, Colorado: Paradigm Publishers, 2005, p. 181; Anthony W. Marx, *Faith in Nation: Exclusionary Origins of Nationalism*, New York: Oxford University Press, 2003; Kathryn A. Manzo, *Creating Boundaries: The Politics of*

Race and Nation, Boulder, CO: Lynne Rienner Publishers, 1996; Godfrey Mwakikagile, *Nyerere and Africa: End of an Era*, Atlanta Georgia: Protea Publishing, First Edition, 2002, p. 335. See also Godfrey Mwakikagile, *Nyerere and Africa: End of an Era*, Fifth Edition, Pretoria, South Africa: New Africa Press, 2010, p.509).

He goes on to state:

"While this sketch suggests a portrait of harmony, inclusiveness, and civic nationalism, an in-depth historical analysis offers a much more complex picture. Despite a nationalist master narrative that denies their presence, exclusionary policies based on race and nationality have been persistent features of political contention among Tanzanian nationalist leaders. A close look suggests ongoing conflicts over race and nationality expressed in public policy debates in which Asians and foreigners have actually been targeted for exclusion.[13] Those who portray Tanzania as a model of civic inclusion typically focus on outcomes, such as the inclusive 1961 citizenship legislation, rather than on the process that produced such outcomes.

Nation-building entailed intense divisions among nationalist leaders over exclusionary policies. Exclusionary public policies targeting purported internal and external enemies played a central role in fostering a strong national identity among the territory's culturally diverse population as did inclusionary measures, such as state efforts to provide schools, clinics, and clean water for all citizens.

The successful creation of a pan-ethnic Tanzanian nation-state and a strong national identity that transcended ethnic loyalties was predicated in large part on the political construction of internal and external enemies of the nation, defined in terms of race and nationality." – (Ibid., p. 6. See also R. Aminzade, footnote 13, p. 6: "I use the term *foreigners* to refer to the nonindigenous inhabitants of the territory prior to independence and to noncitizens of the nation-state after independence. The term *Asians* is used in the same way that it was popularly used after the partition of the Indian subcontinent in 1947, to refer to descendants of those who migrated to East Africa from India and Pakistan.").

The egalitarian ideals of socialism also played a major role in achieving and consolidating national unity – hence national identity – in Tanzania; an achievement I witnessed. As Ronald Aminzade also states:

"Despite its internal divisions, the socialist state remained deeply dedicated to the construction of national unity in a society that colonial rule had organized to promote ethnic and racial divisions.

The creation of a national identity involved political processes of inclusion and exclusion: to create pan-ethnic and cross-racial bonds of solidarity among all citizens of the nation and to identify – and vilify – internal and external 'others' who posed threats to the political community of the nation.

Socialist efforts to extend the social rights of citizenship played a primary role in the creation of national identity. The vast majority – 95 percent – of Tanzania's population of around 11.5 million lived in rural areas in 1967. Most Tanzanians were impoverished peasants who lacked access to education, health care, and clean water, and socialist policies emphasized the public provision of these basic necessities to all citizens as critical to the achievement of a unified nation and an egalitarian society. Whereas only 20 percent of the population was literate at the time of independence in 1961, by 1983, rapid expansion of primary school enrollment and adult literacy campaigns that reached 5 million people had left 90 percent of the population literate

– one of the highest rates in any developing country. Between 1970 and 1979 the proportion of children attending primary schools increased from 34 percent to nearly 100 percent.[111]

Rural health care services and medical aides helped increase life expectancy from thirty-five to fifty-two years between 1961 and 1985.[112] And although the government failed to achieve its ambitious goal to provide clean and safe water to everyone, by 1985, clean water had been provided to 42 percent of all households.[113]

But the socialist government also continued to pursue and deepen early postcolonial public policies designed to foster national integration and depoliticize ethnic solidarities. It was during the socialist era that Swahili became the dominant language, spread rapidly via the establishment of universal primary education.

At the time of independence in 1961, the year in which Swahili was declared the national language, only about half of the country's population spoke Swahili. In March 1967, shortly after the Arusha Declaration, the socialist government declared Swahili the language of primary school instruction, and in August 1967, Tanzania's Parliament established the National Swahili Council, whose task was to promote the development and use of the language.

By the end of the 1960s, about 90 percent of the population spoke Swahili with varying degrees of fluency, and it had become the primary language of national institutions, including the legislature, primary schools, national service camps, and army and police barracks.[114]

In most post-colonial African states, the tensions generated by distributional issues, such as the allocation of schools, clinics, piped water, and public employment, exacerbated ethnic tensions. In Tanzania, then, socialist planners were careful not to privilege any one ethnic group, instead distributing scarce public resources across the entire national territory in a manner that did not heighten ethnic tensions.

State policies to prevent ethnic tensions and foster national identification also informed the recruitment and training of personnel. For example, when the socialist government embarked on a major development project, the 1969 – 1974 construction of the TAZARA(Tanzania-Zambia Railway Authority) railroad, it emphasized it as a national rather than a regional project and recruited construction workers from around the country.[115]

Although the assignment of officials to regions other than those of their origin fostered national consciousness and the use of Swahili rather than local languages, the lack of local knowledge on the part of those posted to areas far from their home districts may have had a negative impact on the socialist state's efforts to organize and direct rural production.[116]

In an effort to counter the underpinning of ethnic inequality in uneven regional development, the seat of government was moved from Dar es Salaam to the remote inland rural area of Dodoma, a poor, relatively isolated region. Although some criticized the move as a waste of scarce government resources, the selection made a public statement that even the poorest tribes living in the most remote and impoverished regions were as entitled to public goods as those regions of export agriculture that had been privileged by colonialism." (Ibid., pp. 162 – 163. See also, cited by R.Aminzade, W. Edmund Clark, *Socialist Development and Public Investment in Tanzania*, Toronto, Ontario, Canada: University of Toronto Press, 1978, pp. 186 – 187; McHenry, *Limited Choices*, p. 85; David L. Horne, "Passing the Baton: The Presidential Legacy of Julius K. Nyerere," *Journal of African Studies* 14, 1987, p. 92; ibid., p. 91; M.H. Abdulaziz, "Tanzania's National Language Policy and the Rise of Swahili Political Culture," in Lionel Cliffe and John S. Saul, eds., *Socialism in Tanzania, Volume I: Politics*, Nairobi, Kenya: East African Publishing House, 1972, p. 171; Jamie Monson,

"Defending the People's Railway in the Era of Liberalization: TAZARA in Southern Africa," *Africa 76*, 2006, p. 123; on the absence of local knowledge as a key factor in the failure of state-directed development projects, see Scott, *Seeing Like a State*).

The choice of Dodoma as Tanzania's new capital also had highly symbolic significance. Centrally located in the heart of Tanzania, it was meant to be equally accessible to all Tanzanians, in terms of distance from all parts of the country.

It was this sense of equality which also partly inspired the establishment of the National Service. Enrolment in the National Service was non-discriminatory. Young people from all walks of life, and from all parts of the country, were enrolled regardless of their social status and education. They all did the same work and stayed in the same tents – those who finished secondary school and college graduates together with those who had very little or no formal education.

They were united by their common identity as Tanzanians, committed to nation-building and radical transformation of Tanzania into a socialist nation, and inspired by egalitarian ideals which formed the basis for a just society across the spectrum.

I was one of them. I went to Ruvu National Service camp in the Coast Region a few miles from the capital Dar es Salaam in January 1971, and later in July to another National Service camp in Bukoba near the western shore of Lake Victoria in the North-West Region which was later renamed Kagera Region.

Even national leaders went to National Service. President Nyerere himself had a National Service uniform which he wore when he worked on farms in the villages with the peasants. He also wore the same uniform on many other occasions when he visited different parts of the country to work with the people and address mass rallies. I remember what one news editor at the *Daily News* in Dar es Salaam, Costa Kumalija, said one day in 1972 when I worked there as a news reporter. He said, with pride:

"The elite are here in Dar es Salaam, living in comfort, while Mwalimu (Nyerere) is working with his peasants in the villages."

He did that numerous times in different parts of the country.

When died, the people, especially the masses, paid him the highest compliment when many of them said: "He was one of us." Simple, humble, and poor. And he died poor.

Tanzania may never get another leader of his stature in terms of humility and dedication, especially commitment to the well-being of the masses.

Among those who joined the National Service was Second Vice President Rashidi Kawawa; so did a number of cabinet members. As Ronald Aminzade states:

"The National Service played a key role in fostering national consciousness and the identity of citizen among the nation's youth during the socialist era. President Nyerere called in the nation's youth to be 'the vanguards of the socialist construction' as well as the 'enemies of our enemies.'[117]

A number of prominent political leaders, including Second Vice President Rashidi Kawawa and several government Ministers, joined the National Service for several weeks in 1968 to demonstrate their commitment to this important nation-building institution.[118]

In 1969 the socialist state affirmed its commitment to the nation's youth by lowering of the voting age from twenty-one to eighteen. In a March 1971 speech on the role of the National Service, Kawawa highlighted its goal to 'promote among the youth a sense of nationhood' and acknowledged the potential danger that 'outsiders will come and try to divide our people and to create suspicions between them on the basis of tribe and religion.'

In speaking about racial minority citizens, he acknowledged that the same danger existed on 'a much smaller scale, though perhaps with greater intensity' and urged people to 'act positively in strengthening the TANU doctrine of human equality so as to avoid the possibility of racialism, which South Africa propagates.'[119]

The need of the socialist government for highly qualified and educated personnel and the legacy of a colonial policy that had fostered regional inequality through uneven educational opportunities meant that charges of ethnic discrimination persisted throughout the socialist era.

Complaints about the persistence of ethnic divisions were expressed by those who saw Swahili as the language of *ujamaa* and equality and regarded the continuing use of local languages in public places as exclusionary and antithetical to socialist development." – (R. Aminzade, op. cit., pp. 163 – 164. See also, cited by R. Aminzade, "Focus on the Marchers," *The Nationalist*, 18 September 1967, p. 3; "2nd VP and Four Ministers to Join National Service, *The Nationalist*, 9 January 1968, p. 1; "NS: Training Ground for Socialist Living: Kawawa," the *Standard*, 29 March 1971, p. 5).

Young people in the National Service were some of the most politically conscious Tanzanians – so were secondary school and college students – and some of the biggest supporters of the liberation struggle in the countries of southern Africa, including Namibia, which were still under white minority rule.

Everyday during marches to work on the farms and back, we sang revolutionary songs condemning apartheid South Africa and other white minority regimes and pledged to give up our lives along with our brethren in southern Africa to liberate the white-ruled countries. It was a level of political consciousness that inspired other young people in the country to support the liberation movements and played a big role in fostering national unity and consolidating national identity among the youth.

Speaking tribal languages in public was frowned upon; that is still the case today. Even in the privacy of their own homes, many people in Tanzania, especially the youth, spoke Swahili and still do. Many of them, especially those who grew up in towns and cities, don't even know their tribal languages well, if at all. Swahili has helped to promote and foster national unity, and has given Tanzania a solid national identity, in a way that is unparalleled on the African continent.

Racial harmony has been another great achievement especially under President Nyerere whose legacy of fairness and equality had endured and continues to hold the country together. Blacks who talked about "Wahindi" (Indians) with racial connotations were automatically suspected of being anti-Asian and racist, as some of them indeed were, and still are. The primary emphasis was on a single nation, and one identity, as the attributes of a unified country where everybody had equal rights:

"Race, although discussed in coded ways, was a remarkably taboo subject during the socialist era. After the Arusha Declaration, the government removed all racial categories from national statistical tables. Socialist government policy prohibited candidates for political office from addressing the issue of racial inequality, and the government suppressed the use of racial categories in the 1970 census." (Ibid., p. 164).

In comparing Tanzania with Namibia, it is obvious that the two countries have taken similar approaches towards achieving unity. But there are also some differences. While Tanzania has virtually obliterated ethnic distinctions in order to build a solidly united country with only one identity, Namibia provides room for ethnic identities which co-exist with national identity.

There are also some differences in their linguistic policies. There is no school in Tanzania where children are taught in their tribal language or languages. It is not allowed. Also, Tanzania has chosen an indigenous language, Swahili, as its national language but primarily because it is pan-ethnic and does not belong to one particular tribe. Such a policy would have been counterproductive in the case of Namibia where there is no indigenous language which can be embraced by members of all ethnic groups because it would be identified with one tribe.

Namibia also chose a non-African language to be its national language because she had no other choice; a predicament that has bedevilled most African countries because they don't have indigenous pan-ethnic languages like Swahili.

Hausa would be a good candidate in West Africa. But the language is too closely identified with the Hausa ethnic group and would cause deep resentment among other groups if it were to be adopted as the national language in countries where it is widely spoken: Nigeria, for example, where there are already deep divisions along ethnic, regional and religious lines among the people; so would Oshivambo in Namibia where the Ovambo are also resented by some members of other ethnic groups because they are politically dominant and are accused of practising discrimination against other groups.

Unity in Namibia requires a neutral language, hence the choice of English, but only if it can be learned by the majority of the people of all ethnic groups. The alternative is linguistic sovereignty, giving all languages equal status as national languages. As a multilingual society, Namibia already has ethnic groups which are linguistically sovereign and co-exist on the basis of unity in diversity.

The obstacles Namibia faces in spreading the use of English has led some people to question the wisdom of choosing it as the official – hence national – language in a country where the majority of the people don't even have the opportunity to learn it; even students face enormous obstacles in trying to learn English because they don't have teachers, and the ones they have don't know the language well themselves; also in a country where ethnic languages are an integral part of daily life and will not be replaced by a foreign language or languages.

In addition to being an integral part of culture and the African way of life, indigenous languages are indispensable to learning, any kind of learning including formal education especially at the primary school and middle school levels. They are also repositories of knowledge transmitted to future generations, and are indissoluble bonds of traditional societies.

Ignoring or suppressing them is tantamount to encouraging their extinction. As the Namibian deputy minister of education, Sylvia Ganaone Makgone, stated, it is important to pay attention to indigenous languages in a country where colonial languages are being promoted at their expense. According to Albertina Nakale in her article, "Makgone Calls for More Sophisticated Language Policy," in *New Era*, Windhoek, 19 June 2013:

"The Deputy Minister of Education, Sylvia Ganaone Makgone says the development of indigenous languages can no longer afford to receive meager resources, while settler colonial languages such as Afrikaans and German and to some extent English continue to enjoy inordinately greater support.

She said Namibia is a multi-lingual nation, but language development has always been unequal, including the resources expended on that development. Makgone made the remarks yesterday during a two-day language policy review conference hosted by the National Institute for Educational Development (NIED), a directorate in the Ministry of Education.

The conference is a follow-up initiative on the outcome of the 2011 National Education Conference. She said promoting one language at the expense of others in a multi-lingual country is counterproductive and it is not in the national interest. The theme of the conference is – Language for Teaching and Education for Social Justice.

The language in education policy of Namibia is derived from the country's constitution, which guarantees equal linguistic rights to all Namibian citizens. The constitution states in Article 3 (1) and (2) that the official language of Namibia shall be English and also that nothing shall prohibit the use of any other language as a medium of instruction in private schools or in schools financed or subsidized by the State. This is subject to compliance with such requirements as may be imposed by law, to ensure proficiency in the official language or for pedagogical reasons.

'Despite this consensus, there have been numerous political and educational controversies regarding the implementation of these constitutional provisions. As it appears, Article 3 did not help much to advance the development and promotion of indigenous languages in Namibia. Both Article 3, Section (3) of the constitution, as well as the Education Act (Act No.16 of 2001) are vague on the status and use of indigenous African languages in formal domains,' she said.

According to her, before independence more resources were devoted to the development of Afrikaans and German, and to some extent, English. 'The development of most, if not all indigenous African languages received meager resources. Furthermore, the development of indigenous African languages in Namibia was not done according to plan, but rather in a piecemeal way,' she pointed out.

Consequently, she said some indigenous languages

became marginalised through neglect, adding: 'This state of affairs cannot be allowed to continue in an independent Namibia.'

She noted that English, formerly perceived as the language of a small, educated elite is now in demand from every quarter as a means of progress and the key to a better life. She further said it is interesting to note that the language, which was a 'key part of the mechanism of exclusion,' because of its very unequal distribution in society, is now seen 'as a means of inclusion.'

'It is also interesting to note that the English language in Namibia today is both an admired and a hated phenomenon. There is also an increasing demand for the language, which is associated with progress and development, while on the other hand the language is perceived as a killer of native or indigenous languages,' she indicated.

She said the formulation of a sophisticated language policy is now considered a long-term solution.

Such a policy, Makgone added, would assign official functions to indigenous African languages in the national government, as well as in the regional and local authorities, which would in turn elevate the status of these languages and expand their use. Studies have shown that learners in bilingual schools in a number of African countries such as Mali, Zambia, Niger, Burkina Faso, Senegal and Nigeria fare better in mathematics, sciences and languages, including French and English, compared to learners in monolingual schools.

The purpose of the conference is to establish a balance sheet for language policy formulation in mother tongue education, making use of experiences in Africa and beyond so that relevant strategies for the development of a useful language policy in the Namibian context may be pursued.

'This conference is thus aimed primarily at exploring language policy-making processes in the African context;

implementation issues, as well as the place and role of ex-colonial languages in education,' she said."

The importance of indigenous languages as a medium of instruction was also underscored by Richard Lee in his article, "Should Namibia Stop Teaching in English?":

"At Independence, Namibia chose English as its main national language although it had no history of English as a colonial language and few citizens who spoke it as their first language. The decision has been well supported and there is an expectation among Namibians that learning English as early as possible is important because it will open many doors to the future.

The government implemented the decision through a language policy for schools that sets down that learners should be taught in their home language from grades 1 – 3 and in English from grade 4 onwards. However, despite high levels of spending on education, failure rates as a whole remain alarmingly high. For example, only four in ten (39%) learners starting school in 2009 are expected to reach grade 12.

The Urban Trust of Namibia – funded by OSISA – undertook research to ascertain what impact teaching in English had on Namibian students and whether it was contributing to the poor results.

The literature review suggested that the longer a child learns in his or her home language the more successful she or he will be at school. Meanwhile, the field research showed that a high proportion of learners are confused by the second language (English) in which they are taught. They want to succeed at school generally and in English in particular but do not understand their subjects well enough because of the problems of language.

The research also highlighted that teachers, parents and educationalists do not fully understand the problems learners face with the English language and often attribute poor learner performance to a lack of interest and commitment.

Educationalists are divided as to the correctness of the language policy, with those in the regions seeing the language policy as failing learners, while parents are keen to see their children succeed in English but are divided as to how best this can be achieved.

The research concluded that a major review of Namibia's language policy is needed to help address the continuing failure of so many learners. While there are challenges with mother tongue learning, policy makers should encourage its wider use to achieve better educational results for Namibia's children." – (Richard Lee, "Should Namibia Stop Teaching in English?," Open Society initiative for Southern Africa (OSISA), 24 February, 2012).

The problems the country faces in teaching English were also highlighted by Denver Kisting, in her article, "Namibia's Language Policy is 'Poisoning' its Children," *The Guardian*, London, 10 January 2012:

"Namibia's commitment to English as the main language of education has been undermined by revelations that 98% of the southern African country's teachers are not sufficiently proficient in the language.

Leaked results of government tests carried out last year indicated that all but 2% of teachers need to undergo further training in basic English.

Up to 30 languages are spoken in Namibia, 14 of which have a full orthography, but in 1990, when the country gained independence from South Africa, Afrikaans, which had functioned as a lingua franca, was jettisoned in favour of English. Though spoken by a small minority, the adoption of English as the language of school instruction was seen by the new government as a break with the colonial past and a means of unifying the country.

But experts say that the government has failed to provide adequate training to teaching staff for whom English is a second and even third language.

Andrew Matjila, a retired school teacher and former politician, said that the language policy, in place for over 20 years, had failed to deliver widespread competence. He said public figures, such as politicians, struggled with the language and that the limited language skills of teachers had 'poisoned thousands of children.'

Adolf de Klerk, another commentator on education, said there was a direct link between the low English language skills of teachers and students' exam results. Nearly 50% of 16-year-olds failed the junior secondary school certificate in 2010. He called for 'drastic' action to be taken.

Researcher Priscilla Harris, author of a recent study, claims that 'the medium of instruction used in schools is a major cause for concern which the government has overlooked.'

Harris said the post-independence adoption of English was 'a challenging decision,' because 'only 8% [of Namibians] are English speakers, whereas the rest of the population use their home language and Afrikaans as the language of communication in their daily lives.'

Close to 23,000 teachers sat an English language proficiency test last September as part of an education ministry strategy to identify further training needs.

The test, compiled by the University of Namibia, assessed comprehension, grammar and writing skills. In the writing section, teachers were required to construct four complete sentences.

Results from a leaked report indicate that more than 70% of teachers in senior secondary schools cannot read and write basic English. Among junior secondary teachers 63% have a poor grasp of English, which is jeopardising their teaching, the report said.

Even the 18% of teachers who scored between 75%

and 92% made mistakes with capital letters and punctuation, subject-verb agreement, singular and plural forms and articles.

Another damning finding was that some teachers struggled 'to fill in personal data required on the front of the answer sheet.' This included basic biographic information.

Abraham Iyambo, the minister of education, tried to downplay the results when they were leaked to the press in November.

In a statement to parliament Iyambo claimed that the results had been misrepresented. The test, he said, was not meant 'to fail or pass a teacher. Neither was it a means of firing teachers; it was diagnostic in nature.'

He added that 'the test is intended to determine the training needs of teachers and place them in the appropriate continuing professional development course.'

Matjila called for the immediate provision of training for teachers, saying that without intervention 'the danger that is coming to Namibia is unimaginable.'

Priscilla Harris was the lead researcher on a report publish last month by the Urban Trust of Namibia (UTN), a local NGO, which is highly critical of the current language education policy. The report, called Language in schools in Namibia – the missing link in educational achievement? – claims that the policy in place since 1993 'was essential to drive the strategic decision for English in education. But this massive decision was made without the required resources being in place.'

'Teachers were not ready, could not express themselves and were not trained in English,' Harris said, adding that the curriculum, syllabuses and materials linked to a successful outcome were not made available.

Harris points to higher success rates of school students in South Africa and Botswana, two of Namibia's neighbours, where children learn in their home language.

'The challenge of the decision to use English as the

national language still deeply affects the levels of success in education. Some of these difficulties relate to skills,' Harris said.

She cites evidence of poorer results in maths in classes taught by older teachers who have low English levels, compared to classes taught by younger teachers whose competence in English, thanks to better training, is higher.

'But language stands out throughout the research as a major problem,' she said.

Harris recommends that learners should be allowed to be taught in their mother tongue until at least the end of primary school at age 11.

Momentum is growing behind a challenge to the current language policy. After a national conference on education held last June, calls to revisit the language policy were heard within government circles.

UTN wants education provision to be more closely matched to the needs of learners. It wants 'urgent in-service and pre-service training' for teachers who teach home languages, along with 'access to technical support in those languages with time and resources set aside for study leave.'

The government is yet to respond to UTN's report."

Even if Namibia were to take a multilingual approach, elevating tribal languages to the status of national languages without abandoning English, it still could achieve unity and construct a solid national identity by guaranteeing, in practice not just in theory, equal opportunity to all ethnic groups including the most marginalised.

The problem of language would be solved – would take care of itself – as the people willingly learn the languages of other ethnic groups out of which could even emerge a common language, a *lingua franca*, as is the case when some people from different ethnic groups try to communicate when they don't know each other's language.

That is not ethnic segregation or separation. It is unity in diversity.

As an organising principle, unity in diversity has both prospects and challenges within the Namibian context – whose outcome very much depends on the nature of the heterogeneous society itself and its component units which collectively constitute this multiethnic and multicultural nation.

How close are the ethnic groups in terms of relations? Or how far apart are they? Are there regional rivalries and alliances? Is unity in diversity a practical proposition in the context of Namibia?

Is a federation or even a confederation of autonomous ethnic groups or ethno-regions – for the sake of equality among the various groups – more in tune with unity in diversity than a centralised system under a unitary state as in the case today?

There are many issues which have not been addressed and many questions which have not been answered. As the country continues to pursue its policy of unity in diversity, many questions will be asked about the wisdom of pursuing such a policy under a highly centralised system – also, with a monolingual policy – and whether it is succeeding or not. As Alexactus T. Kaure stated in "Unity in Diversity: Myth or Reality?," in *The Namibian*, 27 June 2008:

"The rallying cry during Namibia's liberation struggle was 'One Namibia One Nation.' Yes, we now have one Namibia. But do we have that elusive one nation yet?

This is a question that many people are now increasingly asking 18 years into our Independence.

Some people are getting a sense of being left out or marginalised altogether – whether at individual or community levels.

The recent subtle cry of discontent from the south of the country might represent many other silent voices across the country.

I'm posing this question as an entry to a much broader discussion.

Are heterogeneous societies prone to divisions and thus to economic and political failure as opposed to more homogeneous ones?

What is the evidence? I'm disregarding deviant cases like Somalia.

The point, however, is that most societies that are torn apart around Africa are characterised by at least two factors: ethnic conflict and class struggle. In such settings, national consensus becomes the first victim.

What is the situation like in Namibia 18 years on? Would it be appropriate to liken the country's situation to the Biblical Towel of Babel story?

We seem to be speaking in different tongues and thus unable to understand each other and therefore unable to reach a consensus on many of the major issues that confront Namibia today. And without a sense of common vision and purpose, we can't do much on the developmental front.

A good part of our time and energy is thus wasted arguing over conflicting priorities – sometimes misplaced ones. What you get then is a highly partisan type of politics.

My sense is that our country is more divided now than it was at Independence. Tribe, race and class are now the defining factors of our society.

In order for a person to get, say, a scholarship, a decent job or tenders, those factors come into play. Examples abound.

The saga at the Social Security Commission, a few years ago, where a white Namibian's appointment as a CEO was withdrawn at the last hour epitomises many other cases of people being appointed (or not) solely on the basis of either tribe or race/colour.

Unfortunately a number of whites think that people are

still being appointed on the basis of affirmative action. This is no longer so.

The criteria for employment now is either tribe or race.

Affirmative action is already dead and even if it was being implemented to the letter, it would be tantamount to some sort of injustice.

Why should someone who returned from exile in 1990, armed with postgraduate qualifications and has been, say, a director since then, be given preferential treatment over other recent graduates? Just because of the colour? The unfortunate thing is that public policy decisions taken with tribe, race or even class in mind, tend to be irrational most of the time.

If the apartheid system had made some rational decisions then, a good part of Namibia would be developed by now, not just some few pockets in urban areas. But unfortunately this was a system based on race.

Put this in our contemporary context.

We all know that the Caprivi and Okavango regions offer some of the best agricultural land in rural Namibia for crop production and other activities yet these regions are given scant attention today in terms of government agricultural policies.

So the government would rather pursue bad policies even though the majority of Namibians would benefit from increased agricultural production in those regions because there are ethnic factors at play.

Again, I always meet people who complain that they didn't get that job or a scholarship because of their ethnic origin – sometimes perceived but sometimes real. And we have seen such cases in practice here.

So, it boils down to the same problem.

When giving out scholarships one has no clue who is going to be the best student or worker but yet those allocating the scholarships or deciding on who to appoint to that specific job don't worry about the best outcome possible. The benefit to the broader society doesn't matter in such a context.

This picture might be different in a more homogeneous society or in a society where ethnic, race and class polarity has been reduced to a minimum.

Thus, many scholars have wondered why public services provision has tended to be low in ethnically polarised societies.

And it has been argued that for the government to supply a public service, ethnic groups have to agree on what kind of public service they want.

If one takes the example of oil-producing Norway and counter-pose that with say Nigeria or Sudan, two other oil-producing countries, one can clearly see how ethnically diverse countries struggle over how resources should be distributed as opposed to the more homogeneous Norway where the rule of the game is understood by all – this is not to say that there are no class issues involved.

Polarisation by tribe is not the only kind of social division that can pull society apart and into warring factions. Class division is another factor.

I have always wondered why India and China, two of the emerging giants of Asia, are today moving at a different pace. I think class and caste in the case of India have made that country's efforts at reducing poverty even harder.

In the case of China, which didn't have a sharp class division, the problem was how to address general poverty, and they seem to be succeeding.

There is thus an inverse relation between class inequality and economic growth.

When a large part of your population is reduced to pauperism, then there is no time for this section of the population to engage in other intellectual endeavors other than foraging for food. Class inequality then, is a sure recipe for continuing underdevelopment.

But do things have to be this way all the time? Not necessarily.

Ethnic diversity need not always lead to conflict or violence. But this depends on how those differences have been negotiated politically. And it also depends on the quality of democracy and its institutions and the leadership."

One solution that has been tried in a country with deep ethnic divisions is ethnic confederalism. Ethiopia has taken that approach, although in practice it remains a centralised state with power concentrated at the centre, despite professions to the contrary. But adoption of ethnic confederalism was at least a concession, and a confession, on the part of the government that there is an imperative need for unity in diversity.

It was also an acknowledgement of ethnic inequalities and injustices in a country dominated by the Amhara and the Tigray and which also led to rebellions by marginalised groups including the Oromo, the largest in the country.

The Ethiopian constitution adopted in 1994 even allows states – formed on the basis of linguistic and ethnic identity – to secede from the federation. But that is only in theory, as the brutal suppression of Oromo nationalism by the central government clearly demonstrates.

Namibia does not have to go that far if all of its groups are treated equally on the basis of unity in diversity. As Charles Tjatindi – using the linguistic context only as an example and as one area of contention – stated in an article about the challenges his country faces in its quest for unity, "Let us Embrace Unity in Diversity," in the *Namibian Sun*, 15 February 2013:

"The diversity in Africa in terms of language, culture and way of living has never ceased to amaze me.

In Namibia for instance, the various languages spoken here create an entertaining plot for a perfect Nigerian movie, where juju screaming is part of the game.

I have always been a proponent of relationships and marriages amongst the various language groups spoken in Namibia. In fact, as we speak, I have my eye on a pretty Oshiwambo-speaking colleague of mine.

The problem, however, is deciding what language to speak at home with the kids, once the relationship has been consummated. This may sound easy, but have any of you ever paid close attention to the different words used in our local languages and how some will leave you more baffled than anything else?

In Oshiwambo for instance, the word for glass, window and bottle is the same. The variation is only between singular and plural. Imagine if you have to tell a kid not to throw the bottle out of the window or not to hit the glass with the bottle? For a kid who is learning Oshiwambo, you will create more confusion than clarity!

The word 'aluka' means come back in Oshiwambo, while in Otjiherero a similar work 'jaruka' means go back. If I have way with my colleague and we attempt the happily ever after, I will be telling my boy to 'jaruka' (go back) to his room, while the mother will think I'm telling the boy to 'aluka' (come back) to the living room.

That poor boy will be running up and down the stairs, clearly confused and not knowing what to do. Well, who said such marriages were a bed of roses?

I also wonder how on earth the word for 'face' and 'forehead' can be the same in Oshikwanyama/Oshindonga. The confusion does not stop there.

In Otjiherero, for instance, the word for nose, heaven and sky is exactly the same word. This is really weird. I mean, what do nose and heaven have in common? Couldn't other words be found for some of this stuff?

Now imagine teaching our child what the Otjiherero word for nose is, only for him to hear the word repeated more often when we pray and make reference to Jesus Christ and God. The poor boy will probably think the Ovaherero have no respect for God. How dare they refer to his nose!

Also, in Otjiherero, the word for leg and wheel is the same. Imagine asking our boy to take his leg off the wheel! Eish.

I am now starting to believe we will be having a tough time raising this boy.

Then comes the culture shock associated with who does what around the house. In Ovaherero culture, for instance, the cows are milked by a woman.

Well, the Ovaherero are apparently also known for loading their women at the back of the bakkie.

I am told it is the exact opposite in the Oshiwambo culture. And yes, the Ovaherero love meat. What else is there to love? Cheese?

Finally, if you get stuck as to who should be in charge of the household between you and your partner, the answer is pretty simple. Let her be in charge! Even if she lets you take charge, we all know who is really in charge of matters.

I remember how a dude at a hangout spot recently bragged the night away about how much of a man he is in his house. 'Gents, you got to show your wife who wears the pants in the house,' he told us.

Just then his wife, angry from having to wait in the car while the brother idled in the shebeen, stormed in. I tell you, I have not seen that dude so afraid in his life.

The giant of 1.85m was suddenly reduced to a midget – and tail between his legs he excused himself from the group, put on a brave smile and joined the madam!

'Mbuae when that woman is that angry... the stories about who wears the pants do not suffice. In fact gents, at such a time, let her wear the pants instead,' were his parting words."

That alone demonstrates the distinctiveness of each group in Namibia. No group wants to give up its language and culture, making unity in diversity a viable option and the only alternative to national disintegration short of totalitarian rule.

Tanzania would have faced the same problem if she did not have the Swahili language to unite her people and facilitate formation of what is probably the most unified and most cohesive nation on the continent and in the history of post-colonial Africa.

There is nothing wrong with ethnic identity or one being proud of one's culture. But ethnic distinctiveness – us versus them – can also lead to ethnic prejudice including favouritism which is an integral part of prejudice. It is a common problem across Africa and Namibia is no exception.

There is no question that diversity is invoked as a cardinal principal in the reconstruction of the Namibian society as the country tries to build a strong national identity embracing all groups. The transformation started soon after independence and is even being hailed as a success.

Yet there is also polarisation. Many people are aware of the problem. They complain about discrimination in employment, education and other areas of life simply because they belong to the "wrong" tribe. Alexactus T. Kaure is one of the Namibians who have addressed the subject. He addressed the subject in his article, "Unity in Diversity: Myth or Reality?," in *The Namibian*, 27 June 2008 and revisited the subject four years later in another article, "A Pluralist Or Polarised Namibia," in *The Namibian*, 17 August 2012, stating:

"Namibia is not just known for its geographical diversity and contrasting landscape but also for its ethnic, tribal, racial, religious, cultural diversity.

In some societies pluralism – read diversity – is regarded as boon yet in others seen as a bane. The question is how do different societies address and balance cultural, religious, epistemological and political diversity? In some societies diversity is seen as creative but in others it is perceived to be a curse.

In what terms do we see our diversity? Yes, we fought for one Namibia. But are we moulding a society built on the pillars of diversity? This is a question that many people are now increasingly asking 23 years into our independence....

Most societies that are torn apart in Africa are characterised by at least two main factors: ethnic conflict and class struggle. In Namibia there are, in addition, divisions based on regionalism and the problematic division based on who stayed behind and who went into exile during the struggle years - giving us a 'special' group of 'war veterans' and 'struggle kids'....

Our country seems more divided now than it was at independence because the glue of nationalism is no longer binding. With time, our society has been evolving into a socio-political direction where tribe, race and class, regionalism and partisan politics are now the defining factors of our society. One might argue that we found these at the dawn of independence and that might be true. But did we do enough to soften the edges of class struggle or to harmonise racial, ethnic and tribal animosity, the policy of national reconciliation notwithstanding?....

Theoretically, we are a plural society which is polarised in practice."

Yet, Namibia's goal of unity in diversity is by its very nature inclusive.

But it is also exclusionary because by trying to build a unified nation with a strong national identity, the government has to clearly define who is Namibian and who is not, including isolating enemies within who might impede progress towards unification of all ethnic groups into a cohesive bloc which constitutes the nation. Language is one of the areas where this unity can be forged.

Namibia's linguistic policy which is critical to achieving unity is similar to Tanzania's in terms of emphasis on having a common language for all Tanzanians. While Tanzania chose Kiswahili, which is already understood almost by everybody in the country, Namibia chose English which is *not* understood by most of its people. And while Tanzania chose an African language to unite its people, Namibia chose a European language to unite its black African ethnic groups as well as its white minorities.

Yet the focus is the same in both cases, Tanzania and Namibia.: to unite all ethnic and racial groups. As Bernadette Müller states with regard to Tanzania in "A Success Story of Creating National Identity in Tanzania: The Vision of Julius Kambarage Nyerere," in *Crossing Borders, Shifting Boundaries: National and Transnational Identities in Europe and Beyond*:

"Besides the personal integrity and charisma of Nyerere, concrete political actions of his socialist government have led to overwhelming national unity, namely language policy, education policy, rural development policy – ujamaa villages – and a movement strategy to send young people and public servants into different areas throughout the country....

After independence, Nyerere upraised Swahili as the sole mode of political discourse (Askew 2002, 47). The language was used to unite people, to impede tribalism and to empower ordinary people to participate in the political process.

In his last speech as a chairman of the (ruling) Chama Cha Mapinduzi – CCM – in the year 1990, Nyerere talked about the motives of his language policies:

'Making Kiswahili Tanzania's language helped us greatly in the battle against tribalism. If every Tanzanian had stuck to using his tribal language or if we had tried to make English the official language of Tanzania, I am pretty sure that would not have created the national unity we currently enjoy. Although I am personally of the opinion that we should continue teaching English in our schools because English is the Kiswahili of the world, we have, however, an enormous duty to continue to promote and enhance Kiswahili. It is a great weapon for our country's unity.' (Nyerere, quoted in Topan 2008, 258).

Nyerere did not see English and Kiswahili as competing languages, but rather as complementary to one another. While the second was used for creating an national identity and enabling communication with the masses, the first should advance progress and enable participation around the world.

The use of language in education is discussed controversially and a debate is going on whether English or Kiswahili is more appropriate for instruction (Sigalla 2010, 118; Topan 2008, 261).

However, in general, Swahili is used in primary schools and for adult education, whereas English is the language of instruction in secondary and higher education. Language use and education are deeply linked in the creation process of national identity." – (Bernadette Müller,"A Success Story of Creating National Identity in Tanzania: The Vision of Julius Kambarage Nyerere," in Franz Hollinger, Markus Hadler, eds., *Crossing Borders, Shifting Boundaries: National and Transnational Identities in Europe and Beyond*, Frankfurt-on-Main: Campus Verlag, 2012, pp. 131 – 132).

That is also the case in Namibia where English is taught in order to make it the "national language" – like Swahili in Tanzania – although it is a herculean task in a country where even the majority of the teachers themselves who teach English in secondary schools don't know the language well, thus making the task of creating

Namibia's national identity through a foreign language probably a bigger challenge than the government expected it to be.

In the case of Tanzania, national integration was facilitated by strong national leadership, especially President Nyerere himself; egalitarianism under socialism; widespread use of Kiswahili as the national language; and by the absence of tribal antagonism partly attributed to the fact that there are no large ethnic groups which could dominate the rest in a country of about 130, almost all relatively small and therefore politically and economically weak at the national level even if a few were to mobilise forces against the other groups. Instead, they all were mobilised to form one solidly united country, virtually a monolithic whole as a nation, with a national identity whose legitimacy few would question.

With regard to Namibia, some of the problems the country has faced in identity construction – critical to national unity and allegiance – can be attributed to apartheid and racial oppression since the advent of colonial rule when Germany conquered the territory. As Sandra Düsing states in her book, *Traditional Leadership and Democratisation in Southern Africa: a Comparative Study of Botswana, Namibia and South Africa*:

"Namibia's specific historical conditions of divisive colonial experience, have resulted in the absence of a single, common national identity and culture.

The Apartheid system preserved white privilege in a divided society, segregated and invented divergent ethnic cultures and truncated the growth of a common national identity. Thus, Namibia lacked any facilitating conditions for unitary nation building, such as a national identity and loyalty undisturbed by interethnic group rivalries, a common accepted and spoken language as a national medium of communication, and effective, generally recognised territorial borders.

In order to solve the Apartheid imposed legacies of ethnic segregation, and to integrate and harmonise the different ethnic groups – Ovambo, Kavango, Damara, Herero, Whites, Nama, Coloureds, Caprivians, San, Rehoboth, Basters, and Tswana – within a single nation state, Namibia adopted a multiculturalist approach of democratic state and nation building. Similar to South Africa, Namibia adopted the 'unity in diversity' approach, which intends to pacify conflicting group interests through the recognition and protection of cultural and ethnic identity and the development of a strong sense of national unity, cohesion and consciousness deriving from the national value of cultural diversity.

Ethnicity as diversity, nation building as the objective to improve the lives of all citizens, and democracy as the chosen political system, characterise the three important strands that shape the Namibian nation.

Prime Minister Hage G. Geingob identified the reconciliation of the different ethnic groups in Namibia as an integral part, requirement and precondition for democratic state and nation building, and characterises, as a major goal in this process, the development of a historical consciousness, encompassing the entire nation with all of its ethnic and cultural groups: 'You can be a Herero and Namibian, or Ovambo and Namibian, or Nama and Namibian...conflicts will not arise if the national identity and cultural identity are in harmony.'" – (Sandra Düsing, *Traditional Leadership and Democratisation in Southern Africa: A Comparative Study of Botswana, Namibia and South Africa*, Münster, Hamburg, London: LIT Verlag, 2002, pp. 122 – 123).

Historical experience has also shaped perceptions of ethnic and national identities among the different groups which collectively constitute Namibia as a nation. While they share a common national identity which essentially binds them as one people, some groups are more conscious of their identities because of their "subordinate" status although they are equal to the rest in terms of rights as citizens of Namibia, including the right to effectively participate in the political process to determine their own destiny.

The emphasis is on assertion and affirmation their identity in a heterogeneous society because of its multiculturalist nature where no cultural fusion has taken place as it would or might have in a "melting pot." Even the United States which claims to have one dominant culture – the culture has historically been Anglo-Saxon – no such fusion has taken place, prompting Nathan Glazer, one of the leading American scholars and author of *Beyond The Melting Pot*, to say, "We are all multiculturalists now," which is also the title of one of his books. He contends that racial integration in the United States has failed, leading to multiculturalism, because of "the fundamental refusal of other Americans to accept blacks." – (Nathan Glazer, *We Are All Multiculturalists Now*, Cambridge, Massachusetts, USA: Harvard University Press, 1997, p. 95).

The Herero are one example in the context of Namibia of how some people view their ethnic identity in relation to – and in contrast with – the national identity they share with the rest of their fellow countrymen. As Hildi Hendrickson states in her book, *Clothing and Difference: Embodied Identities in Colonial and Post-colonial Africa*:

"Some Herero people in Namibia recently joked that if you squint at the multicolored national flag adopted after independence in 1990, you will see only the DTA or NUDO colors – that is the red, blue, and white associated with these two Herero-based political groups. As the Namibian flag's actual dominant colors are red, blue, and green – colors associated with the mainly-Ovambo-speaking, SWAPO-aligned (South West Africa People's Organization) majority – these pundits are asserting that if they try, they can find themselves in this image of the new nation.

The joke implies that Herero identity is not plainly represented in the flag, but that it is submerged there, that it must be sought after, and that it can be found.

The imagination of Namibian identity, the struggle both to choose representations of the polity and to assign lasting meaning to them, has been developing since the Germans claimed colonial control over the territory of South West Africa in 1884." – (Hildi Hendrickson, *Clothing and Difference: Embodied Identities in Colonial and Post-colonial Africa*, Durham, North Carolina, USA: Duke University Press, 1996, p. 213).

This historical experience continues to shape perceptions and even determine reality not only for the Herero but for other Nambians as well. They were equally conquered, subjugated, oppressed and exploited by the Germans; next by the apartheid rulers of South Africa whose injustices against the indigenous people of Namibia also affected and even shaped group identities to the detriment of national unity.

Although the struggle for independence united Namibians against a common enemy and helped the people to submerge their differences in a larger body, Namibia as a single national entity comprising all ethnic groups in the country, there were some groups which were not comfortable when the goal was finally achieved. The reasons for that were ethnic, racial and the privileged status of some Namibians during the apartheid era. As Felix Mukwiza Ndahinda states in "Marginality, Disempowerment and Contested Discourses on Indigenousness in Africa":

"The Rehoboth Basters are said to represent a population of 35,000 peoples. Niezen portrays the Rehoboth Basters as: 'descendants of *indigenous* Khoi and

Afrikaans (sic) settlers who claim that, with Namibia's independence in 1990, they were deprived of their traditional form of self-government, had their communal land expropriated, thus losing their means of subsistence based upon cattle raising, and were denied use of their mother tongue in administration, justice, education and public life.'

Some analysis considers the Rehoboth Basters as a formerly privileged group under both German colonisation, and South African mandate over Namibia. Throughout this pre-independence period, they enjoyed a relative autonomy; a status which was formally recognised under Act No. 56 of 1976 passed by the South African Parliament and granting them a 'right to self-government in accordance with the Paternal Law of 1872.'

Labelled as 'coloured peoples,' they enjoyed a relatively privileged position vis-à-vis the black masses under South Africa's apartheid practices – as extended to their administered Namibian territory – characterised by a hierarchy of the races.

The advent of Namibian independence resulting in a transfer of power by South Africa to – mainly elites from – the black majority was not necessarily a happy occurrence for all as it led to a subsequent loss by the Basters of their previously enjoyed 'privileged' position. In fact, they strongly objected to the exercise of a wide range of powers by the new authorities in the wake of the country's independence. The Rehoboth Basters leadership undertook a number of initiatives including unsuccessful legal battle(s) in domestic and international – quasi – judicial bodies.

In addition to legal battles, the community strategically endorsed indigenousness as a new identity through which the struggle for communal land rights could be channelled. In a formal declaration, dated 10 October 1992, they proclaimed themselves an indigenous people and, accordingly, demanded 'all rights to which autochthonous

[sic] and indigenous peoples are entitled to according to international practice and conventions.'

The following year, in 1993, they took their case to the UNWGIP where their representative made an impressive statement 'on the discrimination of the Rehoboth Basters: an indigenous people in the Republic of Namibia.' They further established contacts with other claimant indigenous groups in the sub-region – namely the Griqwa and Nama – aiming at sealing the 'First International Treaty between Indigenous Khoisan First Nations in Southern Africa.' From their initial participation until 2005, community representatives participated in all sessions of the UNWGIP, and appeared before the subsequently created United Nations Permanent Forum on Indigenous Issues (UNPFII).

The Rehoboth Basters' move was emulated by the Afrikaner Volksfront, an umbrella organisation formed by a number of right-wing Afrikaner groups hostile to the democratic transition in South Africa." – (Felix Mukwiza Ndahinda, in Kristin Henrard, ed., *The Interrelation between the Right to Identity of Minorities and Their Socio-Economic Participation*, Leiden, The Netherlands: Koninklijke Brill NV, Martinus Nijohoff Publishers, 2013, pp. 346 – 348. See also, cited by F.M. Ndahinda, Ronald Niezen, *The Origin of Indigenism: Human Rights and the Politics of Identity*, Berkeley: University of California Press, 2003, pp. 21 – 22; F.W. Krüger, "Identity Building and Social Transformation: The Cases of Namibia and Botswana Compared," *GeoJournal*, 46, 1998, p. 81).

The demands by the Rehoboth Basers in Namibia amounted to a quest for ethnic self-determination within the context of Namibia. Carried to extreme, it was a call for independence, although they were probably realistic enough to know that secession would not be tolerated by the Namibian government to allow them to form their own "nation within a nation."

But the mere fact that they voiced such demands and articulated their position very clearly demonstrates that being an integral part of Namibia does not mean the Rehoboth Basters or any other ethnic and racial groups should sacrifice their ethnic identities and rights for the sake of a larger entity: the multiethnic and multicultural nation. It means the two identities, ethnic and national, have to be reconciled in peaceful existence which guarantees the continued existence of both. That is why the principle of unity in diversity which has been embraced by the Namibian government is probably the best foundation for peace and harmony as well as prosperity in a country where the salience of ethnicity is an integral part of national life.

There are times in African nationalist discourse when the role of ethnicity is ignored or dismissed as irrelevant. Such analysis should be contextual. There are many countries in Africa where suppression of ethnic identities and aspirations of ethnic groups can wreak havoc. The Hutu majority in Rwanda can not be ignored when they are marginalised under what is essentially a Tutsi ethnostate despite government claims to the contrary and that there are no Hutus or Tutsis in Rwanda anymore – only Rwandans.

The people of the Niger Delta in Nigeria is another example. The legitimate demands of the Ogoni and other groups in that region can not be ignored if Nigeria is to continue to exist as a stable political entity; nor can the demands of any other group, in any country, if the demands are legitimate and do not interfere with the rights of others.

Most of those demands can be met under a government whose governing principles include unity in diversity as is the case in Namibia – in practice not just in theory.

Ethnic identities do matter; so do national identities which are a product of multiple identities – ethnic, cultural, racial and so on – constituting a heterogeneous or a monolithic whole: Kenya and Nigeria, in the former case, and Tanzania and Botswana, in the latter, to give only a few examples in the African context.

In the case of Namibia where just one group, the Ovambo, constitutes almost 50 per cent of the population, there may be a tendency among smaller groups to feel and believe that they are marginalised even if that is not always or necessarily the case.

Usually in such cases, there are many times when smaller groups do have legitimate demands and their fear is justified. It is rare for minorities to be as powerful as the majority except when they conquer and dominate the majority as was the case during colonial rule in Africa and elsewhere.

In most cases, the majority do not need protection; it is the minorities who do because they are usually powerless or marginalised. They can not continue to be marginalised or dominated if they are going to be an integral part of the nation and collectively, with the rest, form a single national identity. As Karena Korostelina states:

"The central problem of national identity formation concerns the inter-relations between the majority and the minority, between dominant and small minorities, and between natives and immigrants. The core question for the national identity concept is the the position of ethnic minorities within the nation, that is, whether the minority will be oppressed by the majority or whether members of the minority will have opportunities to maintain their ethnic culture.

The analysis of relations between ethnic groups shows that people can have three different concepts or ideas of national identity: an ethnic concept, a multicultural concept, and a civic concept.

People with an ethnic concept of national identity perceive their nation as built around a core ethnic community into which ethnic minorities must assimilate. They see their nation as monoethnic and monolingual, and they believe that those who have inherited or assimilated the values and attributes of the ethnic core should have higher status within the nation.

Those with a multicultural concept of national identity view their nations as offering equal rights – and even some elements of autonomy and self-governance – to all ethnic groups. They see their states as societies within which ethnic minorities should be guaranteed resources to maintain their ethnic cultures and communities. The different ethnic groups must have an opportunity to receive education in their native language, and their cultural heritage must be part of the country's heritage.

Those with a civic concept, finally, perceive their citizenship as a contract between the people and the state that involves rights and obligations. They view the constitution, the rule of law, and civic responsibility as the main features of the nation, and they see ethnicity as insignificant. They perceive their nation as built on a distinctive nonethnic civic culture into which all citizens must integrate." – (Karena V. Korostelina, "Readiness to Fight in Crimea: How It Interrelates with National and Ethnic Identities," in James L. Peacock, Patricia M. Thornton, Patrick B. Inman, eds., *Identity Matters: Ethnic and Sectarian Conflict*, Oxford, New York: Berghahn Books, 2007, p. 57).

One of the biggest problems African countries, including Namibia, have faced is to try to build nations after states were formed, instead of the reverse being the case. The states were the governing structures and institutions African leaders inherited at independence from the departing colonial masters.

The colonial rulers left the colonial structures intact, and African leaders inherited them just as they were to govern their countries. In most cases, they have not worked well because they have not been restructured to accommodate and reflect African realities.

In order to build nations, Africans had to transcend ethnic or tribal loyalties to create a new identity for all. And that required subordinating their tribal or ethnic loyalties to a higher loyalty; that is, loyalty to the new nation that they were building under a highly centralised state.

In most cases, it is a task that has not been completed, and it may never be, because of conflicting loyalties: tribal or ethnic versus national.

Decentralisation or devolution all the way to the grassroots level may be one of the best ways to accommodate conflicting loyalties by allowing the people to decide what is best for them instead of the central government making decisions for them. Members of ethnic groups who feel they are marginalised will then be able to exercise their right to "self-determination," in their own context, and within prescribed limits in order to maintain national unity.

While Namibians – at least theoretically – are united by a common identity as fellow Namibians and pledge allegiance to the nation, not to their ethnic groups, the lingering effects of colonial rule and apartheid which sanctioned, institutionalised and enforced tribal and racial separation and segregation, continue to haunt the nation. Paradoxically, it is these same effects which have facilitated the construction of nationhood on the basis of unity in diversity.

Without trying to build the nation on such basis, it would be very difficult, if not counterproductive, to attempt to achieve uniformity in such a heterogeneous society with a long history of institutionalised segregation. Yet constructing a genuine national identity is a goal worth pursuing, however elusive it may be. As Minette E. Mans states in "State, Politics and Culture," in Henning Melber, ed., *Re-examining Liberation in Namibia: Political*

Culture Since Independence:

"Even though the state in Namibia calls for a national identity inclusive of different cultural identities, the notion of an all-inclusive national identity is not as simple or defined as might be expected. The deeper the perception of difference is embedded, the more difficult it is to create a sense of national identity. As a result, the major structuring institutions, such as the legislature and education, appear to move into the domain of 'way of life' and the state 'interpenetrates civil society and limits its deliberative space' (Du Pisani 2001: 6). Cultural difference, which may lead to increased differentiation and emphasis on value differences, is seen as a potential political danger.

National identities themselves may also be exclusionary and based on membership – or not – of a political cadre or shared experience, such as the armed liberation struggle. Should one not be a member of this group, one's loyalty as a citizen is also brought into question.

Further, the implementation of democracy in Namibia initially brought about a great sense of patriotism. Namibia's citizens are said to be 'defining, negotiating and legitimizing their identities in a new Namibian nation' (Markusic 2000: 1). Some of the (re)defining is most noticeable in terms of national identity, and some in terms of cultural and ethnic identities, not necessarily in terms of heritage or language. According tor research in one district, people whom Markusic describes as Oshiwambo-speaking, identified themselves as Namibian first and foremost, and as liberators of the country. Those described as Damara, on the other hand, identified themselves primarily as Damara and tended to ascribe many of the present problems of poverty, crime and unemployment to oppression by the Owambo majority.

Thus, in one way and another, certain social divisions on the grounds of ethnic or cultural boundaries of difference remain drawn." – (Minette F. Mans, "State, Politics and Culture," in Henning Melber, ed., *Re-examining Liberation in Namibia: Political Culture Since Independence*, Uppsala, Sweden: Nordic Africa Institute, 2003, p. 120).

Although these differences do indeed exist, they can be harmonised to build a just, stable and productive society in which all members have equal access to opportunities and the nation's resources even in a country such as Namibia where different groups, not justs the Damara, complain about domination by the largest ethnic group, the Ovambo. The best way to address grievances of marginalised groups, or which perceive themselves to be on the periphery of the mainstream, is to institutionalise multiculturalism, but within limits to make sure it does not lead to Balkanisation of society.

Even the Ovambo themselves are not a monolithic whole. They are a collective group which comprises 12 sub-groups, each with its own identity, thus making unity in diversity as the basis for nation-building and reconstruction of a common national identity the best organising principle. The people of Namibia are organised not simply as a single unit but as units within a larger unit in order to satisfy the aspirations of all groups.

That is in sharp contrast with a country like Tanzania where tribal identity has become virtually meaningless because of the government's relentless effort through the years, especially under the first president, Julius Nyerere, to build a highly cohesive and just society in which no single tribe or group of tribes will be able to dominate others. The policy succeeded in ending tribalism in Tanzania, a rare achievement on a continent where this form of discrimination is the norm rather than the exception.

Namibia is one of the countries where there is a strong perception – evidence exists, according to critics – that tribalism is used by powerful individuals and groups to deny opportunities to others in spite of the government's commitment to building a just society on the basis of unity in diversity. Co-existing with tribalism is regionalism which is a higher form of tribalism when members of some tribes from a particular region work together to discriminate against members of tribes from other regions. As Catherine Sasman stated in her article, "Speaker Warns Against Regionalism, Tribalism":

"The Speaker of the National Assembly, Theo-Ben Gurirab, says Namibia's body politic is 'slowly but surely entering a slippery terrain which is encouraging disunity and regionalism spurned (sic) by tribalism and nepotism of the old fashion kind.'

Addressing the National Assembly yesterday, Gurirab said these tendencies are 'very dangerous' for nation building, political tolerance and mutual respect of public officials at all levels. He said Members of Parliament have to make laws that change the socio-political environment, but added that there is a failure on the fronts of corruption, public administration and service delivery.

Gurirab urged MPs to re-read the Namibian Constitution alongside that of the Swapo Party that addresses nation building and social restructuring, and calls for the combating of retrogressive tendencies of tribalism, ethnicity, nepotism, racism, sexism, chauvinism, regionalism, personality cults, and so on.

'We must walk in tandem with the letter and spirit of the Constitution in particular the preamble. That is what must inform our thinking and temper our public actions as national leaders at all times, otherwise we would be like imposters and wolves in sheep's clothing. Dignified and sustained upliftment is what all our people yearn for all the time and everywhere,' said Gurirab.

He said the process of democratisation of the Namibian society requires that the National Assembly, more than

Cabinet or the courts, must meet the challenges of sustainable social development and 'all-round empowerment.'

After Minister of Youth, National Service, Sport and Culture, Kazenambo Kazenambo's outburst against 'stupid and hungry Ovambos' that he said are 'worse than the Boers,' both President Pohamba and other leaders in a veiled manner took him to task – in public – by warning against the divisive nature of tribalism, ethnicity, and regionalism.

Sources within the Swapo Party circles said Kazenambo has been 'dealt with' within the party, but was so far not publicly castigated by the party's leadership over his utterances.

Opening the fifth session of the fifth Parliament on Tuesday, President Pohamba stressed that leaders must provide exemplary leadership, uphold respect for human rights and equality.

Pohamba also impressed it upon MPs that they are not only tasked with the legislative function, but also have the 'sacred duty' to pass fair, just, well-researched and thoroughly debated laws.

'I personally understood the President not only to have affirmed our collective mandate and duty to serve the public interests but actually saying to the House to do more so that the citizens are truly satisfied and acclaim service delivery and outreach contacts.'" – (Catherine Sasman, "Speaker Warns Against Regionalism, Tribalism," 30 January 2012, on Namibia-Botschaf; and in the *Namibian*, 16 February 2012).

There have been other complaints of tribalism. They are mainly directed against the Ovambo – Owambo – who not only constitute the largest ethnic group in the country; they are the backbone of the country's largest political party, SWAPO, which led Namibia to independence and which continues to rule today. The founders of SWAPO were, in fact, mostly Ovambo. According to their critics, they are disproportionately represented in government and exercise power virtually in every area across the spectrum.

This inequity of power is rooted in tribalism, critics contend. As Charles Mubita stated in his article, "Political Tribalism and Ethnicity" in the *Namibian Sun*, 17 October 2013:

"Namibian politics has long been among the most 'ethnic' in Africa. The majority, if not all of our political parties, businesses, and other establishments, have their origins in one or the other tribe or ethnicity.

Our total outlook at national development is primarily shaped by and premised on the benefits of our tribes or ethnic groups. Politicians have become used to seek support from their ethnic or sub-ethnic groups with the promises to divide the 'national cake' among the constituent ethnic groups equally. Most leaders are elected and embraced, first and foremost, on the basis of their tribes. The merits and proven track records of national leaders are usually not considered.

The root of tribalism is bare and does not need telescopes or intellectual sophistry to see it. It is promoted by the most educated and powerful among us, embraced by the young and the old, passed from generation to generation, and has now publicly crept into our elections campaigns.

The recent decision by UDF (United democratic Front) President and Damara Chief Justus //Garoeb to mobilise all Damaras to vote for Swapo candidate and Prime Minister Hage Geingob in next year's presidential election is music to all Swapo members. It is good news in that it shows the popularity of Geingob, whose credentials to ascendency to the National presidency of Namibia is not only long overdue but unquestionable.

Geingob's popularity, grounded in his proven record as a national leader, may lead to many other opposition leaders pulling out of the presidential race for fear of being resoundingly defeated. Others may pull out for the mere respect they have for Geingob as an indefatigable national leader. Among the many strong characteristics of Geingob is his abhorrence for tribalism, nepotism and ethnic segregation.

It is therefore sad that within a space of a year his glorious name has been dragged into tribalism, the very vice that he deplores with passion, by people who purport to support him and his ideals. Firstly, before, during and after the Swapo party congress, some (not all) of his supporters used a 'non-Owambo candidate' label as a launching pad for his election to the position of Swapo party vice-president. They failed to acknowledge the fact that his credentials as a national leader, coupled with his track record in government, far outweighed those of his comrades who also contested for the same position as per Swapo party democratic traditions. He was ultimately elected by the majority of those who attended congress, irrespective of their tribes – Owambos included.

Calls for 'a non-Owambo president' have now been joined by the utterances of Chief Garoeb that 'We decided to support Geingob because he is a Damara. The Owambos have been leading this country for very long. It is time for another tribe. This country belongs to all Namibians and not to the Owambos alone.'

Using the logic of Chief Garoeb, it would be fair to suggest that we put in place a tribal roster showing which tribe should occupy the Namibian presidency and when. This author is willing to challenge Chief Garoeb to prove, first and foremost, whether Geingob agrees that he deserves to be elected as President of Namibia solely because he is Damara. It would surprise Chief Garoeb that Geingob regards himself as a Namibian national leader and not a tribal quisling.

The question we need to ask ourselves as Namibians is what is responsible for this tribal obsession? Is our history to blame? Are our leaders, present and past, responsible for this? Is it caused by greed, corruption or competition?

Tribalism breeds nepotism. Once people feel that their tribesmen are better than people from other tribes they tend to surround themselves with their tribesmen when they get into positions of trust.

The tribalists are willing to hire people from their tribe who may not otherwise be the best candidate for the given job. Such actions deprive the nation of the right people for the right job.

Tribalism affects national cohesion. To the tribalists their allegiance is first to their tribe before the nation. They do not see themselves as Namibians but as a member of tribe A or B. Therefore they do not look for ways that can benefit the whole nation but rather they look for ways that will strengthen their tribes at the expense of the nation. And this does not bode well for the nation. To some extent they try as much as possible to create hegemony when they have power or are put in a position of trust.

It should be borne in mind that petty tribal conflicts divert national attention and resources. The amount of money and personnel that are used to quell such tendencies could have been used for other pressing and important needs. Above all tribalism can be a prelude to a civil war, the result of which will be disastrous."

The cancer of tribalism and regionalism has almost destroyed a number of African countries. It has deprived them of highly talented people who could have served in positions of leadership and in other capacities but have not been allowed to do so because they are not members of the tribes of the people in power, and because they belong to to the "wrong" tribes. Namibia is no exception despite genuine attempts by some leaders and other people in general to fight the vice.

Yet, as a continental phenomenon, tribalism, inextricably linked with regionalism, has gained legitimacy in some circles – of tribalists and regionalists, of whom there is no shortage – simply as an African way of life which requires Africans to help their kith-and-kin.

Tragically, it is done at the expense of other people who, as fellow Africans, are no less related to you than your fellow tribesmen if you are a true Pan-Africanist and humanist.

Even devolution of power to the regions, and decentralisation all the way down to the grassroots level, does not mean members of other tribes who live in those areas should be excluded from the decision-making process or denied opportunities simply because they are not indigenous to the areas and regions in which they now live. It simply means giving more power to the people regardless of who they are, to let them decide for themselves what is best for them without waiting for instructions or policy blueprints from higher authorities telling them what to do.

In the case of Namibia, as in other African countries, unity in diversity can go a long way not only in keeping the people united but also in ensuring opportunities are available to all on equal basis if such an approach is complemented with decentralisation and devolution which is also one of the best ways to fight tribalism. When power is concentrated at the centre and members of one tribe or just a few tribes are the ones who exercise power, there will always be complaints of tribalism, many of them – if not most – being legitimate.

There are many Namibians who do not believe the government has done enough, if anything, to combat tribalism. They see it as a pervasive phenomenon that has permeated the entire social fabric. As Alfredo Tjiurimo Hengari stated in his article, "Tribalism is Real, Not Imagined," in the *Namibian*, 13 April 2007:

"NAMIBIA is not far from exporting tribal refugees because authoritarian tribal sensibilities which subordinate the 'ordinary other' to crumbs are now commonplace.

In so many ways, we have become (maybe we have always been) a bunch of cold-hearted tribalists through the choices we make on a daily basis – our choice of barbers, the lawyers we choose as parastatals or as individuals; our BEE partners must be fellow tribesmen – renting a 'darkie' is no longer enough for that coveted Government tender; the secretaries and assistants we choose must come from our villages etc."

He went on to state:

"The most depressing feature of a free Namibia is its spineless lack of urgency when dealing with tribalism. This crystallises the predictable inability of our leaders (and ourselves) not only to talk candidly about tribalism but also to develop responses against this malaise.

Heated concerns around tribalism are raised, debated in villages and shebeens and certainly permeates a general angst about the place of each ethnic group in the politico-economic make-up of the state.

That explains, sadly, why it has now taken on a rudimentary discourse with unimpressive formulations of 'Kwanyama-axing' supposedly reaching in recent months discussions of the Swapo Politburo.

My contention is that a conversation at that level was misplaced and is an insult to our half-hearted attempts to deal with tribalism. Because the issue of Kwanyama-axing replaces and obscures what ought to be a much more robust debate about tribalism in the ruling party and the country.

Our captivity to tribal reasoning is accentuated in such subtle, yet perceptible ways that we have come to accept a dangerous tribal consensus in the way we conduct our politics. It is this tribal consensus – which in recent years lost its progressive potential and has cowed us into submission to the extent that we don't question the quality of appointments as long as they are drawn from our villages.

We all knew that Tsukhoe was not well suited for a SADC posting, but chose to be silent, even if such an appointment as rooted as it were in the tribal consensus, occurred at the expense of many competent Damara-speakers. And when towards the end of last year a local economist Martin Mwinga analysed shockingly in a government newspaper our contributions to the economy through a tribal lens, arguing for instance that Owambos and Hereros contribute more to the economy based on 'innate' entrepreneurial acumen and 'savoir-faire' in farming respectively, no politician raised objections to such simplistic reasoning.

Our national silence was also a revealing admission that we entertain the possibility that these tribal stereotypes may indeed be true.

Let me hasten to add that when Swapo fielded three candidates for the internal presidential nomination, it did not vex those who sought a discussion in the politburo about 'the fate of Kwanyamas' that all three candidates came from the North, with two of them being Kwanyama speaking.

Such hypocrisy is edifying of how our political parties have developed a tendency of creating self-styled guardians of tribal constituencies.

Being a politician cum tribal-guardian has now become the only gateway for a ruling party politician to become state President.

Conversely, I think we should rather deify leaders like Dr Hage Geingob, Dr Libertine Amathila, Theo-Ben Gurirab or Ben Amathila for their noble refusal to play at great political cost the guardianship of tribal constituencies.

We were (are) ignobly quick to refer to them as lacking constituencies irrespective of their principled positions against tribal reasoning – (similar to Martin Luther King

Jr. who refused the racial label of 'leader of black America,' emphasising being an American leader).

Alas, minorities in the ruling party also displayed a failure of nerve by not calling into question frameworks of tribal reasoning. They easily acquiesce and for some their support for presidential candidates was born of the scandalous admission that they will always be second-rate cadres negotiating from the gutter for the PM or Speaker positions with those they support on the pedestal.

I don't want to appear alarmist but there are cogent reasons that suggest tribalism is real and not imagined in Namibia. Indeed the broader question that should have been raised and be discussed now has to do with what we are doing against tribalism.

What example is the State President, Swapo party president and politicians en masse setting for us to follow in the daily choices we make? I am afraid, not much.

Renowned Afro-American scholar Cornel West in his classic *Race Matters* (1992) writes:

'Where there is no vision, the people perish; where there is no framework for moral reasoning, the people close ranks in a war of all against all.'

Tribal reasoning discourages any form of the moral reasoning West talks about and it is utopian to think that through the deceptive policy of national reconciliation tribalism will just quietly fade away.

Essentially, the best of our leadership and society must recognise the truth that tribalism is one of the most underrated, yet most serious threats to our peace and democratic order. Moral reasoning and vision is urgent on this matter because there is need for a new mature Namibian identity that transcends tribalism."

Tribalism can even lead to Balkanisation on a larger scale where smaller tribes form alliances against bigger and powerful ethnic groups to safeguard their interests and pursue a common agenda to get their fair share of the "national cake."

It happened in Kenya in the early sixties when Ronald Ngala, a member of a small tribe from the Coast Province, together with his compatriots from different parts of the country who were also members of smaller tribes, formed a political party, the Kenya African Democratic Union (KADU), to protect the interests of smaller ethnic groups against the dominant Kikuyu and Luo tribes.

It has happened in other parts of Africa.

The danger is that such alliances, although a product of marginalisation, can fracture society along ethno-regional lines which could eventually become permanent, thus weakening national identity and even making it virtually meaningless. You end up having "micro-nations," or "nations within a nation," to the detriment of national unity. Such disunity may spell doom for the nation, although Namibia has not reached that stage; nor have most African countries.

But prospects for such disunity are real if tribalism or regionalism is not neutralised or contained by instilling in the minds of the people a true sense of national identity. As Ndapewoshali Shapwanale stated in her article, "Tribalism, The Cancer That is Slowly Eating Namibia Away," *Confidente*, Windhoek, Namibia, 6 September 2013:

"When talking about disunity among Namibians, we tend to conclude that racism, black and white, is the root cause of this scourge when in actual fact tribalism is the biggest root of disunity.

The cry for national reconciliation is a sermon to the choir; national reconciliation is not needed among the black and the white, it is much more needed among the different tribes in our country.

The way tribalism has taken a turn for the worst, I

deem it a great insult to the earliest Namibian nationalists, the likes of Chief Hosea Komombumbi Kutako, Anton Labowski, Herman Andimba Toivo ya Toiva and Hendrik Witbooi, to name a few.

These leaders are some of the first idealists of seeing Namibia as a united nation, they diligently engaged for the future of Namibian independence.

When these nationalists, from their different tribal backgrounds, fought for independence, they did not fight to liberate their respective tribes but to liberate the whole Namibian nation, whether Damara, Oshiwambo, Herero, Nyemba, Nama, to name a few.

We keep going on about how Namibia needs to develop and we forever hear that Namibia is a rich country but we cannot understand why our development is crippled, why it took us 23 years to strictly apply the universal free primary education policy.

What we as Namibians need to understand is that our trivial tribal fights and feuds are doing nothing for us but dragging us down, the feuds and competing will not assist us in reaching the so called 'Vision 2030' or realize the dream of those who started the revolution to liberate the land of the brave as an independent nation.

With the assistance of various English dictionaries, nation can be defined as a group of people organized under a single, usually independent government, inhabiting a country or territory.

Now unless my English teacher failed to do her job or sense has left me, I believe Namibia and its people fall perfectly into the definition of a nation.

Being a nation entails, among various other things, the need to identify as one, being Namibian. It necessitates inhabitants to work together towards the development of their country regardless of ethnicity.

Although we are governed by a Swapo-led government, opposition parties and the ruling party have the duty to share expertise and ideas for the betterment of the country, instead of pointing at each other's mistakes and shortcomings. Politics should be about developing a nation and not monitoring each other's mistakes to score cheap political points.

With that said, Namibia has reached great milestones, but sadly we struggle to find success in facets in which we are united but have little trouble attaining success in individual platforms. Michelle McLean, Frankie Fredericks, Johanna Benson and now Dillish are a few examples.

I congratulate these champions and am grateful for what they have done for Namibia but, to borrow from a very smart young man, Veruka:

'In order for Namibia to become a winning country, we must be more Namibian and less Herero, Ovambo, Damara, Swapo or RDP.'"

One of the best ways to fight tribalism is by sending children from different tribes to the same schools. It is best to start early when the children are very young. But it can also be done when they go to secondary school. It was done in Tanzania under President Nyerere. Nyerere went even further by having people assigned jobs in districts and regions where they did not come from in order for them to work with the people of other tribes in those areas to eliminate ethnic barriers and achieve national unity. As I state in one my books, *Tanzania under Mwalimu Nyerere: Reflections on an African Statesman*:

"Our school was also fully integrated. We lived in the same hostel with Asian and Arab students. We also had African, Asian and European teachers, most of them Tanzanian citizens. Other schools across Tanzania were also fully integrated - student and faculty. At our school, students came from all parts of the country and from many different tribes. We were not encouraged to attend school

– except at the primary school level – in our home districts, which were usually inhabited by members of our own tribes. We were, in fact, assigned to schools and jobs after graduation far away from our tribal homelands in order to live and work with members of other tribes.

It was a deliberate effort by the government to break down barriers between members of different tribes and races in order to achieve national unity. And it worked. This was probably Nyerere's biggest achievement - the creation of a cohesive political entity unique on a continent rife with ethnic tensions and torn by conflict caused and fueled by ethno-regional rivalries in the struggle for power and for the nation's resources. Our schools were a microcosm of what Tanzania became: a united, integrated, peaceful and stable nation." – (Godfrey Mwakikagile, *Tanzania under Mwalimu Nyerere: Reflections on an African Statesman*, Pretoria, Dar es Salaam: New Africa Press, 2006, p. 124).

People from other countries have also noticed the strong national identity Tanzanians have, in contrast with other Africans. As Keith Richburg, a black American news reporter who travelled across the African continent when he was the bureau chief of *The Washington Post* in Nairobi, Kenya, for three years from 1991 to 1994, stated in his book, *Out of America: A Black Man Confronts Africa*:

"One of my earliest trips was to Tanzania, and there I found a country that had actually managed to purge itself of the evil of tribalism.

Under Julius Nyerere and his ruling socialists, the government was able to imbue a true sense nationalism that transcended the country's natural ethnic divisions, among other things by vigorous campaigns to upgrade education and to make Swahili a truly national language. Swahili today is widely spoken everywhere and has become the medium of instruction at Tanzanian universities, where I met a professor of Swahili studies who was busy translating the latest American computer program into Swahili.

Tanzania is one place that has succeeded in removing the linguistic barrier that separates so many of Africa's warring factions.

But after three years traveling the continent, I've found that Tanzania is the exception, not the rule. In Africa..., it *is* all about tribes." – (Keith Richburg, *Out of America: A Black Man Confronts Africa*, New York: Basic Books, Harper Collins, 1997, p. 240).

Kenyan journalist, Philip Ochieng, who is also a prominent socio-political analyst, articulated the same position. He once worked in Tanzania as a columnist at the country's main newspaper, the *Daily News*, in the early seventies. As he stated in his article, "Mwalimu Nyerere's Bequest to Mkapa a Tall Order," in one of Kenya's main newspapers, the *Daily Nation*, Nairobi, 16 October 1999:

"Tanzania (is) the most united country in Africa. This unity and sharp national consciousness was contributed to by (the) life-works of the Teacher (Mwalimu Nyerere).... He insisted on uniform Kiswahili throughout the Republic. During the three years that I worked in Dar es salaam I rarely heard any tribal language spoken."

He stated in another article, "Africa's Greatest Leader," in *The East African*, Nairobi, 19 October 1999:

"(Under President Nyerere) Tanzania became the African country with the highest degree of national self-consciousness and has almost annihilated the bane of Kenya that we call tribalism....

At a time when Nairobi was drowning in crude elite grabbing, Dar es Salaam was a Mecca of the world's national liberation movements, and a hotbed of global intellectual thought....

Mwalimu Julius Kambarage Nyerere is the most successful leader that Africa has ever produced since the European colonial regime collapsed 50 years ago."

Some African countries have tried to fight tribalism with varying degrees of success. In many cases, tribalism is simply ignored, accommodated and accepted as an African way of life. It is also encouraged and used as a weapon against political opponents.

One of the solutions proposed in fighting tribalism in Namibia is detribalisation, including stripping traditional rulers of their political power. It happened in Tanzania when President Nyerere abolished chiefdoms to build a strong, united nation without ethnic enclaves as centres of power.

A similar approach has been proposed in the case of Namibia, although abolishing chiefdoms would be a radical proposition and probably unacceptable in a country with such strong traditional rulers and institutions. Curtailing their powers would be more acceptable, as Gerson Sindano stated in "How Best to Fight Tribalism: An Academic Perspective," in the *New Era*, Windhoek, Namibia, 3 September 2013:

"Brow (2008) defines tribe as a grouping of people whose loyalty to their group is greater than their loyalty to a nation. It is against this background that tribalism should not be allowed to rear its ugly head in our beautiful country, Namibia.

Tribalism should not only be viewed as an African curse but rather a global curse. Belgium is currently in trouble, the country is likely to rupture into Flemish and French speaking.

Canada is in a similar tribal conundrum in the French Québec. In the past tribalism caused chaos in

Czechoslovakia, resulting in Czechoslovakia breaking into Czech Republic and Slovakia. If tribalism thrives in Namibia, the repercussions are too ghastly to contemplate.

Studies have revealed that we can only fight tribalism effectively through nation building.

By nation building I am not talking about the common knowledge of shaping behaviour, values, languages, social institutions and physical structures, but I am talking about nation building at the emotional, spiritual and psychological level.

We should understand that nation-building does not only involve physical infrastructure development but rather fundamental principles of humanity that promote social equality and core existence. Studies have further revealed that a nation can only be built if the backbone of tribal powers of the state is broken.

Get me well, I am not saying annihilate the tribal authorities in Namibia, my argument here is reduce tribal powers to strengthen nation building. It becomes too dangerous for a state to function properly if some tribes or groups of people feel they are loyal to themselves than to a nation. The hard question that arises from this argument is what could a state do in a situation where a certain group of people feel differently than the whole nation?

Well, studies have again revealed that we should introduce educational institutions to help council and educate the most radical members. Additionally, encourage intermarriage, encourage citizens to work in different parts of the country other than their own, restructure language policy in such a way that each learner is encouraged to take an indigenous language other than their own, as a minor subject - this should be compulsory.

If the above suggestions are fully implemented, nation building would be realised.

And in the long run our democracy will become viable and stable. We need to stop bickering about trivial issues such as tribalism, which do not grow us.

We should rather focus all our energy in promoting development and equal economic opportunities for all our people regardless of their colour, creed, race and sexual orientation. Capable young professionals should be given equal opportunities in the job market and they should not be judged based on the language they speak or surnames they carry.

Some social studies carried in sub-Saharan Africa have established that at least half of the educated young African professionals who do not belong to the tribes of those in power occupy strategic positions in governments.

It is too painful and disheartening to note that such things are still happening in certain parts of an independent Africa. We must fight tribalism tooth and nail. Africa has come a long way, we cannot afford to tribally divide ourselves now.

Finally, I should commend the Namibian government for its tremendous efforts in establishing national paraphernalia (national flags, anthem, holidays, army, national stadia etc.) but a lot should be done to unite our people at the emotional and spiritual levels."

Although few, Namibia's ethnic groups are some of the most well-known on the continent; for example, the Herero, partly because of their history when they were almost exterminated by the Germans; and the Ovambo because they constitute almost an entire half of the country's population.

The Ovambo also played a major role in the struggle for independence, with Ovamboland being the origin of the liberation movement itiself: SWAPO. As Iina Soiri, director of the Nordic Africa Institute, states in her book, *The Radical Motherhood: Namibian Women's Independence Struggle*:

"Why is this study concentrating on a certain area of Namibia and on a certain group of Namibian women?....

[They were] at the core of the liberation movement in many ways.

Ovambos are the biggest population group in Namibia. Their culture is quite homogeneous and the area of inhabitancy has remained the same for centuries. Most of the Ovambos themselves feel that they belong to the Ovambo community, so their group identity is strong.

The most severe effects of the liberation struggle were felt in the northern areas of Namibia, among others in Ovamboland. SWAPO was initiated by migrant workers and was long regarded as an Ovambo party.

This is not to undermine the importance of any other Namibian women – or men. Neither is it to be seen as following 'divide and rule' policy in Namibia, which was the main approach of the supporters of apartheid. Besides, the 'Namibian' identity is still very weak which is understandable taking into consideration the young age of the nation." – (Iina Soiri, *The Radical Motherhood: Namibian Women's Independence Struggle*, Uppsala, Sweden: The Nordic Africa Institute (Nordiska Afrikainstitutet), 1996, p. 12).

The Ovambo also clearly have determined and shaped the national agenda more than any other ethnic group or groups because of their numerical preponderance and the dominant role they played in the liberation struggle as the founders of SWAPO which they also overwhelmingly supported. They still support SWAPO more than any other political party in the country. SWAPO is still dominant as the ruling party which also enjoys support across the country.

What has happened in Namibia has also happened in other African countries where one or only a few ethnic groups have dominated and continue to dominate their countries. It happened in Kenya where the Kikuyu became dominant since independence in 1963. The first president of Kenya, Jomo Kenyatta, was a Kikuyu himself who ruled with an iron fist. He established what virtually became an ethnocratic state dominated by his people, the Kikuyu, and dominated Kenya until his death in August 1978.

Even after his death, the Kikuyu remained powerful because they were well-entrenched in almost all areas, although their power was curtailed by President Daniel arap Moi who succeeded Kenyatta and went on to establish his own ethnocracy dominated by his people, the Kalenjins.

In Nigeria, it was the Hausa-Fulani from the north who dominated the government for almost 40 years since independence in 1960.

In Rwanda, the Hutu were dominant for 32 years since independence in 1962; in Burundi, it was the Tutsi until 2005 when a Hutu president was elected after a power-sharing agreement was reached between the two ethnic groups who had been virtually at war since independence in 1962.

In Malawi, it was the Chewa who were dominant when their fellow tribesman, Dr. Hastings Kamuzu Banda, was president for almost 30 years since independence in 1966; in Togo, it was the Kabye for almost 40 years since 1967 when Gnassingbe Eyadema, their fellow tribesman from the north, seized power in a military coup. In Ivory Coast, it was the Baoulé when their kith-and-kin, President Felix Houphouet-Boigny, ruled the country since independence in 1960. He was succeeded by another Baoulé, Henri Konan Bedie, his hand-picked successor.

All these dominant groups determined the destinies of their countries for decades because they controlled the government. It is they, with the support of their allies and members of other ethnic groups, who determined the national agenda – what policies the countries pursued and so on – and who had the upper hand in the decision-making process because of their dominant position.

In Namibia, it is the Ovambo who are dominant. They

have the power to determine the country's destiny more than any other group. As William Lindeke states in "Participation and Democracy," in Bryan M. Sims, Monica Koep, eds., *Unfinished Business: Democracy in Namibia*:

"A large dominant ethnic group also can build support for the larger national project. In many respects the dominance of the Oshivambo-speaking group – 50% of the population – and its overwhelming 90% plus voting for the ruling SWAPO party and government, predetermine stronger nationhood values and participation in support of government than might otherwise be the case. SWAPO also receives a majority of the other voters as well.

Indeed, both SWAPO supporters and Oshivambo speakers express a slightly stronger preference for democracy than do others....

Long-term hegemony by a single party or ethnic group has a tendency to fossilise people and policies around the dominant positions, thus creating excessive and unhealthy uniformity, while choking off creativity and diversity." – (William Lindeke, "Participation and Democracy," in Bryan M. Sims, Monica Koep, eds., *Unfinished Business: Democracy in Namibia*, Pretoria: Idasa, 2012, p. 24).

He goes on to state:

"...In its long history, apartheid colonialism attempted somewhat successfully to graft a rigid character of ethnic separation onto Namibian society. One important consequence of this structuring has been the common experience of monocultural life for many rural people. Ethnic issues have not disappeared and, indeed, seem to be simultaneously resurging.

On the whole, however, over the past 21 years Namibia has managed to avoid repetitive collective violence and destructive dissent around ethnic identities. Public participation in the political process revolves around common institutions and policies, and not around whether one desires to be in or out.

Namibia is not very different from other African countries in terms of these identities....

Fully 80% of the (Namibian) respondents in 2008 report(ed) either 'equal or more national identity' (equal with ethnic or more national). This measure of identity has changed slightly since 2006, which might reflect the increase in new ethnic political parties in the lead-in to the 2009 election. Again these are neither large nor dangerous changes and may only reflect the pre-election influence.

The 2009 election outcome did see a small increase in the share of votes for the more ethnic-based parties, but this growth was mainly at the expense of the opposition Democratic Turnhalle Alliance (DTA) rather than the ruling party. Nationhood remains the dominant theme in Namibia which keeps political participation within appropriate constitutional and democratic bounds." – (Ibid., pp. 24 – 25).

There is also a generational difference in the way Namibians identify themselves, with younger ones being less ethnic or tribal than older ones. Modernisation, which includes urbanisation and education, has played a major role in shaping the attitudes of young people who have the opportunity to meet and interact with members of other tribes – especially their peers, for example in school and at work – than older people do.

Preference for national identity over ethnic is more noticeable among younger people than older ones, a trend common in other African countries as well. As Lindeke states in the context of Namibia:

"Examining the issue of identity from a generational perspective, one finds that younger respondents have a slight bias of a very few percentage points toward national identity, with older ones being slightly more ethnic, but without any dramatic difference or clear hierarchy of age differences, as most differences remain within the margin of error. This situation around ethnic and national identity is unlikely to change dramatically in the future.

Even so, government leaders are somewhat ambivalent about identity, repeatedly beseeching the public to remember their roots on the one hand, while launching a new public 'nationhood' promotion campaign in 2011 on the other.

....The Most 'ethnic' regions are in the east, where Hereros support traditional ethnic parties such as the National Unity Democratic Organisation (NUDO), and in the Omusati area of founding President Sam Nujoma's origin. This is interesting in the sense that supporters of Nujoma's faction of the ruling party – referred to by opposition politicians as the 'Omusati Clique' – were accusing their rivals from other regions of being 'tribalist' and of fomenting 'tribalism.'

Party and government leaders have warned traditional leaders against becoming involved in party-political activities, but never shy away from including them in big events, and the government provided all recognised traditional leaders with new 4x4 vehicles and a driver just before the election in 2009.

When the question of identity is broken down by self-reported ethnic identity groupings, only a few of the smaller groups are less national in identity than average. Among the larger groups, only Namas have weak national-only responses. However, they make up for it with a larger than average equal identity at 60%. Only marginal, smaller groups with some history of grievance – San, Baster, Mafwe – show majority 'ethnic' responses, indicating again that Namibians have strong national identities in general, with 80% claiming 'equal or national identity'....

Namibia has the third highest national identity score, behind Tanzania and South Africa.

Leaders and ethnic brokers have created some isolated

problems. For example, Baster leaders fought to maintain a separate sovereignty in 1990 and were even threatening violence. This issue was negotiated successfully by the then prime minister and has not recurred." – (Ibid., 25 – 26, and 27).

On average, it seems the majority of Namibians have embraced dual identity – ethnic and national – without one being necessarily in conflict with the other. The two co-exist peacefully – Ovambo and Namibian, Damara and Namibian, and so on.

Besides ethnic identity, racial identity also is strong because of years of domination by whites. Collective suffering solidified collective black identity which also helped to mobilise forces during the struggle against racial oppression when the country was ruled by apartheid South Africa. Even the slightest sign of racial insult or mistreatment evokes bitter memories of suffering under white minority rule during apartheid.

Demographics reinforce that identity. Almost 90 per cent of Namibia's population is black African. Different groups also live in their own areas which are considered to be their traditional homelands, a phenomenon common throughout the continent.

Although racial oppression served as a catalyst towards mobilisation of forces across ethnic lines to fight for independence, ethnicity is still an integral part of national life even though many Namibians are uncomfortable with such compartmentalisation into ethnic categories and consider themselves to be Namibians first before anything else.

The country is sparsely populated. It has only about 2 million people in a vast expanse of territory. Namibia also has one of the lowest population densities in Africa and in the entire world. That is in sharp contrast with Rwanda and Burundi which have some of the highest population densities on the continent and in the world, prompting

Julius Nyerere to suggest that African countries should relax their borders to allow resettlement of people from countries which were wracked by conflict over land; specifically Rwanda and Burundi. No other African countries are overpopulated besides the two twin nations in East Africa.

Demographically, Namibia is lopsided. About 60 per cent of Namibians live in the north, contrasted with the southern and coastal regions which are thinly populated. The inhospitable Namib desert has claimed a large part of the coastal area, although there are some groups of people who live in the region. They are mostly pastoral: the Nama in the central part, and the Herero and the Himba, both in the northern part. The Himba are related to the Herero.

The country is composed of 11 ethnic groups: the Ovambo, Kavango, Damara, Herero, Nama, Caprivian, San, Tswana, Basters, Coloureds, and whites who are mostly Afrikaner, German and British. There also many whites of Portuguese origin who migrated from neigbouring Angola.

Namibia has the second-largest population of whites in sub-Saharan Africa after South Africa. Most of them speak Afrikaans, like the whites in South Africa, and have basically the same culture; so do people of mixed race – Coloureds and Basters.

About 30,000 whites are descendants of German colonial settlers. They have retained German culture and continue to preserve it by having their own institutions including schools and a newspapers. Their German identity is an integral part of their identity as Namibians in a country that will probably continue to have strong ethnic and racial identities, given its history of racial segregation and ethnic separation. It is a case of racialised ethnicity – for other white groups as well, including Afrikaners. They are not just an ethnic group; they are white, different and distinct from black Namibians. As Janet M. Fuller states in "Language and Identity in the German Diaspora," Mathias Schulze, James M. Skidmore, eds., et al, *German Diasporic Experiences: Identity, Migration, and Loss*:

"In Namibia, the racial aspect of German identity was even more apparent and explicit. Settlements began in 1884 when German occupied Namibia and, although many left in 1919 when Namibia became a mandate of the League of Nations, a settlement of some thousands has remained.

Research from the 1990s describes German schools and use of the language in school, church, family, and friendship domains, indicating a robust Germany identity. The link between whiteness and German identity was firmly established by the early twentieth century, and children born of the illegal union of a white German and a black African were denied an entry in German birth registries by a 1908 Berlin law.

However, racialized ethnicity does not necessarily mean that whiteness is used for a group to align with other white groups. In some cases, language is used to draw boundaries between racialized social groups. Despite widespread trilingualism in German, English, and Afrikaans, the German language is used by white Germans in Namibia as a symbolic tool for maintaining their positions of power in society, and separates them from white South Africans.

The identity of Germans in Namibia as 'südwester' is in many ways a hybrid one, stressing both their German identity and their sense of belonging in southwest Africa, even though they cannot be integrated into Namibian society. Similar to the Fredericksburg Germans in Texas, their identity is tied to both their German heritage and their experience in the diaspora." – (Janet M. Fuller, "Language and Identity in the German Diaspora," in Mathias Schulze, James M. Skidmore, David G. John, Grit Liebscher, and Sebastian Siebel-Achenbach, eds., *German Diasporic*

Experiences: Identity, Migration, and Loss, Waterloo, Ontario, Canada: Waterloo Centre for German Studies and Wilfrid Laurier University Press, 2008, pp. 13 – 14).

The are other people who belong to various groups and constitute the multicultural mosaic of the Namibian society include immigrants from Angola and Chinese who have migrated to Namibia to work or start businesses.

The influx of foreigners into Namibia has added to the cultural mix of the country but not to integration. Various groups maintain their distinct identities.

Although English is the official language, it is not the most widely spoken; Afrikaans is, which is also the most widely understood language in the country. Most whites speak Afrikaans and German, not English. But there is a great interest among many young Namibians of all races to learn English and many of them use it.

About 60 per cent of whites speak Afrikaans, and 32 per cent of them speak German which is also an important commercial language in a country that was once a German colony, although the Germans lost it about 100 years ago. English is understood or spoken by about 7 per cent of Namibians but by only about 1 per cent as a first language. Portuguese also has a significant number of speakers, including blacks, because Namibia borders Portuguese-speaking Angola; also because of the Portuguese who migrated to Namibia from Angola during the struggle for independence in that country and after the country won independence and was engulfed in civil war.

All those factors have played and continue to play a role in shaping a new Namibian identity. As in most African countries soon after they won independence, it is an identity that is new and fragile in spite of its acceptance by the people as a common bond which unites them as Namibians.

Forging a strong national identity will take a long time and on compromise basis because it is must be a product of consensus and concessions. How many people are willing to sacrifice their ethnic identities or subordinate them to a higher common identity? You don't find that in most African countries. National identity is still secondary to ethnic identity.

Ask the Kikuyu or the Luo, the Luhya or the Kamba and others if they are Kenyan first; or the Yoruba, Hausa-Fulani, and the Igbo if they are Nigerian first. It goes on and on.

More than 50 years after independence when national identities of the new African nations were proclaimed although not fully constructed, ethnic identities remain as strong as ever, impeding national unity and the evolution of an artificial common identity. As Minette E. Mans, a Namibian, states:

"Clearly, there is no 'essential Namibian,' as there is no essential Damara or Omuhimba....

The colonial history, and particularly the period of South African occupation in Namibia, had a profound impact upon the way people perceived one another – especially across racial and ethnic boundaries. Further back, this permeated even the missionary introduction of a form of Christianity in which God was partial to the white race.

In the recent past, racism in its strongest form was consolidated in apartheid policies, but permeated local societies in many other more subtle forms, whereby ethnic differences were targeted so as to isolate groups from one another and create distrust and division among the people of the country – the classic 'divide and rule' policy. Difference in all its guises – physical, historical, cultural and economic – was always emphasised, creating a strong perception of 'them' versus 'us.'

It is therefore not surprising that the current government, which came into power after the long and and bitter armed liberation struggle, is determined to stamp out all references to apartheid's focus on difference. For this reason, the call for unity, one nation, is constantly emphasised. This qualified not only educational and cultural policy, but the entire environment of identity formation. Among the people, however, this unity is evidently going to take far longer to achieve than those in power might like to admit." – (Minette E. Mans, "State, Politics and Culture," in Henning Melber, ed., *Re-examining Liberation in Namibia: Political Culture Since Independence*, op.cit., pp. 114).

She goes on to state:

"Partly as a result of the historic emphasis on defining and maintaining difference, many Namibians continue to describe themselves in terms of their ethnic group rather than nationalist. Namibia, with its composition of eleven main language groups, is often describes as a cultural 'mosaic.' To me this term implies disparate pieces fitted together loosely to create an impression of a larger picture, rather than a clear and defined unity. Perhaps this is an accurate portrayal of contemporary Namibia.

In both urban and village settings, cultural background and ethnicity are spoken about in various ways, ranging from conscious pride to self-conscious ambivalence. Certain cultural and ethnic groups align themselves with one another, but tend at times to be united only in feeling threatened by the ruling majority.

Thus, while the growing sense of national identity is strengthening in sport, regional politics and business, the pretence that there exists a real unified nation is misleading.

The building of a nation represents a process that cannot be forced. The prominent anthropologist Clifford Geertz stated some thirty years ago:

'Nationalist ideologies use cultural devices to

demonstrate the process of collective self-definition, to provide feelings of pride and hope connected with symbolic forms so that these can be consciously described, developed and celebrated' (1973:252).

Is the Namibian government going to develop the strategy of using cultural devices to speed up this process?" – (Ibid., pp. 114 – 115).

The complex nature of nation building and constructing a national identity are underscored by Minette Mans when she states:

"The primary aim of nation building is usually to create an environment where there is a shared linguistic, religious and symbolic, therefore, cultural, identity. It, therefore, involves 'a process that seeks to unite different, unrelated and sometimes incongruent population groups into an integrated and identifiable nation' (Du Pisani and Lamb, n.d.:6).

Since independence, this has meant that the government has stressed the importance of national unity, for example, by implementing an official 'shared language' through the institutionalisation of English. Instant national symbols were created – a flag, an anthem, a national airline, armed forces, a television network and a university. However, nation building is a long and tedious process, in the course of which Namibians are expected to forget historical and cultural differences through the policy of national reconciliation, avoid discourse on race (Kober 1997) and unite under the new national symbols. The liberation struggles of the past and the entrenched racism are not forgotten, yet are rarely brought out into the open. For true reconciliation, our history requires deconstruction before national identity can really evolve.

If asked what constitutes 'the' Namibian culture or personality, people are unable to supply the answer

because there is as yet no 'Namibian culture' or identity."
– (Ibid., p. 118).

It also applies to most African countries where there are many cultures identified with ethnic groups. There is no single culture, and no culture that is dominant and acceptable by most people to provide a focal point for national identity construction.

If you ask a Cameroonian or a Ugandan, "What is your national identity?" He or she will probably give you the obvious answer: "Cameroonian" or "Ugandan." But if you asks them: "What constitutes your national identity?" They will be hard-pressed for an answer.

Ask them: "What are the positive attributes of your national identity?" You may get these answers: "Unity," "We are a peaceful country," "We treat each other fairly," "We are hardworking," "We have equal opportunity for all," "We are tolerant of other people," even "We welcome strangers"; answers which could come from anybody in any country on any continent.

They are not unique to any country. Yet countries, or nations, have specific national identities – Zambian, Malawian, Nigerian, Angolan, Tanzanian, Ethiopian, Ghanaian, Mozambican, and so on.

The same applies to Namibia, the focus of this study.

What is obvious and clear is that there are many cultures and identities – essentially ethnic – which collectively constitute Namibia as a multiculturalist nation that is being built on the basis of unity in diversity.

There is also geographical diversity in terms of where the different groups are located, thus reinforcing distinctive identities and cultures. Each group has its own area. This is not unique to Namibia. It is a pattern common throughout Africa where each tribe or ethnic group has its own homeland.

Although the traditional homeland of the Ovambo in Namibia is in the north, many of them live in towns in different parts of the country, drawn by employment and other opportunities. Members of other groups are also scattered in different urban areas throughout Namibia. But the vast majority of the members of each group live in their own traditional homelands, with their own cultures.

And although the Ovambo collectively constitute an ethnic group, their ethnicity is a product of other ethnicities – related groups – constituting a "micro-nation" within the larger nation as is the case with other groups, all of which had their own traditional institutions of authority and ruled themselves before they were conquered and colonised by Europeans. As Allan D. Cooper states in his book, *The Geography of Genocide*:

"Most ethnic groups constitute sub-national entities....

There is much debate over what defines ethnicity. Some scholars claim it is a group with a common genealogy or ancestry. Other note that ethnic groups share 'cultural properties, consciousness, and boundaries' that shape communal identities that are 'situational, circumstantial, and contingent.' Ethnic identities are said to be rooted 'in perceptions of differences between lifestyles, and the *others* are held to represent lifestyles and values which are regarded as undesirable'....

There is an increasing consensus among scholars studying ethnicity that this category of identity also is a product of relationship, and not a primordial or inherent characteristic....

Many ethnic groups are the product of administrative structures created by colonial authorities to rationalize political control over a territory. For instance, German colonists in Namibia established an administrative district called Ovamboland to demarcate a territory where Ovambos lived. Prior to this development, the people of the region had not thought of themselves as Ovambo, but rather one of several communities including Ukuanyama, Ondonga, Ukuambi, Ongandjera, Ombalantu, Ukualuthi,

Okolonkuthi, or Eunda. Related communities residing across the Kunene River in the Portuguese colony of Angola were exempt from being considered Ovambo. It has been argued that the term 'Ovambo' was first used by neighbors of the Ovambo to identify them.

Colonial authorities considered anyone living in Ovamboland to be an Ovambo, even if they were recent immigrants from another community who spoke a different language. Likewise, an Ovambo who left Ovamboland and lived in another region of the colony for for some period of time would then be considered the ethnicity of the group dominating this region." – (Allan D. Cooper, *The Geography of Genocide*, Lanham, Maryland, USA: University Press of America, 2009, pp. 26 – 27).

What is critical to understating the validity of the categorisation of the Ovambo as an ethnic group is that the groups which constitute this larger group are related and were related before the coming of the Germans.. Their cultural and genealogical relationship was not a product of colonisation or administrative fiat by the German colonial rulers to categorise them that way – as one group: Ovambo.

The same applies to most African tribes or ethnic groups, not just a few. They existed before Europeans came – and "created" some of them. They had a common history, the same origin, from a common ancestor or ancestors, the same culture and spoke the same language. Colonial rulers did not create all that – the cultures, the languages, and common origins, of different African tribes. Tribal members already knew they had their own separate identities when they waged war against members of other tribes whom they knew were different from them. They all had their own identities before Europeans came.

The Ashanti were Ashanti before being conquered and colonised by the British after one of the bloodiest wars in British colonial history. They were not created by the

British; nor was their culture and language. The Mandinka were Mandinka before the French came. The Yoruba were Yoruba before they were colonised by British; so were the Kikuyu in what later came to be known as Kenya, the Igbo in what became Nigeria, the Hehe and the Zaramo in what is now Tanzania, the Chewa in former Nyasaland now Malawi, and others elsewhere across the continent. They were what they were, with their own separate identities, before the advent of colonial rule.

Common ancestry is one of the most important features of ethnic identities in Africa, including Ovambo. As Anene Ejikeme states in her book, *Culture and Customs of Namibia*:

"Today most Ovambo are Christian....The pre-Christian religion of the Ovambo included belief in a supreme deity and veneration of ancestors....Linguists divide the Ovambo into two broad groups; the two main languages spoken by the Ovambo are OshiNdonga and OshiKwanyama. According to some, the Ovambo and the Herero are descended from two brothers; thus some consider these two communities as siblings.

The area in northern Namibia that the Ovambo consider their ancestral home was formerly known as Ovamboland.

The area is known today by the names of the districts into which it is divided: Omusati, Ohangwena, Oshana,and Oshikoto, popularly known as the four O's." – (Anene Ejikeme, *Culture and Customs of Namibia*, Santa Barbara, California: Greenwood, 2011, p. 9).

Besides common ancestry as an ethnic bond, linguistic ties also constitute a strong basis for ethnic solidarity among the Ovambo and members of other groups.

Even in this era of modernisation in which some ethnic distinctions have been blurred among some groups because of intermingling including intermarriage, ethnic loyalties are still strong across Africa, except in a few countries such as Tanzania.

Ethnic solidarity of the Ovambo has raised some concerns among some groups in the country because, as the numerically dominant and politically powerful group, they are in a very strong position to favour their own people in employment and other areas of national life at the expense of other Namibians. But it is a continental phenomenon:

"Ethnic identities are almost as strong in Namibia as in Nigeria, where Ovambo are particularly prone to adhere to a shared solidarity along linguistic lines.

Ethnicity also retains above-average importance as a basis for self-ascription in Malawi, Mali, and Zimbabwe, where it bests other modes of subjective solidarity. Thus, while many East Africans say they eschew ethnicity, many Africans in West and Southern African countries continue to cling to family, clan, and language as key aspects of identity.

One would expect that ethnic minorities, who risk being sidelined by a dominant culture, would be especially protective of communal identities. To our surprise, however, we find no overall difference in the prevalence of ethnic identities between members of majority or minority ethnic groups. Any such effects are country specific.

In Nigeria, for instance, Ijaw-speaking minorities from the Niger Delta and Tiv and Igbo speakers from the Eastern zone express an intense sense of ethnic awareness. These groups are liable, more so even than Yoruba speakers, to cluster defensively around cultural identities (79 percent). By contrast, ethnic minorities in Namibia are less likely than the majority Oshivambo speakers to fall back on the expression of kin-based connections. Most members of the Silozi minority on Namibia's northeast border with Zambia, for example, describe themselves in terms of their occupations as farmers (70 percent).

Perhaps what matters most is whether ethnic minorities feel discriminated against economically in their relations with others, as do Nigeria's Ijaw over oil revenues, Tiv over land, and Igbo over opportunities for trading.

Adding to the economic interpretation, we note that, for all Afrobarometer countries, individuals who are unemployed are almost twice as likely as others to define themselves in ethnic terms. We take this as evidence that ethnic attachments are often constructed, situational, and derivative of economic distress....

In most of the African countries we studied,...new regional identities – for example, 'northerner,' 'southerner,' – have not superseded more primordial ethnic attachments." – (Michael Bratton, Robert B. Mattes, E. Gryimah-Boadi, *Public Opinion, Democracy, and Market Reform in Africa*, Cambridge, UK: Cambridge University Press, 2005, pp. 188, and 189).

This means the Ovambo are not necessarily allies of members of other ethnic groups who are also indigenous to the northern part of Namibia, simply because they are fellow northerners. They include the Kavango, the second-largest group in the country, who are native to the northeastern part of the country.

Their identity has also been partly shaped and influenced by their geographical location as an ethnic group that straddles the Namibian-Angolan border; so do the Ovambo, the Herero and others.

Their identity as Kavango transcends the boundary between the two countries, while their identity as Namibians precludes identification with their brethren across the border who are Angolan. But that is only at the national level or when enforcing national laws. Locally, multiple identities – Kavango, Namibian and Angolan – have functional utility.

Also the impact of war – the Namibian war of independence and the war in Angolan after apartheid

South Africa invaded that country – had a profound impact on them and how they identify themselves. Their experience had parallels elsewhere on the continent. As Bridget Hynes states in *Children of the Borderlands: Young Soldiers in the Reproduction of Warfare*:

"It cannot be said that certain cross-border configurations of identity are either protective or inflammatory....

Factors in the cross-regional landscape made the Mano River and Kailahun regions (in Sierra Leone) more explosive than in Kavango.

The complexity in defining the 'other' seen in the Kavango region, with insiders and outsiders considered by length of familial tenure and geographic proximity, rather than through a singular ethnicity, limited violence, where a similar system of norms did not suffice in southern Sierra Leone, due to the strength of generational and class-based cleavages....

Also, norms around sovereignty, borders and belonging also emerge as influential. Given tendencies toward ethnic animosity in warfare, care needs to be taken with local normative limits, not to encourage the xenophobic. In the Kavango, the construction of borders that extend beyond borders, yet are delimited, offer post-colonial options to a challenge endemic in Africa.

Moreover, in presenting a sovereignty identity framework that is creative and non-targeting in the formation of protective boundaries, its local norms offer something to Western societies grappling with new external threats.

Though, structurally not autonomous within Angola or Namibia, traditional leaders and regional actors acted in a 'semi-autonomous manner' in their social field along the Kavango, defining the terms of their norms and values over treatment of, and disputes between, one another....

'Most of the people that I know in the Kavango are people that came from Angola, if I have to say that. Mostly, let me say about ninety percent of the population in the Kavango are people that came from Angola long, long ago, so this sense of culture that they have is the one that keeps them. The most population that's in there are definitely from Angola.' – Kavango Youth interview#3.

In the Kavango, local norms contested national interpretations of boundaries. As part of a long-standing tradition (with regular patterns of interchange), crossing the border in a *wato* to work the field (Namibians generally crossing into Angola where lands are better and more familial lands are tilled) or go to the market (Angolans into Namibia where more goods are available) was no more eventful, in the absence of active war, than a drive to work or the store for an average American.

Given the years of war that marked the region, and the absence of a formalized border (during many parts of the 20th century), intermigration into the Kavango from Angola has been high.

As a result, the social and commercial edge of the nation is defined differently on the national level than locally. In the Kavango, the normative understanding of boundaries does not exclude a national identity; it simply allows for several levels of identity: Kavango, Angolan, and Namibian simultaneously. Often, the connections of locality take priority over national differences through the porousness and interconnections of day-to-day life.

In the Kavango, multiple layers of identification exist. Nationalism is given an expansive twist in light of daily realities. In local parlance, national borders are not the formal borders that national and international officials designate." – (Bridget Hyne, *Children of the Borderlands: Young Soldiers in the Reproduction of Warfare*, doctoral dissertation, Graduate School of International Studies, University of Denver, 2008, pp. 216, 217, and 218 – 219).

In spite of the multiple identities which are acknowledged by some people as we have seen in the case of the Kavango, and the dual identity – ethnic-national – that is common to all Namibians, there is another aspect of this issue that needs to be addressed.

In trying to understand the conception of a nation – the idea of nation is usually conceived by the elite including politicians – it is also important to understand that nationhood and national identity, which embrace all groups, are nebulous concepts to many ordinary people. They mean little in their daily lives and are irrelevant to the way they define themselves. One good example comes from a segment of the Herero. As John T. Friedman states in his book, *Imagining the Post-Apartheid State: An Ethnographic Account of Namibia*:

"During my stays in Opuwo, I rarely heard Otjiherero-speaking Kaokolanders invoke 'Namibia,' the idea of the Namibian nation, or a strong sense of national identity, especially among those who had spent most of their life in the region. There are many reasons not to expect otherwise.

Apartheid conditioned people to think in terms of pre-defined ethnic categorisations, and forced them to live within those confines. Furthermore,...Kaokoland was not politicised during the nationalist struggle, and the inroads that the liberation movement did make in the region were eventually rolled back by the South Africans and their aggressive anti-SWAPO propaganda campaigns.

Even today, two decades after independence, those in Kaokoland have limited means through which to imagine 'Namibia.' In this sense, the fact that one cannot purchase a newspaper in the regional capital is particularly significant. As Benedict Anderson has argued, a shared newspaper readership is central to the imagining of community, for it creates an 'idea of steady, solid simultaneity through time' (1983: 63).

But how did 'Namibia' and Namibian-ness appear to those in Kaokoland during the course of my stay there? Most commonly, people associated 'Namibia' with *ehi* (the land, in Otjiherero), and as such, the concept denoted little more than a geographically delimited area.

Many people argued that it is impossible for someone to be Namibian because 'Namibia' references a place, not people. 'I am a Herero, and not a Namibian,' explained one young person. 'Namibia is a country, and Herero are people.'

Others expressed a similar understanding when they suggested that if they were in fact Namibian, then they would have known it all along, even prior to independence in 1990.

For many of the old Otjiherero-speaking people in the region, 'Namibia' manifested itself as a vacuous and confounding notion, a term that was of such recent origin that it had yet to acquire signification. 'I don't know anything about that, but it is now on my identity card,' one woman declared. 'Being Namibian is something that I have just come to hear.'

At the opposite end of the age spectrum, young children were more likely to find application for the concept in their everyday lives. They often described 'Namibia' as 'the flag,' or 'singing the national anthem,' or 'celebrating in the name of Sam [former President Nujoma, now officially re-titled Founding Father of the Namibian Nation].' For them, 'Namibia' was practised everyday in the schoolyard or during national holidays.

But the town of Opuwo did, of course, contain some 'Namibians.' Those who expressed a strong sense of national belonging were usually either secondary school children, or government civil servants who had moved to the region because of their work." – (John T. Friedman, *Imagining the Post-Apartheid State: An Ethnographic Account of Namibia*, Oxford, Brooklyn, New York:

Berghahn Books, 2011, pp.198 – 199).

He goes on to state:

"As many scholars have shown (Borneman 1992; McClintock 1993; Delaney 1995), leaders and citizens often draw upon the emotive power of the family in their national discourses, and even conflate the nation with the family. However, the Otjiherero-speaking Kaokolanders that I met almost never drew upon or promoted such images in direct relation to the Namibian nation. Even though they readily invoked the family as a metaphor, I hardly ever heard anybody suggest that the Namibian nation was 'like family,' or that it even had the capacity to become one.

Kaokolanders were more likely to treat the Namibian nation as a collectivity of families. In this conception, numerous ethnic groups were considered united in their sharing of a single geographical space, and nothing more, not even a common history.

In relation to the Namibian nation writ large, Otjiherero-speakers in Kaokoland were much more likely to root themselves in the Herero nation, a 'community' that extends from southern Angola, through central and eastern Namibia, and into Botswana. Ethnic self-consciousness almost always trumped a national one.

The 'nation-as-a-family' discourse was thus reserved for use in relation to nations that people constructed on the basis of ethnic, and sometimes racial, categorisations. It was when one of Namibia's component groups was put into discursive play vis-à-vis other such groups that the family idiom surfaced. Issues relating to the policy of national reconciliation, for example, often sparked such imagery. In this respect, one woman equated the independence war with a struggle between two families, one White and one Black, each fighting to inherit a deceased person's wealthy estate; while a young boy explained that White people were not fulfilling their obligations under the new policy because they refused to treat their fellow Black citizens as they would a member of their own family: 'A White can just posses something without giving it to the Black person. It happens with things such as food and clothes. Whites are supposed to give these things to Black people. They must give, and if they don't, then there is apartheid. Whites and Blacks are people from the same house because now they are staying together.'

....A similar language is often deployed by Otjiherero-speaking Kaokolanders when they reflect on relations between Herero and Ovambo 'families' vis-à-vis the new independent government. In addition to the Namibian nation and the Herero nation, a third national 'family' is now coming into discursive play throughout Kaokoland. Some of the region's more progressive leaders are working to transcend the ongoing factional dispute between the Otjikaoko and Thom houses by promoting a regional based identity, or what is being termed the Kaoko nation (cf. Miescher 2000). 'I want to say this: When are we going to be one people who are going to work for the Kaoko nation?' asked a local headman during an annual chief's commemoration ritual in Opuwo.

'We teach [this] division to our children, the ones that are being born. Until when? They are going to regard us as different nations, which is not like that at all. We are not different people. No, we are just the same people. Now we have to find the thing that divided the people, so that we can be what we used to be from far back....For how long is it going to be like this? Who is going to build this nation if it is like this? You are the same people; then you divided yourselves into groups, which is not necessary. Please try to come together and make an agreement.'

The Kaoko nation construct is a relatively new political

development, and for some, a most welcome one, particularly because it offers a model based on something other than the notion of shared substance. In trying to bridge the factional dispute, though, the idea of a Kaoko nation does indeed generate another layer of political segmentation. Who will be part of the Kaoko nation, and who will be excluded from it? What will be the relationship between members of the Kaoko nation and the ever-fragmenting Herero nation? Will new regionally based 'nations' serve as repackaged versions of tribal identities that were constructed and inculcated during the apartheid era? The question remains, then, as to whether or not such a healing strategy will generate a different set of tensions in its wake." – (Ibid., pp. 199 – 201).

The apartheid regime also took advantage of the situation that already existed. Ethnic groups existed before apartheid was imposed on the people of Namibia. But the white minority government used ethnic differences to facilitate and consolidate white control over the country by keeping the people divided and trying to make them believe they had nothing in common – although it was obvious they did as Africans, as black people, and as victims of racial injustice.

Affirmation of ethnic identities – and whatever political power, including votes, ethnic groups have – is one of the strategies different groups sometimes use to extract concessions from the central government which tries to submerge such identities in a supra-body, the nation (be it Namibia, Kenya, Zambia or Nigeria), at their expense.

Namibia also has a history of political mobilisation on the basis of ethnic solidarity similar to what happened in Nigeria where the country's three main political parties were dominated by the three main ethnic groups: the Hausa/Fulani of northern Nigeria who dominated the Northern People's Congress, the Yoruba who formed the

Action Group in the southwest, and the Igbo in the southeast who overwhelmingly supported the National Convention of Nigerian Citizens (formerly the National Council of Nigeria and the Cameroons). That was even before independence when they could have formed a united front – under one political party – against the British colonial rulers in their demand for independence. And it continued to be the case until January 1966 when the federal government dominated by the Hausa-Fulani was overthrown in a military coup masterminded by young Igbo army officers to end northern domination of the Nigerian federation.

In the case of Namibia, ethnicity played a major role in the formation of the first political parties which wanted to end apartheid rule:

"The first attempt to create a *national* liberation movement was in 1957 when a group of Herero ex-students joined forces with the Herero Chiefs' Council to found the South West Africa National Union (SWANU). Its goal was national independence. While linkage with the Chiefs' council broadened its appeal among the Hereros, the move also led to SWANU's identification as an ethnic Herero organization, thus diminishing its appeal for the rest of Namibia's people, for most of whom ethnic identity is the primary basis for political allegiance.

Meanwhile, by 1960, the OPO (Ovambo People's Organisation) had reconstituted itself as the South West Africa People's Organization (SWAPO) so as to attract support beyond its Ovambo base and thus be in a position to lead the national liberation struggle. In political gatherings held throughout the territory, SWAPO stressed national unity, self-reliance and non-alignment in foreign affairs.

By then, however, the profusion of ethnically-based political parties, together with the minority groups' suspicions that SWAPO could become a vehicle for

Ovambo domination, became major obstacles to SWAPO's ambitions to lead the national movement." – ((The International Institute for Strategic Studies (IISS), *Africa Volume II, Adelphi Papers*, op.cit., p. 224).

Acknowledgement of the continued existence of ethnic groups in Namibia – they are going nowhere – and their solidarity on ethnic basis is one of the justifications for the imperative need to pursue a policy of unity in diversity in Namibia and why the government itself has decided to build a multiculturalist society in which the different groups continue to affirm their identities while at the same time being Namibian, a dual identity that has helped the country to maintain peace and stability.

As a young nation, it is understandable why Namibia has some people who question the concept of national identity and are reluctant to identify themselves as 'Namibian' but would rather be identified with their ethnic groups. It is a problem almost all African countries face. They are young, and their national identities are also new. That is in sharp contrast with countries which have existed for hundreds of years with well-established institutions of authority whose legitimacy is hardly questioned; nor is the concept of nation or national identity.

But even in young African nations such as Namibia, there is a relatively strong sense of nationalism when, for example, there is an external threat if the people think their country is going to be invaded; or when they are insulted or attacked in various ways by outsiders. They mobilise forces to form a united front to defend their country. They all become very patriotic and don't even question their national identity; they are proud of it. They themselves show they do have the same identity. But some of them just don't acknowledge it all the time.

Yet there is still a lot to be done to instill a true sense of nationalism in the minds of the people across the African continent in order to build countries which are truly united and fair to all their people.

In the case of Namibia, as in other African countries, the geographic-ethnic configuration also can be an asset in creating a truly unified nation that takes into account its ethnic and geographical diversity as a basis for unity. The configuration provides a landscape on which national leaders of different political persuasions can try to mould the identity of the nation, using regional clusters of ethnic groups as a basis for a stable and united country – a unitary state under highly centralised authority, as is the case today, or as a decentralised system if members of different groups and regions feel the central government under a unitary state does not serve them well.

Besides the Ovambo and Kavango in the north, other groups of Namibia are:

The Herero in central and eastern Namibia as well as in the western part of the country north of the capital Windhoek. They are the third-largest group after the Ovambo and the Kavango.

The Damara, the fourth-largest, live south of Ovamboland and east of the desert coastal region. Their traditional homeland is northwestern Namibia. Before then, they lived in the central part of the country but were forced out by the Herero and the Namaqua. Like other Namibians, many of them also live in different parts of Namibia. They are of Bantu origin and speak the Khoikhoi language like the Nama but are not related to them.

Forced relocation of the Damara by the apartheid regime in a semi-arid region, Damaraland, caused them a lot of hardship. Many of them could not live in the area and sought employment in towns. Damaraland is now occupied by only a minority who constitute about 25 per cent of the Damara population nationwide. The rest live mostly in towns.

The Nama live in the south; Caprivians in Caprivi Strip in the northeast – they belong to different ethnic groups including the Lozi who straddle the Namibian-Zambian border. Lozi is the main language in the region.

The Khoikhoi live mainly in southern Namibia although they are also found in different parts of the country, mostly in dry areas.

Whites live mainly in the central and southern parts of Namibia including Windhoek where they are concentrated. They live mostly in urban areas. And they constitute a vast majority in Swakopmund, a coastal city.

Coloureds live in Windhoek and other urban areas. Although Coloureds and the Basters are related in terms of origin and share cultural similarities, including Afrikaans as a common language for members of the two groups, they have separate identities whose distinctiveness is emphasised by members of both communities.

The Basters live Rehoboth and its surroundings, south of Windhoek, and in other urban areas. But their homeland is Rehoboth in central Namibia. They are also known as Rehoboth Basters. Besides speaking Afrikaans as their native language, they also uphold Afrikaner culture and live as Afrikaners because of the culture and traditions the two groups share in spite of their distinct separate identities.

The Himba who live in the north are related to the Herero. Although they are a branch of the Herero, they are culturally distinct from them but speak the same language.

The Nama who live in southern Namibia are related to the Khoikhoi and affiliated with the San.

The Tswana live in the eastern part of Namibia. They are the smallest ethnic group in the country and share ethnic identity with the Tswana across the border in Botswana.

Geographical diversity has played a role in the evolution of the identity of the different groups in Namibia, as it has elsewhere in Africa, reflected in their cultures which are partly a product of the environment in which the people live. That is why rivers, lakes and mountains, for example, feature prominently in the cultures and religious beliefs of many ethnic groups in Africa; so do some animals and other creatures.

If they did not exist in the areas where the people settled, the beliefs and cultures of many groups would have been different in many respects. Their identities and way of life are inextricably linked with the environment, hence geography. Thus, the Batonga worship the river god of the Zambezi. The Kikuyu pray facing Mount Kenya. There are river goddesses among the Yoruba and the Igbo. There are also sacred lakes in which the gods and spirits of some tribes reside; for example, Lake Fundudzi among the Venda. The river which flows into the lake, the Mutare, is home to a giant python which is the god of fertility for the Venda.

Different groups in Namibia also have their own sacred places, and even creatures as is the case with the San.

Almost all the members of the black ethnic groups or tribes in Namibia trace their origin to East Africa. They share cultural and linguistic similarities with the members of other groups in East and Central Africa who collectively constitute the "Bantu" family. There are even some words in Namibian languages which are a part of the Swahili vocabulary or very similar to Swahili words; for example, *mama* which means "mother" in Otjiherero/Himba also means "mother" in Swahili; *meme* for "mother" in Oshiwambo is similar to *mama* in Swahili; *ovita* which means war in Otjiherero/Himba is *vita* in Swahili; *indjo* which means "come" in Otjiherero/Himba is *njoo* in Swahili.

Even the San, so-called Bushmen, are related to the Sandawi of central Tanzania and migrated to southern Africa from the eastern part of the continent.

What gives all these groups in Namibia a collective identity as Namibians is colonial conquest and domination which defined them as one colonised people within the boundaries of what came to be known as South-West Africa, later Namibia. But, basically, they are not different from other black Africans, for example, in Zambia, Tanzania, Congo, Zimbabwe, Uganda, Botswana. Mozambique, South Africa and elsewhere.

When we talk about national identity in Africa, we are talking about an identity derived from artificial boundaries and nations created by Europeans who conquered and colonised Africans. They are the ones who gave Africans national identity reflected in the existence of the countries they created.

There was no country or political entity called South-West Africa – renamed Namibia – until Europeans came and created the boundaries of the countries we have today. Therefore, there were no South West Africans as a collective unit under one government. There was no Nigeria, therefore no Nigerians, before Europeans came; no Guinea, hence no Guineans, no Kenya, hence no Kenyans, no Tanganyika, hence no Tanganyikans, no Sierra Leone, hence no Sierra Leoneans, no Gambia, hence no Gambians, before Europeans came and partitioned the continent.

Before then, we were just Africans (although without such a name), with tribal identities, yes, but Africans nonetheless as one people without being constrained by artificial identities imposed on us by our European conquerors and confined to our new countries which we could not leave without travel documents or passports issued by the colonial authorities.

That is why before the advent of colonial rule, Africans were able to migrate from one part of the continent to another and settle in new areas without being asked any questions. That is why members of Bantu ethnic groups were able to migrate all the way from West Africa (what is now Cameroon and east-central Nigeria) to central, eastern and southern Africa including the area that is now Namibia. There were no restrictions then, no passports.

We did not have disputes over natural resources such as lakes and rivers. People on one side of the lake did not say the whole lake belonged *only* to them. It belonged to none and therefore belonged to all; so did land – it belonged to the community.

But when Europeans came, they said: "This is the boundary. The lake belongs to Nyasaland. People on the other side of the border in Tanganyika no longer own part of the lake."

We were more united then than we are now. We did not have the boundaries which we have now. That was when we were simply a people, Africans, an identity we are reluctant to accept or reclaim besides pious and rhetorical professions in the name of African brotherhood.

We defend the sanctity of borders – colonial boundaries – which gave us our national identities we cherish so much. The boundaries define us. And we hold them sacrosanct in the name of territorial integrity. Each to his own.

Nyerere put it succinctly in his speech in Accra, Ghana, on 6 March 1997 as an official guest at Ghana's 40th independence anniversary celebrations when he said:

"We are all Africans trying very hard to be Ghanaians or Tanzanians."

It is a dilemma we are still caught in. Because we inherited the colonial boundaries, we also inherited not only the identity that came with those boundaries but also European ways of life to de-Africanise ourselves.

The task for us now is to shape the identity we inherited to reflect African realities and values, cultures and traditions, not necessarily to reclaim everything from the past but to construct an identity that is inclusive embracing all groups regardless of who or what they are; and to make sure there is no group which dominates others as our conquerors did.

We are all Africans, whether we like it or not, united by common bonds and intrinsic values of our African-ness which can never be dissolved because they are natural. That is what collectively constitutes the African personality: diverse yet indivisible, more spiritual than material.

Appetite for material civilisation at the expense of humanity is one of the worst vices we inherited from our Europeam conquerors. And it has distorted our vision of building just societies, hence nations, in which everybody is treated equal based on traditional African values of hospitality, love, compassion and tolerance which even led us to welcome and embrace strangers who went on to conquer and subjugate us until we reclaimed our independence at an enormous cost.

Conclusion

Although separation of ethnic groups has its own attributes because it has helped to preserve the traditional way of life and ethnic identities since the majority of the people live in their own areas, thus making the task of creating a distinctive Namibian identity much more difficult, it should not be seen as an insurmountable obstacle in the quest for national unity and in the construction of a common national identity.

In the absence of a dominant culture, which everybody else is expected to adopt and which gives a nation an identity, for example the Anglo-Saxon culture in Britain, there are other means which be used to forge a distinctive national identity. One example is the way in which the different national characters – hence national identities – of Kenya and Tanzania have evolved along different paths in spite of the many things the two neighbouring countries have in common including history and culture.

Strong national leadership and policies played a critical role in creating and shaping the separate national identities of the two countries. As I state in one of my books,

Kenya: Identity of a Nation, which is also a comparative analysis of the national characters of the two countries:

"Like most African countries, Kenya is plagued by tribalism. It is a nation fractured along ethno-regional lines.

Yet it exists as a single political entity whose identity has been forged on the anvil of diversity. And it is identified by certain attributes which collectively constitute what can be called its national character.

The concept of national character is nebulous, and highly controversial, especially in young nations like those of Africa which are often dismissed as no more than a hodge-podge of different and antagonistic ethnic groups lumped together with very little in common in terms of identity except their 'African-ness' as a people who share the same continent.

Yet, it is a concept that exists in reality and can be demonstrated by empirical evidence. And it has been given concrete expression in the establishment of nations which assume their own distinctive identities, hence national characters, as they evolve through the years.

In the case of old nations, it has taken centuries for them to solidify their identities and national characters.

Still, all nations have their own characteristics shaped by their beliefs and values including moral values, traditions and customs, learned and taught – individually and collectively – from childhood through adulthood from generation to generation.

Sometimes, inculcation of those beliefs, ideals and values takes the form of indoctrination. And they shape individual characters and collective attitudes which are an integral part of national character.

The concept of national character has even been attributed to a grand design by the Divine. For example, German nationalist philosopher Johann Fichte defined a nation as a manifestation of divine order. Another German philosopher, Johann Herder, argued that The Creator – in his guidance of human destiny – had separated nations not only by physical features such as rivers and mountains but also by languages and national characters.

In his *Addresses to The German Nation* he delivered as lectures at the University of Berlin, Fichte contended that the German people – with their common identity distinct from those of other people – existed as a natural collective entity constituting an indivisible organic whole and spoke a language, the German language, which had naturally evolved and been structured to express the truth. Their language, together with their history, culture, traditions and works of literature constituted their German-ness, giving them a distinct identity as Germans.

And since Germany did not have natural frontiers (mountains or large rivers or an ocean around its borders), like her neighbour France, for example, did; he argued that the German language itself formed inner frontiers – uniting the German people while keeping foreigners out – and thus constituted natural boundaries for the German nation. Tanzanians and Kenyans can probably say the same thing about Kiswahili!

Nations can indeed exist without land and physical boundaries. The case of the Palestinians is a typical example in contemporary times. They don't have a country as a sovereign political entity, yet they do exist as a nation. Before then it was the Jews until the establishment of Israel as a political entity in 1948 at the expense of the Palestinian Arabs.

Fichte's concept of the nation as a manifestation of divine order, combined with his fanatical patriotism, stimulated German nationalism.

Among Italian nationalists like Mazzini and Garibaldi who sought the unification of Italy, Italy's natural (physical) frontiers defined the Italian nation as a natural entity inhabited by Italians with their own national character.

Mazzini even invoked the shape of Italy – with its physical barriers as borders – to argue that it was meant to define the Italian nation with its own distinctive identity and characteristics different from those of other nations.

Italian nationalists also argued that God had intended for them, as Italians or as an Italian nation, to occupy that land The implication was obvious. The land was intended exclusively for them as Italians with their own distinctive identity and attributes as a people.

And in many fundamental respects, especially in terms of inner frontiers, not necessarily with regard to national language as defined by Fichte but mostly in terms of their own characteristics including collective attitudes and values which distinguish them, African nations are no exception as entities with their own unique characters.

For example, it is common to hear quite often people talk about Nigerians, what kind of people they are. Among their best attributes is that they are very ambitious and are high achievers. And there are quite a few bad things said about them, of course, just like any other people.

Ghanaians also have their own characteristics. Under Nkrumah, they were able to achieve a degree of unity, as one people, unheard of in most African countries because of Nkrumah's ability to fight tribalism and regionalism. And he instilled in his people a sense of national pride in a way most African leaders did not or were not able to, besides Nyerere and very few others.

Even today, many Ghanaians identify themselves first as Ghanaians, not as Ewe, Fanti, Ga, or Dagomba; while it is not uncommon to hear Nigerians say, "I'm Yoruba," or "I'm Igbo," before they say "I'm Nigerian"; or Kenyans say "I'm Kikuyu, Kamba, Luo, or Luhya" before they say, "I'm Kenyan."

Also, many Ghanaians are some of the most Pan-Africanist-oriented people because of what Nkrumah taught and the role Ghana – under his leadership – played in supporting the African liberation movements the way Tanzania did under Nyerere.

It is an enduring legacy, left by Nkrumah, which has played a critical role in shaping Ghana's identity and national character.

All those are attributes or characteristics of national character – whether Ghana's, Kenya's or Nigeria's or of any other country.

While it is true that African countries don't have solid national identities like the old nations of Europe and Asia whose identities have been forged through the centuries and have had the benefit of time – many centuries – to take shape, there is no question that they have individual attributes which distinguish them from each other in a number of ways; although they also have a lot in common as fellow Africans and as young nations or political entities which attained sovereign status only a few decades ago, mostly in the sixties.

One of the fundamental differences between European nations and African nations is that the establishment of nations in Europe preceded the creation of states – which are institutions of authority over a well-defined area or territory called a country – while in Africa, the reverse was the case.

States preceded the establishment of nations – they were established even before countries were formed and before the people developed a sense of loyalty to the country they shared as 'one people.'

In Africa, states as instruments of authority were created by the colonial powers to bring different tribes together into a cohesive whole, the nations and countries we have today, to facilitate colonial administration. And there is a lot that still has to be done to weld these ethnic groups together into truly cohesive entities transcending ethnic and regional loyalties and be able to establish truly united nations.

But even in their infancy, as entities which have existed as independent nation-states only for the past 50 years or so since the end of colonial rule, they do have their own identities. And these identities have largely been shaped by the political leadership which assumed power on attainment of sovereign status in the sixties and in a few cases (like Ghana and Guinea) in the late fifties.

Thus, you had Jomo Kenyatta, The Burning Spear, whose formidable personality had such a profound impact on the development and evolution of the modern state, hence nation, of what we know as Kenya today that it is virtually impossible to think or talk about Kenya without also at least thinking about Kenyatta at the same time. He ruled with an iron fist, shaped his country in his image, and preferred continuity rather than change.

He left almost everything virtually intact after the British officially relinquished power on independence day, 12 December 1963, as if nothing had changed.

Preservation or continuation of the status quo, the way the British ran the country, played a critical role in shaping Kenya's national character to the point where even today, it is not unusual to hear some Africans from other countries say, 'Kenyans are very British,' they 'worship' the British, or that they are 'subservient' to the white man. And the country remained solidly capitalist after independence.

Stereotypes sometimes correspond to reality, and not all characterisations are stereotypes. Perceptions of Kenyans – and other Africans – as to what type of people they are sometimes reflect reality.

But it does not mean that Kenyans are really subservient to the white man or are 'very British'; what it really means is that many Kenyans admire British achievements in many areas especially in terms of education and material civilisation, although there are some people – not just in Kenya but in other African countries as well, including my home country Tanzania – who think that they are 'civilised' if they copy the manners of their former colonial masters, British or French, or 'act white' and even sound British or French; and ape the consumption proclivities of their former imperial masters whom they see as the paragon of virtue and the embodiment of what is best in mankind.

That is colonial mentality at its worst. And it is typical of many Africans, especially among the elite, who not only admire and even 'worship' our former colonial masters; they are mesmerised by the glitter and glamour of the West, the same place our conquerors came from, and whose nations continue to exploit us.

Even today, there are many Africans who try to be carbon copies of our former colonial masters and are more 'British' and more 'French' than the British and the French themselves.

The same people who conquered us and who continue to exploit us are glorified by some of us as our heroes as if we don't have our own heroes, and as if we never even had any before the coming of Europeans. Glorifying our conquerors as our heroes is the worst form of colonial mentality and mental slavery.

The British are among those who are glorified by a significant number of Kenyans and other Africans who were once ruled by them.

This kind of admiration and glorification also fuels imperial arrogance, best exemplified by an old English lady who once asked Tom Mboya on a street in London: 'Which one of our possessions are you from?'

These are the kind of people who already have an inflated ego. So glorifying them, and admiring them so much, only makes things worse.

There is no question that British influence is still very strong in Kenya even today more than 50 years after independence. And all the governments which have been in power in all those years have chosen to maintain the status quo instead of opting for fundamental change across the spectrum in the way the country is run and how the country's wealth is shared.

It is clear that the British played a major role in shaping

Kenya's national character.

It could even be argued that the people of Kenya and Tanganyika differed in national character even before independence; with Kenya's national character having been partly, if not largely, shaped by the British settlers who settled in Kenya in very large numbers during colonial rule.

They were highly visible, they spread their values – directly and indirectly – and were seen by many Kenyans, not just by the elite, as role models to be emulated. And there are still many whites of British descent still living in Kenya today, including some members of the aristocracy. Many of them are citizens, others are not and have no interest in becoming citizens.

Tanganyika, on the other hand, had far fewer settlers than Kenya did. There were about 66,000 settlers, mostly British, in Kenya during the fifties not long before the country won independence. Tanganyika had between 21,000 and 23,000, also mostly British.

If the former British colonial rulers were to return to Kenya today, they would notice very little change in the way the country is run in terms of institutional arrangements, attitudes, values and even moral traits which are some of the characteristics which collectively constitute national character. They would also notice that many Kenyans, black Kenyans, are indeed 'very British.'

It has been an entirely different experience in neighbouring Tanzania where Julius Nyerere, a charismatic personality, dominated the political scene for almost 40 years from independence in 1961 until his death in 1999. A former secondary school teacher, he was popularly known as Mwalimu, which means "teacher" in Kiswahili.

He sought fundamental change in his quest for radical socialist transformation of Tanzania in order to build an egalitarian society and successfully welded almost 130 different ethnic groups and racial minorities into a solidly united and peaceful nation unparalleled in the history of post-colonial Africa, giving Tanzania and Tanzanians a unique national character.

The egalitarian ideals he instilled in the people of Tanzania played a critical role in shaping their national character.

They not only transcended tribalism under his leadership; they also came to accept each other as equals in terms of rights and dignity as fellow Tanzanians and as fellow human beings in a society where no one was better than another simply because he or she was rich or belonged to a certain tribe. They addressed each other as "ndugu," which literary means "relative," "brother" or "sister." It also means "comrade." They saw themselves as one family.

In Kenya the entrepreneurial spirit under capitalism went long ways in shaping Kenya's national character. Kenyans are said to be more "aggressive," more "enterprising," and more "daring" than Tanzanians.

By remarkable contrast, Tanzanians, shaped by the egalitarian ideals of ujamaa (familyhood) and compassion and respect for fellow man taught by Nyerere, are known to be "humble," "more reserved," "trustworthy," "more patient," "compassionate," and "non-tribalistic" unlike their Kenyan neighbours who have a reputation for being very tribalistic, "very individualistic" and "selfish."

And the fact that tribalism was institutionalised under Kenyatta has meant that this vice – or virtue depending on who the beneficiary is – has played a critical role in shaping Kenya's national character distinctly different from Tanzania's.

In Kenya tribalism is accepted as a way of life, a way of doing things or of getting things done.

Therefore, tribalism has not only shaped Kenya's national character; among many Kenyans – not all but many – tribalism is celebrated as a virtue and is not seen as a vice to be despised. It is not only a way of getting ahead in life; it is also a means to promote and protect the interests of "my people," that is, of "my fellow tribesmen," at the expense of other Kenyans, of course.

So, Kenya exists as nation, yes. But it is a nation that is divided from within, fractured along ethnic and regional lines.

Yet its weakness, tribalism, is one of the most prominent attributes of its national character. Many Kenyans say "We are one nation, but my tribe comes first." Otherwise it is not the Kenya we know if we contend otherwise.

That is in sharp contrast with what goes on in Tanzania where tribalism is not a major problem. It has not been eradicated but it has been effectively contained, and has even been virtually neutralised in many areas of national life.

To most people in Tanzania, tribalism is not a virtue; it is a vice. It is not glorified; it is despised. It is not something to be proud of.

Even speaking one's tribal language in front of members of other tribes is frowned upon in Tanzania. That is not the case in Kenya.

All that is part of Tanzania's national character. Most Tanzanians see themselves as Tanzanians first; not as Digo, Nyamwezi, Kerewe, Nyakyusa, Zigua, Zaramo, Kinga, Chaga, Ngoni, Yao, Makua, Nyaturu, Sukuma, Luguru, Hehe, Ndengereko, Fipa, Safwa, Gogo, Bena, Bondei, Haya, Sambaa, Nyika, Zanaki, Pare, Kurya, or Makonde among many other tribes.

But while Tanzanians have transcended tribalism, the question that now arises in this era of globalisation after the triumph of capitalism over communism and socialism is whether or not the entrepreneurial spirit that has taken hold in Tanzania, after the country renounced socialism as a state ideology, will also re-mould Tanzania's national character and transform the country into a place where the people no longer care about each other and no longer see each other as one and as equal human beings as in neighbouring Kenya.

In Kenya, the entrepreneurial spirit under which the country has thrived since independence as a capitalist society has remarkably shaped Kenya's national character and has radically transformed the country into a nation characterised by ruthless competition.

The emphasis is on competition, not on cooperation or compassion, because raw-naked individualism is celebrated as a virtue. It is a product of capitalism and the acquisitive instinct nurtured in a society which is itself a product of Western material civilisation.

In Tanzania, this highly competitive spirit is not very pronounced even today among the vast majority of the people – at least not as much as it is in Kenya – and was virtually non-existent under socialism; although there is a lot of competition nowadays among the elite and the urban dwellers in general in terms of employment and earning income by various means including self-employment especially in the subterranean economy.

During the socialist era especially in the early seventies when there was so much rhetoric about the virtues of socialism versus capitalism, it was not uncommon to hear some Tanzanians say, "Kenya is a dog-eat-dog society" or a "man-eat-man society"; to which Kenyans responded by saying, "In Tanzania, it is dog eating nothing!"; a statement that was given prominence when it was also made by the arrogant Kenyan attorney general, Charles Njonjo, in 1977.

It was common knowledge among the Kenyan elite that Tanzanian President Julius Nyerere did not like Charles Njonjo and had no respect for him because he saw him as arrogant and callous towards the plight of the poor, as he did other members of the Kenyan elite, of course; an observation also made by Kenyan Professor Ali Mazrui in his moving eulogy – "Nyerere and I" – when Nyerere died in October 1999. As he stated in his memorial tribute to Nyerere:

"With his concept of Ujamaa, Nyerere also attempted to build bridges between indigenous African thought and modern political ideas. Ujamaa, which means 'familyhood,' was turned by Nyerere into a foundation for African Socialism. Ujamaa became the organising principle of the entire economic experiment in Tanzania from the Arusha Declaration of 1967 to the mid-1980s.

His relations with the Kenyan political elite deteriorated further and further. He found Attorney-General Charles Njonjo particularly distasteful and arrogant as a person and reckless in his attitudes towards Kenya's neighbours.

Nyerere was fond of Mzee Kenyatta, but he thought Njonjo exercised disproportionate influence on the old man. Nyerere was not sure whether to be amused or outraged when Njonjo turned any discussion on Kenyatta's mortality into something close to a capital offence!

Nyerere was against turning rulers into gods – 'Like the old Pharaohs of ancient Egypt.' Making Kenyatta immortal was like turning him into a god.

Nyerere and I remembered the proposal which was made in 1964 to celebrate annually the day of Kenyatta's arrest by the British as 'the Last Supper.' There was such a strong negative reaction from Christian churches in Kenya against using the concept of 'the Last Supper' in this way that the idea was dropped....

Tanzania was one of the few African countries which attempted to find its own route to development instead of borrowing the ideologies of the West....

Nyerere's policies of nation-building amount to a case of Unsung Heroism. With wise and strong leadership, and with brilliant policies of cultural integration, he took one of the poorest countries in the world and made it a proud leader in African affairs and an active member of the global community....

In global terms, he was one of the giants of the 20th Century....He did bestride this narrow world like an African colossus....

Julius Nyerere was my Mwalimu too. It was a privilege to learn so much from so great a man." – (Ali A. Mazrui, "Nyerere and I," at Africa Resource Center: africaresource.com/content/view/56/222).

While Nyerere's socialist policies did not succeed in developing Tanzania and did not transform the country into a truly socialist society, the idealism which inspired those policies united the people of Tanzania in their quest for equality across the spectrum in a way they probably would not have been able to pursue the same goal under capitalism.

That was in sharp contrast with what happened in neighbouring Kenya where equality meant nothing. And it still means nothing even today.

And when Kenyan Attorney-General Charles Njonjo ridiculed Tanzania as a "man eating nothing" society – not only because of the failure of socialism but also because it was a society of egalitarian ideals where the people shared poverty and whatever 'little' they had as a country, instead of encouraging individuals to accumulate personal wealth at the expense of others – he epitomised Kenya's national character and one of its best or worst attributes: selfishness.

And it is an attribute that still defines Kenya today. It is an integral part of Kenya's national character and psyche in a country where ruthless competition is glorified as a virtue and where tribalism – which is itself a form of competition and selfishness – is the very essence of national life and one's well-being.

In fact, greed can be seen as an incentive to production, hence a catalyst for economic development. Where there is competition and selfishness, there is also high productivity. That is the essence of capitalism.

It does not mean that Kenyans in general are selfish; nor does it mean that there are no selfish people in Tanzania – there are plenty, especially among the elite and even among ordinary people.

What it means is that Kenyans, after living under capitalism for decades since independence, are animated by a spirit of individualism and entrepreneurship in a way their brethren in Tanzania are not. That is because this kind of spirit was stifled by socialism among the vast majority of the people in Tanzania.

You can not thrive under capitalism without being highly competitive. In fact, capitalism is ruthless, and even heartless, by nature. Each to his own.

But it is also highly productive and provides the best incentives to production. Yet it fosters inequality.

In Tanzania, socialism not only stifled individual initiative; it also sometimes compromised standards of excellence which are encouraged under capitalism.

But socialism also had its virtues: the egalitarian ideals which fostered national unity and equality among Tanzanians its antithesis, capitalism, did not and could not in Kenya.

Even today collective consciousness, an attribute Tanzanians share, is rare among Kenyans except in a tribal context.

Loyalty to the tribe takes precedence over loyalty to the nation among most Kenyans.

Individualism and tribalism are deeply embedded in the national psyche. And it is impossible to understand Kenya's national character without comprehending or coming to grips with this harsh reality.

If the existence of nations is indeed a manifestation of divine order, there is an imperative need for all nations to improve and for some even to change their national characters. Kenya is no exception.

And if Kenya decides to do that, the ideals of justice, equality, fairness, compassion and concern for the well-being of others which inspired the struggle for independence and led to the birth of a new nation may one day become some of the finest qualities, and some of the most outstanding attributes, of her national character transmitted from one generation to the next." – (Godfrey Mwakikagile, *Kenya: Identity of a Nation*, Pretoria, South Africa: New Africa Press, 2007, p. 195 – 207).

In the case of Namibia, which has been the focus of this study, the evolution of a distinctive national identity will depend on strong national leadership and the policies the government pursues to achieve unity in diversity without domination by one group, as it happened in Kenya where the Kikuyu established what virtually became an ethnostate under the leadership of the country's first president, Jomo Kenyatta, a perverted policy whose devastating impact on national unity still haunts the country more than 50 years after independence.

Appendix I:

Amid Namibia's White Opulence, Majority Rule Isn't So Scary Now

John D. Battersby, *The New York Times*
Monday, December 26, 1988

The white inhabitants of Namibia celebrated Christmas in this coastal resort (of Swakopmund) with little of the fear and panic that the prospect of black-majority rule evoked in them a decade ago.

"We will have to live with it and make the best of it," said Andries Auret, the chief official of Swakopmund's town council when asked about the likelihood of black nationalists winning independence elections that are to take place next year.

While his views did not reflect those of the territory's more recalcitrant whites, they underscored changing white attitudes after 10 years of internal reforms in race relations and a campaign by South Africa's white rulers to prepare the territory for independence and a sharing of power among the races.

'Way of Life'

"People have been living with the talk of independence for so long that it has become a part of the way of life," said Peter Kittler, a German-descended Namibian who owns a store on the beachfront here.

Blacks and whites mingled freely on the main beach here on the chilly waters of the Atlantic Ocean. A huge waterslide discharged white, black and brown children in a torrent of water.

The prospect of a black-majority government in Namibia came a step closer with the signing of a peace accord in New York last Thursday after six months of American-sponsored negotiations among representatives of Cuba, Angola and South Africa.

Whites are a small minority in Namibia – by one reckoning, only 76,000 of 1.2 million people, the great majority of whom are black.

South Africa gained control of the territory from Germany in 1915 and has ruled it since, for the last 22 years in disregard of United Nations resolutions. Now, the drain on South Africa's economy, the political costs of the war against black guerrillas based in Angola, and the buildup of Soviet-backed Cuban forces in Angola appear to have coaxed Pretoria to significant concessions at the negotiating table.

Its rich mineral deposits, thriving fishing industry and prosperous farms have intensified the international dispute over the status of the former German colony.

After a decade of waiting, the white residents of Namibia – estimated at 46,000 Dutch-descended Afrikaners, 20,000 German descendants of German colonialists, 8,000 English-speaking settlers and the rest of other backgrounds – face the prospect of independence with a mixture of impatience, resignation and uncertainty.

Exodus in Late '70s

The number of whites has diminished from a high of about 110,000 in the mid-1970's. There was an exodus of perhaps 30,000 whites between 1977 and 1981 as a result of South Africa's agreement to a United Nations independence plan in 1978.

Pretoria stalled at putting the plan into practice and was later backed by the United States in its insistence that the plan could not go ahead until a large Cuban force withdrew from Angola, Namibia's northern neighbor.

But this time, there appears to be a philosophical mood to the prospect of change among Namibian whites.

While there are indications that some senior managers of banks, mines and railroads have begun requesting transfers to South Africa, there is so far no sign of a major exodus.

Like many white Namibians, Mr. Kittler, the owner of the beachfront store, is skeptical that the agreed-upon timetable for independence will be met.

"If the independence plan is put into effect and things get bad, then people will leave," he said. "But it won't be like 1978 when many whites left in anticipation of the event."

An Exemplary Life Style

The white minority's position of privilege and prosperity has so far been barely affected by the changes that have taken place. Whites still control the wealth and enjoy a life style matched in few places. Fine hotels serve excellent German cuisine to the mainly white patrons.

The handful of whites who have openly sided with the black guerrillas are treated as pariahs by most of their fellow whites.

Swakopmund, the principal coastal resort about 200 miles west of the territorial capital of Windhoek, is a refuge for Namibians from the hot, arid interior.

Its expanding population of 17,000 more than doubles as Namibians head for this coastal resort through the giant dunes of the Namib Desert.

The relaxed racial atmosphere in this quaint town, a place of German colonial buildings, reflects the progress made in Namibia toward scrapping statutory racial discrimination.

Apartheid Significantly Eased

Apartheid laws such as enforced residential segregation have been abolished, and the interim administration is made up of a majority of blacks. Although vestiges of apartheid remain, there is little of the racial tension found in South African towns and cities.

"We have done a lot of work preparing people for a black government," said Dirk Mudge, an Afrikaner who heads the black-majority transitional administration.

"If independence had been put into effect 10 years ago it would have been a disaster," he said in an interview in his vacation home here. "People are more used to the idea now and I think it will go more smoothly this time."

According to the timetable for independence, a United Nations peacekeeping force will oversee a seven-month transition beginning on April 1, 1989, leading to elections for a constituent assembly by November, 1989.

The assembly will draw up a constitution by April, 1990. One of the main points of concern among the white minority is that the guerrillas of the Marxist-oriented South-West Africa People's Organization will emerge triumphant in one-person, one-vote elections, a prospect considered likely by political experts.

In the seven months before independence, all but 1,500

of an estimated 50,000 South African troops stationed in Namibia will be withdrawn. At the same time, the 50,000-strong Cuban force will begin withdrawing from Angola where it has been helping the Angolan Army withstand attacks by South African and American-backed rebels of the National Union for the Total Independence of Angola. The Cuban withdrawal is to be completed in June, 1991.

Namibia as a Laboratory

South Africa has announced a cessation of aid to the Angolan rebels, but a dispute remains as to whether Angola will, as a reciprocal gesture, cut off help to guerrillas of the African National Congress, which is fighting to end white control of South Africa. Namibia has long been used by South Africa's leaders as a forward laboratory for its own racial problems, and there is a wide belief among South African whites that the destinies of the two areas are inseparable.

Swakopmund's position north of the South African enclave of Walvis Bay, which will remain under Pretoria's control after independence, serves as a reminder of just how dependent Namibia is on South Africa. Walvis Bay is the only functioning port to which Namibia has access.

"It's going to be very hard to stand on our own feet," conceded Mr. Auret, the town council official.

But many whites take solace in the reality that South Africa will continue to wield enormous influence over the territory after independence.

And militant black trade unionists have begun criticizing some guerrilla leaders for cooperating with the peace plan and have started preparing for a new battle on the question of sovereignty over Walvis Bay, a South African enclave that was never a part of Namibia.

Appendix II:

Mass participation limited by English as sole medium

Jerome Mutumba, Lecturer in the Department of English, Ongwediva College of education

Southern Africa, like most parts of Africa, is confronted with complex linguistic problems. There are many languages in Southern Africa that linguists like Pütz (1995:1) observed that the population of sub-Saharan could be measured against. Languages are tools for communication and the medium through which thoughts, values and attitudes are transmitted within and between cultural groups.

During colonialism in Africa, languages were used as tools for perpetuating divisive ideologies and the spirit of hatred among indigenous Africans (Benjamin Jean in Fardon & Furniss 1994:47). Divisive ideologies were promoted through colonial language policies aimed at legitimising the then colonial governments. Language policies during the colonial era in Southern Africa promoted European languages in schools and in most social domains of the sub-Saharan communities at the expense of indigenous local languages. With the advent of political independence, one would expect language policies aimed at reversing the disastrous colonial language policies in Southern Africa.

However, most African countries, upon attainment of political independence, opted for the languages of their former colonisers to be official languages (Matinee 185 in Pütz 1995:1). The Republics of Zambia and Botswana opted for English, the language of their former colonisers, and Mozambique and Angola opted for Portuguese. Later Namibia also joined the Anglophone team. Language choice, in terms of what language had to be accorded official status, was difficult for post-colonial African governments because of the fear of being accused of ethnic or tribal favouritism for one individual language among thousands spoken.

With the advent of independence in formerly colonised countries in Africa, most post-colonial governments attempted to mould so-called 'contemporary national' cultures; cultures that, supposedly, reflect the pride and true identity of the indigenous people. As part of the new cultures in developing countries, creation of national identities is frequently given high priority by the political leadership (Weinstein 1990). During the process of moulding the nations, political leaders felt obliged to accelerate the pace of national reforms in accordance with their political philosophies.

Educational reforms, often integral components of nation-building programmes, have sometimes been results of hasty deliberations in political chambers. Some countries, such as Namibia, exhibit clear discrepancies as well between policy statements and their actual implementation processes.

The Namibian Government, upon the attainment of independence in 1990, through the then Ministry of

Education, Culture, Youth and Sport (MECYS), took three years to produce a guiding language policy document entitled "The language policy for schools". The document was issued in June 1993 (Pütz 1995:169)

By the time the language policy document was issued, however, the MECYS had already implemented the language policy in all state schools. The phasing in of English as a medium of instruction took effect from 1992. Both Grades 8 – 9 in state schools were being taught in English. In fact only two years after independence was the language policy in schools 'ready' for implementation. With the implementation, one would expect that all the required resources such as teachers, textbooks and other relevant materials, would be in order, but this was not the case.

However, despite the problems mentioned, the Namibian language policy made provision for commendable guidelines for implementation. The implementation was planned to take place in phases. From 1992 Grades 8 – 9 were supposed to implement English medium instructions. In 1993 this had to continue to include Grades 8 – 10, 1994 Grades 8 – 11 and finally in 1995 all Grades (8 – 2).

The phasing-in of English in Namibia is in itself a good idea in principle, but the issue is whether it was well-timed. It is hard to judge its successes. I could not find evidence, such as a report or any documented proof by the Ministry of Education and Culture or its implementing agencies that spelled out the successes of the first phase before moving to the second phase.

In the absence of a report or any documented evidence on the application of the language policy for schools, it is difficult to determine whether there is a proper monitoring system in place. The onus is upon the institutions and all other agencies entrusted with overseeing the implementation process to define the success of the Language Policy, the critical issue being in this case the transition to English.

No matter how sound a policy can be, if it is not carefully applied, it is doomed to fail. As stated by Gaelge in Weinstein (1990:143), *the judicious application of a policy by various governmental agencies, such as the ministry of education, is of course its ultimate test, leading towards success of failure, excellence or mediocrity.*

It is imperative at this stage to revisit 'the evolution' of the language policy for schools in Namibia. Though the then MECYS emphasised the democratic nature of its policy formulation (MECYS 1993) and claimed that there was a lengthy stage during the LP process to ensure national consensus, I found no evidence of this. In fact, the nature of the consultation left much to be desired.

The MECYS set up the language development committee that produced a provisional policy for schools in 1991. The provisional draft language policy was distributed in schools with a questionnaire to solicit public response (Haacke 1994). But the results of the investigation were not made public (Chamberlain, in Haacke 1994). In fact, in response to the questionnaire, pressure groups from the Afrikaans and German communities petitioned the MECYS in an attempt to preserve their language privileges.

Haacke (1994:2-45) observed that the majority of the people in the northern part of the country had not input into the draft policy. Apparently these people did not respond to the questionnaire, and therefore their silence was considered approval of the draft language policy for school. This is contrary to the claim made by the MECYS about a 'lengthy consultative' process.

It supports the observation (supported by Haacke 1994) made earlier that political leaders accelerated the pace of the language planning process to fit their political agendas. I consider this act as a total disregard for the needs and aspirations of the people and it is therefore a threat to national unity and language harmony in the country. Fishman (1986) noted that *it is social, economic and political phenomena superimposed on ethnolinguistic, racial and religious differences which explain most language problems.*

The policy document that was drafted in 1981 by UNIN entitled "Towards a language policy for Namibia" laid down the foundation for the Namibian language policy. The document was a product of academic investigations in line with the so-called "International Model" of language planning.

So what role have the indigenous people played in the language planning process? I can only point out that the majority of the indigenous peoples played a mere passive receptive role: digest what was given to them by the ruling elite. This is a sign of the total disregard for mass participation in determining policies which affect the population at large. No wonder there was apathy from the majority of the people in response to questions issued in 1991 by the language development committee.

What differences was it going to make if the people responded to the questionnaire on the draft language policy for schools? Since the majority of the people were not consulted in drafting the 'provisional language policy for schools', it is reasonable to surmise that the input of even the majority of the people could not affect the decision of the language development planning committee which was accountable to the political elite which had appointed them.

This is a bad precedent as Kaplain and Baldauf Jr. (1997:310) observed: *It is likely that in any given environment, political, linguistic and social objectives may be flying off in quite different directions and with different degrees of intensity.*

It is part of the planners' task to try to achieve some coincidence among these disparate goals to bring some order to this chaos as part of the language-planning process. After the language policy was finalised, the

Ministry of Education and Culture, supported by the Overseas Development Agency (ODA) and the British Council, arranged a national conference on the implementation of the language policy for schools (Haacke 1994:244). The Primary purpose of the conference was to *provide a forum for informed debate and a true exchange of ideas to help promote widespread understanding of the language policy for schools and its implementation* (foreword by the Minister of Education and Culture, MEC 1993).

The conference should be seen for what it was, a mere attempt to drum up support from the people and to justify the rationale behind the implementation of the Namibian language policy for schools. Evidently, according to Haacke (1994:244), the most important papers of the proceedings of the conference, but understandably only those in favour of the language policy, were published in a book from (MEC, 1994) and distributed to schools countrywide.

Some problems can clearly emerge as a result of the language planning process and policy. Although the language policy ideally supports mother tongue education, because of inadequate resources, such as teachers and textbooks, it is difficult, if not impossible to implement mother tongue instruction in Grades 1 – 3 in most schools countrywide. This is coupled with what I refer to as the 'reluctance of the elite group' to promote indigenous languages. Haacke (1994) pointed out that during the so-called national language conference on the implementation of the language policy for schools, not one paper was devoted to the African languages. This poses a possible threat to the survival and the status of the indigenous languages.

The shortage of qualified teachers is a very serious threat toward the successful realisation of the language policy goals. As Arthur (1994) and Ridge (1997:173) pointed out in Botswana, issues of pupils' abilities in classrooms are greatly outweighed by those of teachers' competencies because teachers have inadequate command of the medium of instruction.

When the education system that is intended to consolidate the national policies fails to achieve its goals, we can expect failure of broader national policies. The future of the broader national language policy in Namibia might also be in jeopardy. The success of the language policy in schools to promote English and produce students who are proficient in it remains to be seen.

With the language policy that emphasises English as a sole official language, Namibia, like other countries in Africa such as Zambia, will limit the participation and involvement of the majority of its people in economic, political and social development. The education sector will be a vehicle for creating an elite class that empowers the masses.

References

Adegbija, K. (1994). *Language Attitudes in sub-Saharan Africa: A Sociolinguistic Overview.* Clevedon: Multilingual Matters Ltd.

Baron, D. (1990). *The English-only Question: an Official Language for the Americans?* New Haven: Yale University Press.

Beer, W. and Jacob, J.E. (1985). *Language Policy and National Unity.* Totowa, N.J.: Rowman & Allanheld.

Beveridge, M.C. and Reddiford, G. (1993) *Language, Culture and Education.* Clevedon: Multilingual Matters, Ltd.

Bonny, N.P. and Ridge, S.G.M. (1997). *Multilingualism in Southern Africa.* Annual Review of Applied Linguistics. Cambridge: Cambridge University Press.

Clinton, R. (1992).*Language Choice in Rural Development.* Dallas: International Museum of Culture.

Cobarrubias, J. and Fishman, J. (eds.) (1983). *Progress in Language Planning:International Perspective.* New York: Mouton Publishers.

Cooper, R.L. (1989). *Language Planning and Social Change.* Cambridge: Cambridge University Press.

Coleman, L. and Cameron, L. (1996). *Change and Language.* Clevedon: Multilingual Matters.

Eastman, C.M. (1983). *Language Planning: an Introduction.* San Francisco: Chandler and Sharp.

Edwards, J. (1994) *Multilingualism.* London: Routledge. Fardon, R. & Graham, F. (1994). *African Languages, Development and the State.*London: Routledge.

Ferguson, C.A. (ed.) (1996). *Sociolinguistic Perspectives*: *Papers on Language inSociety, 1959-1994.* New York: Mouton de Gruyter.

Haacke, W. (1994a). *Language Policy and Planning in Independent Namibia. Annual Review of Applied Linguistics (19931994) 14, 240-253.* Cambridge: Cambridge University Press.

Kaplan, R.B. and Baldauf Jr. R.B. (1997). *Language Planning: from Practice to Theory.* Clevedon: Multilingualism Matters Ltd.

Jones, G.M. and Ozog, C.K. (1993) *Bilingualism and National Development.*Clevedon: Multilingual Matters Ltd.

Lambard, R.D. (ed.). (1994*). Language Planning around the World: Context and Systematic Change.* John Hopkins University Press.

Lartin, D.D. (1994) *Language Repertoires and State Construction in Africa.*Cambridge: Cambridge University Press.

Ministry of Education, Culture, Youth and Sport (MECYS). (1990a). *Education in Transition: Nurturing our future. A transitional policy guideline statement on education and training in the Republic of Namibia.*

Windhoek: MECYS.

Putz, M. (1995) *Discrimination through Language in Africa? Perspectives on the Namibian experience.* New York: Mouton de Gruyster.

Sandel, L. (1982). *English Language in Sudan: A history of its teachings and politics.* London: Ithaca Press.

Schaffner, C. & Wenden, A. (1995). *Language and Peace.* Vermont: Dartmouth Publishing Company.

United Nation Institute for Namibia (UNIN). (1981). *Towards a Language Policy for Namibia.* Zambia: UNIN.

Weinstein, B. (1990). *Language Policy and Political Development.* New Jersey: Ablex Publishing Corporation.

Wodak, R. & Corsan, D. (eds.). (1997). *Language Policy and Political Issues in Education.* Boston: Kluwer.

Appendix III:

A Muzungu in Namibia

New African, London, 1 March 2004

Martin Rudiger, a German student, studied at the University of Namibia (UNAM) in 2002. This is his impression of a country originally colonised by his native Germany.

"Seek knowledge, even if it would be in China," says an old Arab proverb. Visiting a different country is a good way to learn new things, and to get to know how wealthy other cultures can be. As a German, the first prejudice I had to get out of my mind was that Africa's climate was always hot. When I arrived in Namibia at the end of August 2002 at 7 am, it was quite cold (5 degrees I was told). And I was only in my shorts and T-shirt.

On the other hand, I got to know another prejudice from an African employee at the Hosea Kutako Airport near Windhoek. When my taxi needed three hours to pick me up, he consoled me with a term I would hear many times during my stay: "This is African time."

It was my first time on African soil. I had waited a year for this day. When I was in a taxi to Windhoek city, I received a call from the Namibian embassy in Germany, telling me that my visa had finally been granted and ready for collection--back in Germany.

I spent my first weekend in a bed-and-breakfast run by a German-Namibian owner. She tried to explain the crime rate in Namibia this way: "The black people here are like the Turks in Germany." I would learn later that apartheid was still in people's minds, 12 years after independence.

Her second piece of advice to me was not to move into the university hostel, especially if there were only black students there. If I had followed her advice, I would have missed a very interesting time among nice fellow students.

My aim in Namibia was to improve my knowledge of African history. This was my first subject (Hauptfach) at university. One week before classes started, I went to the campus to complete my admission requirements. The few black students there watched me in bewilderment. The way they stared at me, a white man (muzungu), made me to understand how uncomfortable it was to be stared at just because you had a different skin colour. But I was lucky to meet a Kenyan student who showed me around in Windhoek and introduced me to the lifestyle.

On Friday, 6 September 2002, the president of Namibia, Sam Nujoma, himself visited the campus. He is also the chancellor of UNAM. Looking at Namibia superficially, it appears the country is making progress.

I had to get used to the environment. The whole campus is surrounded by a fence and razor wire and is protected day and night by security guards. The rules are strict: Students have to show their student cards even to enter the campus and hostel.

The way the university system runs in Germany and Namibia differs in many aspects.

The most significant is the level of teaching. Unlike in Germany, the standard of several Namibian schools is poor. The level of general knowledge is weak ("Austria is still a German colony").

School fees are also too high for a lot of Namibians. The university lecturers, though, are highly qualified. For example, in the Department of African Languages, Professor Haacke, a German-Namibian, holds the honour of having published the only Damara-German dictionary. For foreigners, Damara, like Xhosa or Khoi-Khoi, is hard to learn, since it includes several click sounds. Most of the lecturers at UNAM set high standards. Thus students have to work extra hard to obtain their BA-degrees.

UNAM is a magnet for many African students--from countries such as Zambia, Kenya, Zimbabwe, Lesotho, Angola, DRCongo, Sudan and others. They like the idea that classes at UNAM are never interrupted for political reasons and that there is no civil war in the country.

The country

Namibia had been a South African protectorate from 1920 to 1990. It had to endure the scourge of apartheid--and the scars have not fully healed.

You can roughly divide Namibia's population into three categories: black, white and coloured. The white minority does not like to mingle too much with blacks.

Only 5% of UNAM's lecturers are black. Of the university's roughly 8,000 students, there was just one white Namibian while I was there! White students are usually sent to South Africa, Europe or the US by their parents. Ethnicity plays a big role in the country and there are ethnic rivalries. One of the major reasons for this was the invention of the homelands system by the apartheid regime, where each "tribe" had to live separately from the others.

But many people are optimistic that they can overcome the ethnic biases. Says Vincent (20, a business administration student):

"In my region in Caprivi, the older people always warned me about other Namibians and their love for fights. But since I have been here, I have made several friends from all kinds of ethnic backgrounds who are peaceful people. Namibia is about to overcome its ethnic biases."

Prof. Katjavivi, the vice chancellor, is equally optimistic: "In the near future, we will have more and more white Namibian students," he says. He is also working on a programme to include San and Himba people as students. Both ethnic groups play a marginal role in political life. There is also disrespect for women in the country.

At UNAM, some students looked suspiciously at the three white students in their midst (two from Finland and me). Although most students were poor, I was often invited to share their meals or to spend my time playing chess or simply discussing many topics. Some of the topics were hot: HIV and how to defeat it. Students wore T-shirts saying: "Sex thrills, Aids kills--I want to finish with a degree, not with HIV."

Political issues are big on the campus. For example, do the Owambos (Namibia's biggest ethnic group) push other groups out of politics? Do white people own too much land in Namibia? Is it good that Nujoma supports Mugabe politically? Not everyone is content with Nujoma's performance as president, though.

My history class visited the Heroes Acre. This huge national symbol, finished in August 2002 by a North Korean firm, is in memory of the struggle for independence and the heroes who paid for it with their lives.

I got to know the real Namibia. Soon I recognised that my tourists' guide books were not very helpful. As a resident, I was able to have a look at the Namibian mentality, and picked up some inside knowledge. For example, one restaurant in Windhoek is praised for its nice location, attractive outdoor area and good atmosphere, especially in the evening. But I was told by some students that this restaurant practised "racism." I went there twice with my black friends, and each time we were not served-- black people are not welcome in a restaurant in their own country and continent?

UNAM facing reality

Crime, naturally, found its way onto campus. Rumours spread of rape cases among students, and some students tried to steal all kinds of utilities from fellow students. Therefore each hostel window on the ground floor had to be secured with bars. The new hostel is called Katutura, a cynical hint of the former black township in Windhoek by the same name.

But most students were optimistic of the future. From UNAM, they would apply for scholarships to study in Germany or Sweden. Many of them wanted to become teachers and lecturers.

Money was always a big issue. At the end of the term, students did not like being told that they had to pay the fees they owed to the university. When the students demonstrated against this order, soldiers had to come in. But it all ended peacefully, and the students got a grace period to pay up.

But it was not enough for everybody. Several students had to wait one whole year to write their exams because they could not pay their fees. Each course cost around N$400 (about 50 euros) or around N$14,000 a year. For foreign students, it is higher, sometimes double what the locals pay.

Tourists' paradise

When I started to enjoy my stay in Namibia, I even forgot about the rich fond of tourist attractions the country had to offer. I only made three trips: to Cape Town (South Africa), to Swakopmund on the coast, and to Rundu. I had been told that I would find Swakopmund like a "Little Germany". The weather is cold in Swakopmund, and it is full of European houses built in the style of 100 years ago.

One of my student friends invited me to his family home in Rundu, the capital of the Kavango region in the north. With its 20,000 inhabitants, Rundu is considered a big city. His family was happy to see me.

Outside the town, my friend showed me kraals and the mighty Kavango River. I learned that it was an honour in Namibia to be a student. Romanus (23, a history student), also from Rundu, proudly told me:

"In my village, I'm going to be the second person to have finished university."

But I replied that--seen internationally--UNAM standards were still low, for example in comparison to say Germany. In defence, they said it might be because Namibia was still a developing country. But I didn't totally agree. No country is really "fully developed," just look at the challenges (unemployment, weak economies, etc) facing countries such as France, USA or Germany.

Although UNAM can be proud of its achievements, especially during the last 10 years, there is never a pause on the way to make the world a better place or for Africa to make progress.

Tuomas from Finland, who shared UNAM life with me, summed it all up: "The people here have a great social life. Looking back I know I would love to come to UNAM again."

Appendix IV:

Averting Namibia's own holocaust

By Windhoektoivo Ndjebela,
Namibian Sun, 7 June 2013

It is no longer breaking news that Namibia is engulfed in a blanket of tribal and racial tension - both of which are seemingly rooted in a battle for resources and territorial control.

It can in fact be argued that tribalism and racism have picked up significantly since President Hifikepunye Pohamba launched the fading 'My Namibia, My Country, My Pride' campaign in 2011, which was meant to unite us as a people.

This campaign, which was launched amidst pomp, fanfare and curious anticipation, has not helped defuse racial and tribal consciousness, just as it has failed to teach us how to discuss culture in a manner that would not spark feelings of tribalism and racism.

Last week, prominent Oshikwanyama-speaking people farming in the Ondonga district were served with eviction orders, effective from July 1, 2013. They have been told to vacate their land and drive out their animals.

When Namibian Sun published the story on its Facebook page, an infuriated Oshikwanyama-speaking user commented on our story - and in his vernacular - that: "Endonga limwe lopoushiinda shetu olina oku nina nge nena aike. Itandi teelele nokuli omafiku afike kaa!"

Roughly translated, this user is saying: "I have a Ndonga neighbour and he'll sh*t. I won't wait until the eviction is effective."

Reacting to the same story, an Oshindonga-speaking subscriber said: "Nayazemo mOndonga yetu, otaya manapo uulithilo wiimuna yetu (They must leave our Ondonga district because they are finishing our grazing). Ndongas were also chased out of Kavango Region, fair enough they must also go."

The two remarks above, one uttered by a Namibian studying medicine in Russia, are the tip of the iceberg of tension between tribes in this country.

They further suggest that every ethnic community should have its own territory, which reinforces ethnic competition.

Initially, tribalism was attributed to arbitrary pre-independence boundaries that forced different communities to live within artificial borders. But we have been independent for 23 years now and must therefore claim our fair share of blame. Biologically, we cannot change our racial and tribal identities - but we can change the mindset and perceptions that accompany cultural differences.

Some Facebook users, especially those that commented on our article about the eviction of Ovakwanyama, are fairly illiterate. And that's how dangerous this situation is because their understanding of civil matters is shallow – and understandably so.

Tribalism dwarfs reasoning and fairness. In the land of tribalists, there exists no logic or justice. There is no recourse. Even the wrong are defended at all cost. But we are perplexed by the fact that even some leaders have jumped on the tribal bandwagon, in pushing for the "us-and-them" agenda, a dangerous precedent for a country trying to unite its people.

In recent weeks, we have been bombarded with talks of tribally influenced death threats, tribally fuelled eviction bids and tribally inspired propositions for new political regions to be established.

Already, a national leader has publicly apologised for racially abusing two police officers in the South in January, amongst a string of other similar incidents.

This is a demonstration that tribalism is not only an agenda driven by the least educated. The literate and the affluent have also joined the party. What a shame! Nowadays, Namibian politicians are using tribal issues to get votes. It's currently happening that when the president of the country comes from a particular tribe, people from that tribe believe they're superior to the rest of the population.

Civil wars and social fragmentation are but some of the consequences Namibia can expect if the government continues to rest on its laurels and wait for tribalism to fade on its own. This is a human-made catastrophe that would need human action to address it.

Racism

In the Omaheke Region, the town of Gobabis was brought to a standstill because of a racial incident that has landed one person in hospital and another in jail.

As of March 21, 1990, we'd thought by this time racism would be in the evening of its life.

The Gobabis incident, in which the alleged assailant is to appear in court again today for his bail application, proves that racism is still a fact of life in Namibia. The end of apartheid might have removed the legal framework allowing institutionalised racism, but racism in Namibia both predates and encompasses more than just the institutionalised racism of apartheid.

Racial relations remain highly polarised in Namibia, although this is hidden behind pretence and fake smiles. This, despite many policies aimed at redressing the bitter legacy that apartheid left in this country.

The Gobabis incident, involving a white bar owner who allegedly assaulted a black patron because his bar is exclusively for whites only, sparked marathon debates on social networks.

Such exchanges confirmed what many of the citizens already know: that there is a general lack of trust and respect between many black and white citizens.

What also unfolded this week was confirmation that egos and feelings of racial supremacy are alive and well in our country.

Commenting on the matter on Facebook, a white compatriot said: "…Give people space to do whatever they like to do. I stay away from shebeens, as I don't know what a few drunk black people would do to me and I am not going to bother them." His remarks sparked anger among other users, including non-racist whites. Some black Namibians too, some of them political leaders, have been racist in their remarks - including one Malcolm X Matundu, who was charged some years back for holding a placard at a demonstration, that read "Kill all the Boers."

Over the years, the police, prison service and the defence force have all been successfully shown to be guilty of institutional racism, as they are predominantly black.

But also, black people still get on average lower pay than whites, worse jobs than whites and worse housing than whites.

Racism was at the centre of the Holocaust – the mass murder of about six million Jews by the racist German government. In *Mein Kampf*, written in the fortress

Landsberg in 1923, Adolf Hitler (1889-1945) already expressed the fundamentals of the Nazi policy of racism, which was put into action after 1933.

If tribalism and racism are allowed to whirlwind in Namibia without any countermeasures to contain them, it would get to the very core of this society and paralyse us as a people. With tribalism and racism, the prospects of bloodshed cannot be overruled.

Appendix V:

Land claims turn tribal in Namibia

Catherine Sasmann, 15 April 2012
Open Society Initiative for Southern Africa (OSISA)

Omaheke in Namibia

Namibia's reputation for harmony is coming under more and more strain as disputes over power and influence are increasingly tinged with tribalism – including recent conflicts over land.

In one example, in March, an angry group of around 150 Herero communal farmers armed with knobkerries, pangas and guns put up a roadblock on a rural road in the Otjinene constituency in the eastern region of Omaheke. Their aim – to stop Stefanus Gariseb, the Damara-speaking chief of the /Gobanin Traditional Authority, from proceeding to an area within the constituency where he was intending to allocate 20-hectare plots to more than 100 beneficiaries.

Police averted the potentially explosive situation by persuading Gariseb and the potential new land owners to leave the area until leaders of the conflicting groups had discussed the matter. Nonetheless, fearing for his safety, Chief Gariseb fled to Windhoek and only returned a week later after police assured him that he would be safe.

But the heart of the problem has not been resolved. The Otjinene constituency is largely populated by Herero communal farmers, who feel that Gariseb's planned land distributions will infringe on their grazing area. In addition, they are infuriated by the fact that many of those slated to receive land are Oshiwambo-, Kavango- and Tswana-speakers.

And just as importantly, the Ovaherero Traditional Authority (OTA) under Herero Paramount chief Kauima Riruako contests Gariseb's jurisdiction over the area, arguing that – in accordance with the Traditional Authority Act of 2000 – a traditional authority chief has no control over land, but only over the members of a particular tribal community.

Gariseb claims that he does have the necessary authority since the /Gobanin clan was given permission to live in the area in 1947 by Herero chief at the time and because he has been recognised by the current government as the official representative of the /Gobanin.

In the end, further conflict was temporarily avoided when both parties agreed that any future land allocations would be done with the consent of the Herero communal farmers in the region – an unlikely prospect. So the current calm is likely to be just a lull before another storm since the demand for land will not simply disappear.

Meanwhile, politicians have – unsurprisingly – jumped on the bandwagon. The leader of the Communist Party in Namibia, Attie Beukes, said that the 'deliberate immigration' of 'other Namibians' – like the Damaras, Owambos, Okavangos, Tswanas and San – into the Omaheke, which has historically been occupied by the Herero, was "politically reckless and socio-economically irresponsible."

The country's constitution clearly states that Namibia is

a unitary State. But this concept is coming under increasing pressure, particularly in relation to competing demands for land.

Indeed, Beukes said that the Namibian government is enforcing the concept of 'one Namibia, one nation' and that it is time for greater self-determination – even perhaps for a federal arrangement. "This democratic right demands [freedom] from oppressive Owambo dominance and the freedom of oppressed and exploited and marginalised ethnic minorities to agitate by means of a referendum in order to secede in a peaceful manner," said Beukes.

However, Beukes' view remains the minority. Political commentator, Phanuel Kaapama, speaks for most when he says that this would be a very dangerous route for Namibia to take as it amounts to the total nullification of both the Namibian State and its constitution. But he did agree that the Otjinene incident has once again shown that there is a growing trend of 'ethnicification' of issues in Namibia – and particularly so in relation to land, which still provides around 60 per cent of Namibians with their livelihood.

Appendix VI:

Insult reflects tribal division in Namibia

John Grobler, *Mail & Guardian*,
Johannesburg, South Africa,
10 February 2012

A minister's inflammatory comment about his Ovambo colleagues sparks minorities' sympathy.

An intemperate outburst by Namibia's youth and sport minister, Kazenambo Kazenambo, in which he lashed out at some of his senior Cabinet colleagues as "stupid Ovambos" who are "just like the Boers—worse, because you are hungry, stupid", has ignited a political storm and posed sharp questions about Namibia's policy of national reconciliation.

The comments, allegedly made during an interview with a local vvsenior reporter from news magazine *InsightNamibia*, has also laid bare the deep political divisions in the Swapo-led government.

A senior reporter at the magazine, Tileni Mongudhi, demanded to know whether "KK", as the fiery-tempered former political reporter is better known, had not acted more as a Herero than a national minister in his conduct during a recent trip to Germany to collect 20 Herero and Nama skulls from an academic museum.

The question seemingly so provoked KK that he physically threatened Mongudhi and seized his voice recorder as "evidence", an action he later justified as confiscating an "enemy tool."

"In battle, if you capture an enemy tool then you keep it," KK told the newspaper, after the reporter laid a charge of theft against him.

In a later response to the *Namibian* newspaper KK defended his comments as a justified response to what he perceived as tribal bias against him.

The subtext here, however, is the fact that KK hails from the minority Mbanderu tribe, as a segment of Herero-speaking survivors of the German colonial war are known. General Lothar von Trotha's brutal "extermination order" in 1904 was aimed at wiping out the Herero.

Survivors fled and settled in Botswana

A small number of survivors fled the genocide and settled in Bechuanaland (now Botswana). In 1999 the descendants of the genocide survivors who had fled to Botswana were repatriated to Namibia.

KK's inclusion in Namibian President Hifikepunye Pohamba's Cabinet is widely seen as part of the political balancing act among Namibia's 40-odd tribes. Tellingly, Pohamba is yet to publicly call KK to order. As the smallest group among Namibia's Herero-speaking people, the Mbanderu punch above their political weight because of their tragic history.

KK's outburst—just the latest in a series of perceived racial incidents in which he has been involved over the past year—amounted not only to a political but also a cultural faux pas. Most of his Cabinet colleagues are both older and from the Oshiwambo-speaking tribes of central northern Namibia, the country's largest population group.

But his comments have bolstered his reputation for speaking out about what many non-Ovambo Namibians perceive to be a definite bias in favour of the Ovambo people.

Although KK later denied making those comments (but so far has not released the confiscated recorder), they found a lot of sympathy, especially among the unemployed youth who are not fortunate enough to belong to what has become known as "the executive tribe."

As proof of this bias, many point out the rapid urban development in the so-called "four Os"—Omusati, Oshikati, Ohangwena and Oshikoto—the area comprising the former Ovamboland, while most towns in the east and south have become increasingly run-down and desperate for development.

What KK's outburst signalled most clearly was that national reconciliation among Namibia's political classes was a "sham", said Tjiurimo Hengari, a lecturer at the Rouen School of Business in France and a regular local political columnist.

"Namibia is still peaceful, not because its people have overcome racism and tribalism, but because economic conditions have not yet deteriorated to a state in which the ethnic frustrations will boil over," Hengari said.

Patience wearing thin

But patience among minorities—who amount to about a third of the population—was fast wearing thin over the uneven allocation of national resources, Hengari warned.

"You can't have a policy without raising issues of national concern. It is a policy that is not accompanied by any substantive mechanisms checking on the efficiency of the policy and the process of national reconciliation.

"As a shallow policy in terms of its content, it has never been accompanied by any exemplary acts on the part of many of our politicians. It is therefore not a document that has been translated in exemplary citizenship and political leadership," Hengari said.

The outburst is regarded as an example of the power struggle in Swapo. KK has previously upset many in the leadership by calling for a non-Oshiwambo person to become the next president of Namibia.

This person, KK has made clear, is Trade and Industry Minister Hage Geingob, whose lack of a tribal constituency is widely seen as his political Achilles heel.

Geingob's most obvious competition for the top job is Justice Minister Pendukeni Ivula-Ithana, who also occupies the powerful party secretary general position. The succession race will be settled at the Swapo congress later this year

In the end, political insiders speculate, Ivula-Ithana will be the one to decide KK's political future, but a move against him could alienate the party's Herero voters, who have helped Swapo hang on to a two-thirds majority in Parliament since 1996.

Appendix VII:

SWAPO retains power

President-elect Geigob

By Werner Menges,
The Namibian, **Windhoek, 2 December 2014**

THE crushing defeat that the Swapo Party and its candidate Hage Geingob inflicted on their electoral rivals in last week's Presidential and National Assembly elections has taken the ruling party to new levels of popularity and political dominance never seen before in Namibia.

The 86.7% of the votes Geingob received in the presidential election outstrips the level of popularity that both the founding President Sam Nujoma and President Hifikepunye Pohamba enjoyed in Namibia's previous presidential polls, and also shows that Geingob has received substantially broader support at the polls than his party did.

At the same time, Swapo's share of the vote in the National Assembly election has increased to 80% – also the highest level of support the ruling party has received from the Namibian electorate.

He has received a heavy responsibility with his electoral victory, Geingob said in brief remarks made after the announcement of the election results yesterday evening.

"I'll be the President for all the Namibian people," he said, adding that it would be his mission to ensure that no Namibian is left out.

After keeping Namibia's electorate, which endured long queues and a slow voting process at polling stations on Friday, waiting for another three days, the election results were announced by the Electoral Commission of Namibia at about 19h20 yesterday.

ECN chairperson Notemba Tjipueja declared the Prime Minister as having been duly elected as Namibia's next President after announcing that Geingob had scored 772 528 of the total of 890 738 votes cast in the presidential election.

Geingob's closest rival, DTA leader McHenry Venaani, received 44,271 votes (4.9% of the total), followed by RDP leader Hidipo Hamutenya, with 30,197 votes (3.4%).

Nujoma won the 1994 presidential election with 74.4% of the vote, while his support increased to 76.8% in the 1999 election. In 2005 and again in 2009, Pohamba was elected President with 76.4% of the vote.

"Democracy remains incomplete without losers," Venaani said in a short concession speech after Tjipueja's announcement of the results. "Democracy is a cycle of winning and losing."

Namibia's democracy is safe and sound, he said.

Addressing Geingob directly, Venaani said: "As leader of the official opposition-elect I will keep you on your toes."

By winning 715,026 of the 893,643 votes cast in the

National Assembly (NA) election, Swapo will fill 77 of the 96 seats for elected members of the expanded NA from 21 March next year.

While the ruling party has risen to a new height of popularity and dominance, opposition parties have seen their share of the votes in the NA election drop. The DTA of Namibia, the All People's Party, and the Workers Revolutionary Party have managed to buck this trend, though.

For the Rally for Democracy and Progress and the Congress of Democrats (CoD), the 2014 elections had been a disaster.

Five years after the RDP won eight seats in the National Assembly with 11.3% of the vote in the 2009 election, the party has suffered a major setback at the polls, with its share of the vote falling to 3.5% (31,372 votes). The RDP will have only three seats in the next NA. The number of votes that the RDP received this year is about a third of the 90,556 votes it had won in the 2009 election.

The CoD, which entered the National Assembly with seven seats after winning 10.05% of the votes cast in the 1999 NA election, will not be returning to parliament next year. Its share of the vote imploded to only 0.38% this year.

For the DTA, 20 years of electoral decline have been halted and reversed this year, but the party is still far from the levels of support it had during the 1990s. The former official opposition, which had two seats in the NA after the 2009 election, in which it scored only 3% of the vote, won 42 933 votes (4.8% of the total) in the NA election this year. That gives the DTA five seats in the next NA and the status of official opposition.

The APP's electoral fortunes have also improved since 2009, when the party won 1.35% of the votes cast in the NA election. After having only one member in the NA over the past almost five years, the APP will have two

MPs in the next NA. The party received 20,431 votes (2.3% of the total votes) this year.

The UDF, with 18 945 votes (2% of the total), won two seats in the next NA (2.4% in 2009, resulting in two seats), while Nudo won two seats on the back of 17,942 votes (2% of the vote, compared to 3% and two seats in 2009).

The Workers Revolutionary Party will, for the first time, have members in parliament from 21 March 2015. The leftist party, which drew 13,328 votes, has been allocated two seats in the NA.

Although they did not win enough votes to reach the NA seat quota of 9,308 votes, Swanu, the United People's Movement, and the Republican Party have been allocated one seat each as a result of the system of allocating seats to parties based on the number of surplus votes received by the parties.

Swanu received 6,354 votes, the UPM 6,353 votes, and the RP 6,099 votes. About 72% of the country's 1,241,194 registered voters cast their votes in the NA election.

Oh, hug a Geingob!...As RDP lose official opposition status to DTA

By Mathias Haufiku,
New Era, **Windhoek, 2 December 2014**

The ruling party Swapo and its presidential candidate Dr Hage Geingob last night created new electoral records, after mercilessly whipping their opponents – albeit democratically – in the just ended elections.

For the first time since the first democratic elections in 1989, Swapo reached the 80 percent mark in the vote for the National Assembly, while Geingob created his own history by accumulating 86.7 percent, the highest ever attained by a Namibian presidential candidate.

The DTA, under the energetic leadership of McHenry

Venaani, came second with a mere 4.8 percent of the vote. DTA eclipsed the Rally for Democracy (RDP), dubbed the biggest loser in this election, after the former official opposition only managed a paltry 3.51 percent of the national vote.

It was an election of shocking proportions, with Swapo taking 77 seats in the National Assembly, leaving 15 opposition parties to – like eagles on a hare – scramble for the remaining 19 seats in the 96-seat chamber.

DTA took five of those seats, followed by RDP with three seats. But the surprise package of this election, the Workers Revolutionary Party (WRP) shocked all and sundry when it won two seats from virtually nowhere.

Until last night, many Namibians were still asking questions about who WRP are, after the hugely unknown formation defeated the likes of RDP even in Okongo, which is traditionally a home turf of the dislodged former official opposition.

The 893,643 Namibians who voted in the National Assembly elections became the first people to cast their votes electronically in Africa during national elections.

Disappointingly though, 350,456 of the total 1,241, 194 registered voters did not cast their votes in the presidential elections while for the National Assembly, 347,551 voters did not vote.

Many sections of the country were not happy with the newly-introduced one-day polls as they felt the time was not enough for all registered voters to cast their votes.

Others also blamed faulty debutant electronic voting machines (EVMs) as another of the factors that delayed the voting process and in the end deterring voters to stand in long queues.

Each party had to score at least 9 308 votes to qualify for a seat in the National Assembly, the ECN announced yesterday.

The ECN announced that Swapo got 715 096 of the total 893 643 votes.

"I have the honour to and privilege to declare Dr Hage Geingob who has accumulated a total of 772 528 votes in the presidential race, duly elected as President with effect from such a date as determined by the Namibian Constitution. Congratulations, Sir," announced ECN chairperson, Advocate Notemba Tjipueja when she released the results last night.

After Tjipueja declared the results, President Hifikepunye Pohamba, the outgoing Head of State, urged Namibians to respect and honour the results.

"I urge all our people to respect and honour the voice of our people. The nation has spoken. Let us now join hands and put shoulders to the wheel to develop our country, improve the living conditions of our people and take Namibia to greater heights of prosperity," urged Pohamba, who is expected to hand over the presidency to Geingob on March 21, 2015.

"The people have spoken. Democracy is alive and healthy in Namibia. Our country now has a president-elect and members of parliament-elect, who await to be sworn in to serve our people."

When he took the floor, Geingob said his victory is the will of God and thanked Namibians for electing him to lead the country.

"It is proper that you, the people of Namibia, came out in numbers and thought that I should take over," the calm and collected winner said.

"When I look at the numbers of those who attended our rallies, I got worried because what I have deduced is that I have a heavy responsibility that I cannot alone play out. Therefore I will count on you, Mr President, and the guys I terribly defeated."

"Let us hold hands because I will be a president for all Namibians. No Namibian must feel left out," said Geingob.

DTA's Venaani also took the floor and said democracy remains incomplete without losers.

"Leaders must always stand firm when they fall on the battle ground. We ran the most difficult campaigns in many years but we managed to resuscitate our party. Dr Geingob has run a good race, but Africa must also tell the story that ... we must become bigger friends in defeat to build our country," he said.

Venaani, looking in the direction of Geingob, vowed to keep Geingob and his government on their toes by holding them accountable as well as coming up with new ideas.

After delivering his brief statement, Venaani invited Geingob to the stage for a picture as a symbol of unity despite the fact that they both contested to succeed Pohamba.

Namibia currently has nine political parties in the National Assembly but after this election only seven parties are heading to the country's sixth parliament.

All People's Party (APP), Workers Revolutionary Party (WRP), Nudo and the United Democratic Front (UDF) all secured two seats while the Republican Party, Swanu and United People's Movement (UPM) all obtained a single seat each.

Unless an alliance is formed between other opposition parties, the DTA is the new official opposition party after coming second.

The party, an official opposition between 1989 and 1999, obtained 42 933 votes that translated into five seats. DTA won 21 seats in the 1989 election.

RDP's dismal performance saw its parliamentary stake decreasing from eight seats to three.

Nudo, which has admitted it did not recover from the death of its veteran leader, Chief Kuaima Riruako, maintained its two seats.

New kids of the block Namibia Economic Freedom Fighters (NEFF), Christian Democratic Voice Party (CDVP) as well as veteran campaigners Congress of Democrats (CoD), National Democratic Party (NDP) and Democratic Party of Namibia (DPN) all did not win any seats.

Last Friday's elections were held in limbo at the eleventh hour when the RDP and WRP went to the High Court to demand that the elections be postponed because of concerns over EVMs. The matter was dismissed by the court.

RDP in slow death

By Tuyeimo Haidula, Denver Kisting, *The Namibian*, Windhoek, 2 December 2014

THE odds, if the just-ended election results are anything to go by, are that the Rally for Democracy and Progress (RDP) could be heading for the fringes of history.

This is despite the fact that the RDP, which until now, was the official opposition, has participated for the second time in national elections.

There were massive hopes that the RDP president, Hidipo Hamutenya, who quit Swapo to form an opposition party in 2007, would give the ruling party a run for its money.

In 2009, RDP came in with 11,31% of the vote but this year, they lost almost half of their supporters.

RDP secretary general Mike Kavekotora said there are many factors both internal and external.

The RDP vice president, Steve Bezuidenhout, yesterday said the people of Namibia have spoken.

"We respect the decision of the people," Bezuidenhout said, without saying what the party's plan for the future is to revive its fortunes.

"We are not a dictatorship. I cannot speak on behalf of everyone. We have to call our structures to discuss and analyse the results. Only then can we decide the way forward," he said.

Kavekotora said they will conduct a strategic analysis before coming up with a reasonable conclusion.

"Our plan for the future is to re-engineer the party to remain relevant to Namibian politics. We will have a strategic session after all aspects of our performance are clearer to us," Kavekotora said.

RDP secretary of the youth league, Monica Nambelela differed with Bezuidenhout.

Nambelela dismissed the notion that Namibians had spoken and blamed the use of electronic voting machines for the low votes cast in favour of by her party.

"We have seen that the use of EVMs was not logical. Although we are the first to go with EVMs, it was a blunder," she claimed.

She also said those who did not vote left a huge bearing on the results. "Most people did not vote and we do not know who they would have voted for. This should be an eye-opener that perhaps as a nation we did not opt for the best method," Nambelela said, adding they were concerned that although people voted on Friday, the results are not yet out.

She questioned whether people really want to turn Namibia into a one-party state, saying the margins in terms of votes cast for the parties were too wide.

"Namibians woke up to a miscarriage of democracy and this will mean backward development. Opposition parties are a healthy check and balance and if they do not get seats in parliament then we wonder whether this is really democracy."

She said this is the last time she wants a nation subjected to elections that are not credible.

Nambelela also could not divulge any of the party's future plans, saying "our strategy is an in-house thing."

Phanuel Kaapama, a political activist, said the poor performance by the RDP in the preliminary results probably reflects the fact that the party was not active enough in its campaign.

Kaapama said how active the RDP was could also be reflected in media coverage of its activities. "There was not much happening there."

The RDP's State resources for campaigning were four times bigger than that of the DTA, he said. However, one would not say so if one analyses their campaigns, Kaapama said. "We didn't see much of those resources."

Victor Tonchi, another political analyst, said according to him, the RDP had lost momentum.

Moreover, the party does not have any "significant issues" which they are addressing. "They needed to de-link from Swapo to make inroads. This is the mistake they have been making for some time now."

Venaani outlines official opposition's plans

Denver Kisting,
The Namibian, **Windhoek, 4 December 2014**

THE housing crisis is the first issue that McHenry Venaani, president of the DTA, and his team will tackle in the National Assembly as the official opposition of the country.

They are vying to be part of the economic committee of the legislative body. As part of this committee, they intend to launch a probe into skyrocketing house prices, Venaani said. Among others, they plan to call in banks to testify on why the house price situation is so much out of hand.

Venaani said this committee is instrumental as it is the "centre of development."

Another issue which is close to heart and will receive attention is their concern about capital flight. Way too large locally generated profits are still being channeled out of the country. This situation is not sustainable, he said.

Youth unemployment will also be addressed as a "critical issue". "We are not going to parliament to play. We're going to keep the House in a very robust way."

He lashed out at "the S&T raking [in] exercise by MPs". The five DTA members of parliament will not be globetrotters on the National Assembly ticket, he undertook. "We will only go on trips that matter."

These lavish international travels have turned parliament into a mockery, he said.

At the same time, the youthful leader lifted the veil on an allegedly terrorist organisation "which has manifested in Namibia."

This is a concern he would like to personally take up with President-elect Hage Geingob.

Expressing gratitude for the 42,933 Namibians who voted in the DTA's favour, Venaani yesterday said he was however deeply concerned with the overwhelming majority which the ruling party, Swapo, obtained during last week's elections.

This is not healthy for a democracy, he maintained. "Namibia is moving towards a one-party state."

At the heart of the problem is the lack of cooperation among opposition parties, he warned. "Division within the opposition [parties] should be nipped in the bud."

He said there is a need to start working towards a single coalition block.

The business community also needs to play a much bigger role in nurturing democracy, the DTA leader said. He is of the view that entrepreneurs only support the ruling party in anticipation of obtaining contracts.

Venaani emphasised that they have no intention to become government bashers. According to him, they plan to sustain the momentum generated during their election campaign through effective engagement.

However, it is also important to do a comprehensive election post-mortem, the DTA leader said.

Very importantly, they are geared towards running an issue-driven campaign from January next year to 2019, he said.

On a question by The Namibian on what the DTA will do as the official opposition to promote the rights of minorities in the country, particularly gays, Venaani was categorical: "We are not doing enough to promote minority rights."

As far as gay rights are concerned, he said: "I don't support people who say gays must be hanged."

His party undertakes to defend the rights of all Namibians. "I would not want anyone's rights to be trampled upon."

Swapo sweeps elections, Geingob wins presidency

Mail&Guardian, Johannesburg, 2 December 2014

Namibian Prime Minister Hage Geingob and his party, the South West Africa People's Organisation (Swapo), won a landslide victory in presidential and legislative elections billed as Africa's first e-vote, the electoral commission said Monday.

Geingob (73) who ran on a platform of "peace, stability and prosperity", becomes president-elect of the vast desert nation in southwest Africa with a massive haul of 87% of the vote.

"It's the will of God that the people of Namibia came out in big numbers and thought that I should take over," he said.

"I have a heavy responsibility that I cannot do only on my own. I will be a president of all Namibians. No Namibians will be left out." In the race for the legislature, Swapo took 80% of the vote, winning 78 of the 96 seats in the national assembly.

Becoming the strongest opposition party in Parliament, the Democratic Turnhalle Alliance won five seats, with 4.8% of the vote.

The former main opposition, the Rally for Progress and Democracy, saw its percentage of the vote cut from 11% in the last election in 2009 to 3.15%, winning just three seats.

Forged in the anti-colonial and anti-apartheid struggle, Swapo has won every election since Namibia's independence in 1990.

Already an overpowering force in Namibian politics, the party managed to improve on the 2009 elections, when it received 75% of the vote.

Outgoing President Hifikepunye Pohamba said: "The people have spoken. Democracy is alive. I urge all our people to respect and honour the voice of the people."

First e-vote

The African Union (AU) applauded the elections as free and fair.

Ambassador Fatuma Ndangiza, head of the AU election observer mission, gave Namibia a thumbs up for conducting the elections in "a peaceful environment, free from violence and intimidation."

But she suggested Namibia's electoral commission "consider simplifying polling station procedures" and ensuring staff were trained in how the electronic voting machines worked.

Opposition parties complained that thousands of voters were turned away from polling stations Friday because of technical difficulties.

Observers from the Southern African Development Community (SADC) also gave the vote their stamp of approval.

Opposition parties had launched an 11th-hour court challenge just days before the election to stop the electronic vote from going ahead, saying the use of the voting machines could facilitate vote rigging.

But the Windhoek High Court dismissed the application.

About 72% of the 1.2-million eligible voters turned out to cast their ballots on Friday on nearly 4,000 electronic voting machines.

Other African countries have run pilot or limited e-voting, but none have done so on this scale.

Like many of Africa's liberation movements, Swapo has become a big-tent party that spans the political spectrum and often seems more involved with intra-party politics than voters.

Supporters say that allows for continuity, but critics say it brings stasis.

A recent Afrobarometer poll showed nearly two thirds of voters believe the government is doing a bad job creating employment, fighting corruption and improving living standards for the poor

Economic growth is forecast at around four percent for this year, yet one in four people is out of work, according to the government's narrow definition.

The economy remains dependent on diamond and uranium mining.

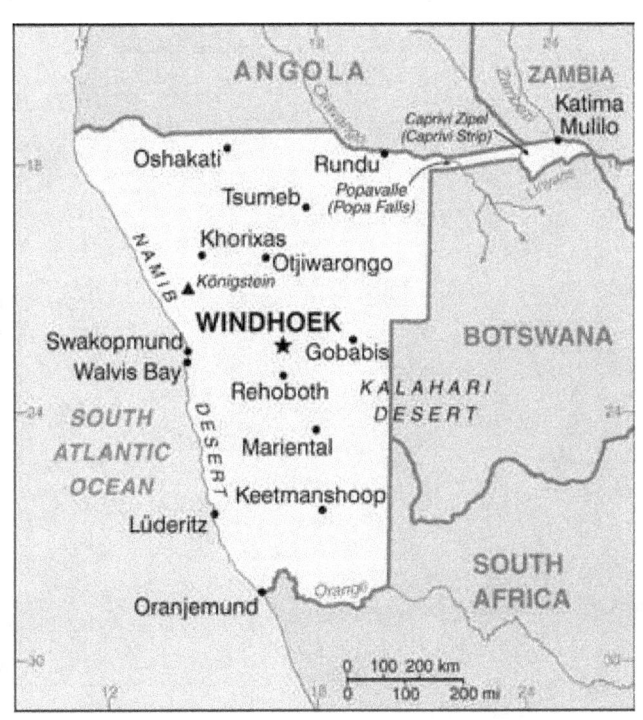

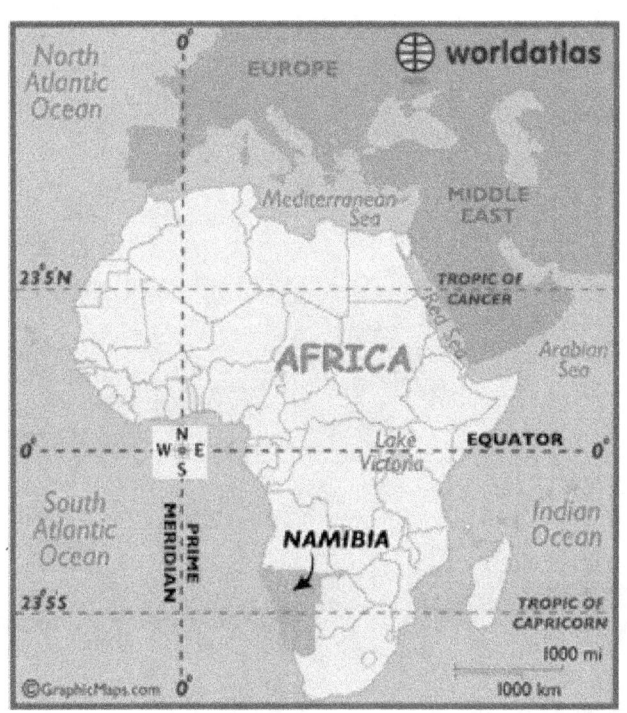

www.ingramcontent.com/pod-product-compliance
Lightning Source LLC
Chambersburg PA
CBHW070735170426
43200CB00007B/532